# Unexpected Treasures

## Running a Mental Health Nonprofit

**Rod Baker**

Copyright © 2020 Rod Baker

All rights reserved. No part of this book may be used or reproduced by any means, graphic, electronic, or mechanical, including photocopying, recording, taping or by any information storage retrieval system without the written permission of the author except in the case of brief quotations embodied in critical articles and reviews.

# Table of Contents

Author's Note ..................................................................... v
Dedication ........................................................................ vii
Recognition and Thanks .................................................. ix
My New Job — October 2004 .......................................... 1
My New Office .................................................................. 4
Meeting the Board of Directors   Unwelcome News ........... 10
Meeting the Staff .............................................................. 21
Stuck on the Monitor ....................................................... 27
The AGM   Fundraiser   Christmas Dinner ..................... 31
Launching the Satellite House ......................................... 42
Shaping the Store ............................................................. 46
The Un-Grand Opening ................................................... 50
Organic Growth ................................................................ 61
Losses and Gains   New Hope   More Losses ................. 70
Searching for a New Location ......................................... 84
The Beginning of a Funny Idea ....................................... 92
Outreach ........................................................................... 108
Problems at Riverside House .......................................... 124
Sheppard House ............................................................... 141
Moving Obstacles ............................................................. 152

Moving our Office & Store   Fine-Tuning Operations........162

Leaving....................................................................................178

England..................................................................................192

Italy........................................................................................198

Bad News   Christmas with Mother   Missing my Tribe....212

Return to Disaster................................................................222

Back to CMHA.......................................................................229

A Sliver of Hope....................................................................240

Restoration...........................................................................244

Gaining Traction..................................................................259

Miles for Mental Health   Team Discord............................269

Everyday Challenges...........................................................274

The Corner of My Desk........................................................300

People Leaving   Women & Wellness   Presentations......316

Life Changes........................................................................331

2012 — Saying Goodbye......................................................345

Afterword 2020....................................................................354

Other books by this author.................................................356

## Author's Note

In this book I wrote about people, locales, and conversations as I remembered them. It may not be an exact record.

I have changed the names and related details of

some individuals and circumstances.

## Dedication

This story is dedicated to all the people who battle daily with the symptoms, stigma, and loneliness associated with mental illness.

## Recognition and Thanks

To the kindness of strangers and clients, who generously volunteered their time in supporting the Simon Fraser Branch as thrift store staff, board members, computer trainers, Comedy Courage comedians, Miles for Mental Health and Women & Wellness event helpers.

\*\*\*

To the citizens of New Westminster who brought their donations to the thrift store and those who purchased them. Without their support, there would have been no thrift store and no story.

\*\*\*

To the staff of Canadian Mental Health Association Simon Fraser Branch whose persistence, creativity, and caring helped support their clients to live better, brighter, and more meaningful lives.

\*\*\*

To the beta readers who made suggestions for this book:

Kathy Bestwick, Wiley Ho, Doug McLeod, Rose Dudley, Neil Loewe, Edyth Anstey Hanen, Elly Stornebrink, Jim Tallman, Joyce Goodwin, Anna Adler, Martha Warren, Cinda Jong, Heather Dawn Gray, Anna Maria Campbell, Matthew Watt, Bette Kosmolak, Barbara Reardon, Cathy Scrimshaw, Katie Chamberlain, Dinah Saleh, and Mariam Saleh.

This book was much improved by the professional help of my formatter and cover designer Sharon Brownlie at aspirebookcovers.com

and my editor Heather Hayden at hhaydeneditor.com

# My New Job — October 2004

I opened the door and slumped into the driver's seat, glad to be back in the comfort of my car. I took deep breaths and exhaled slowly.

A five-person panel had interviewed me for the position of executive director for the Simon Fraser Branch of the Canadian Mental Health Association (CMHA) — a rabbit warren of eight rooms wedged into the steep hillside between a cemetery and the Fraser River. I'd struggled to find the right answers to the panel's questions while trying to smile, appear calm, and knowledgeable.

The cold windshield became foggy. I drew a smiley face on the glass and started the engine, but continued to sit, reliving the interview in my mind: Ada, the organization's president, was a short, intense woman in her forties. After asking each question, she flipped a mop of jet-black hair across her forehead and maintained eye contact as though trying to read my thoughts.

"What would you do if you thought a staff member was suicidal?"

"What are your strengths and weaknesses?"

"Do you have ideas for fundraising?"

"Why do you want this job?"

I slipped the car into gear and eased out of the parking lot. On the drive home, I answered each question more confidently, more eloquently to the rear-view mirror — a passive, non-judgemental listener.

Job interviews make me nervous. I'm more of a doer than a talker. When peppered with a string of questions, I tend to answer in a kind of staccato shorthand as though pressed for time.

I asked to see the previous year's Annual General Meeting (AGM) report, but because the last executive director (ED) had been off sick, one hadn't been compiled. The interview team knew a lot more about me than I knew about their organization, but I wanted the job and ignored the lack of information. They had a staff of 12 compared to 3 at my current workplace — a giant leap forward in my career. An undercurrent of anticipation ran through me for the next few days as I wondered if I'd landed the job.

Four days later, I was painting a kitchen wall in my house and received a call from the board's president.

"Rodney, it's Ada. I'm delighted to offer you the position of executive director for CMHA's Simon Fraser Branch."

My heart pounded. The CMHA was a nationally recognised nonprofit organization with over 120 branches across the country.

"As advertised," she continued, "it's a temporary six-month position but could turn into full time as the current ED may not return from sick leave."

More good news! They had probably heard positive reports about my work running day programs for people with mental illness. That's probably why they sent me a personal email inviting me to apply for the job. My efforts to break into a new career by earning a master's degree in counselling and becoming certified in psychosocial rehabilitation had paid off. After only a year and a half in my field, I'd secured an important job. I gave three weeks' notice at my current workplace and helped the board's president find a candidate for my replacement.

The Simon Fraser Branch was a nonprofit agency that provided housing services for people with mental illness. I'd never worked in housing before. There would be lots to learn. The company offices were on Columbia Street, a double-lane arterial route that bore convoys of trucks hauling goods to and from the Port of New Westminster. There was a sharp corner in front of the office, and two lanes of huge vehicles rumbled by a few feet from the front door, making the ground shake throughout the day. I learned that two years earlier, a truck failed to round the corner and smashed into the front windows of the building. Street parking did not exist, but right behind the office was a large parking lot for staff and visitors.

*The daily armada of trucks passing by our front door*

Mental health clients didn't like coming to this office situated at the edge of town, on a juggernaut truck route, with no bus service. I disliked the location too, especially the noise and remote location. However, my predecessor had signed a 10-year registered lease 2 years prior to my arrival. Changing locations appeared impossible. By reflecting on these deficits, I was following a time-honoured nonprofit tradition of blaming the previous executive director for current problems.

## My New Office

I walked through the door on the first day of my new job and was greeted with a smile from a guy of about 40, sitting at the front desk. He sported a red-and-black plaid shirt and adjusted his thick-rimmed glasses as he looked up.

"Hi, can I help you?"

"I'm Rodney, the new executive director."

He looked surprised and stood up. "A man ED?" he blurted out.

"Yup, that's me." I smiled and extended my hand.

"I'm Jim, the receptionist." He reached over the desk and gave me a tentative handshake. "I'm a volunteer, a client. I'll show you to your office. The coffeepot's in the hall on the way."

I poured myself a cup and added powdered milk. There was no sugar. He opened the door to a medium-sized room with pink walls, a brown linoleum floor, two large filing cabinets, and no windows.

*I should have asked to see my office before accepting the job.*

Ignoring the dismal décor, I slid gingerly onto the wobbly black-leather office chair and stared at the ancient Hewlett-Packard monitor. Pressing the computer's power button, I leaned back and sipped the bitter liquid. A faint odour of burning dust rose from the computer tower on the floor as it whirred to life. I pulled open a drawer while I waited. A tube of lip gloss, pink Post-it Notes, and a Kit Kat wrapper lay scattered inside.

A ghostly barrage of images appeared on the monitor. About 40 files, like an overlapping mosaic of playing cards, filled the screen.

Alice, the executive director on sick leave, was supposed to come back in six months. Rearranging her computer files felt like walking into someone's house and moving the furniture around while they were out. Fixing it wouldn't be like messing up a system, more like system-ing up a mess.

I sipped my coffee, created folders by date, and started dragging in files. Duplicates got deleted. The mosaic chaos lessened, but after 45 minutes, I got irritated and quit.

With the previous ED gone, no one was available to orient me on how to spend my time. I wanted to feel productive, to accomplish *something* on my first day. Swivelling the chair around, I stood up and faced the big beige filing cabinets. I would scan through the files to learn about the organization's past — get a feel for the place.

Unlike the hodgepodge mess on the computer, everything was filed in perfect order. Both large cabinets were crammed to bursting point. Sifting through the bulging folders and three-ring binders revealed the reason why: Since the society's inception in 1958, *everything* had been filed in order by date. Sixteen copies of the 1963 AGM reports almost filled one binder. I reassured myself that discarding surplus copies of ancient files was a worthwhile project. Scanning the files would enlighten me about the organization's history. Dumping duplicate files would make room for more history.

I tossed seven of eight 1984 July newsletters into the small wire wastebasket, filling it up. I needed something bigger and retrieved a large green garbage can I'd seen in the parking lot. Now, I could dump in earnest. The heavy thud of files landing in the garbage can was more satisfying than the whispery "zik" of dumping stuff into the computer trash. Old employee dismissal letters, an eight-year-old payment dispute with the telephone company, and twelve-year-old Christmas cards all whistled into the garbage. Every piece of paper had been meticulously filed, as if time invested in preserving the past would somehow ensure a solid future. Given the run-down feel of the office, and the ED being away on sick leave, it hadn't worked.

Maybe repetitive filing had been calming. As the papers piled up on Alice's desk, she filed them away — pile and file, pile and file, a ritual, like ironing. The new sheriff in town was changing things to read and dump, read and dump. Scrooge-like, I kept no Christmas cards. I assured myself I was doing something useful, tilting the direction of the organization toward a leaner, more focused future.

A tall, red-headed young man in his late twenties walked through the open door of my office and offered his hand. "Hi, I'm Donald, the housing manager."

I gave him a firm handshake. "Good to meet you, Donald. I'm Rod, Rodney. As the new guy on the block, please let me know if there's anything I need to be aware of."

He nodded then shot a surprised look at the half-full garbage can. "How come you're dumping all those files?"

"Trying to sort things out, get an idea what's been going on, and eliminate unnecessary clutter."

"I've never seen an ED do that before," he said, raising his eyebrows. "Alice loved filing."

"Yeah, but not on the computer."

Donald grimaced and agreed that Alice "wasn't good" with computers.

"So, what does your job consist of, Donald?"

He heaved a sigh. I couldn't tell if it was because I should have known or it was a heavy load.

"The housing manager is responsible for ensuring the housing services run smoothly." He explained that we ran three housing programs under contract for the government-funded Fraser Health Authority: a small program to house youth, ages 16-19, who couldn't live at home; three transition houses in the community to help people with mental illness learn the skills needed for semi-independent living; and the largest program that helped about 90 adults find and keep market housing.

"Market housing? Like their own apartments?"

"Exactly." He nodded. "We help them find places to live and troubleshoot any problems."

"What kind of problems?"

Donald gave a wry grin and explained, "Finding landlords that will accept tenants with mental illness, helping our clients deal with paying the rent, cooking, managing their medication, coping with bedbugs, discouraging smoking in their apartments, and keeping the place clean — tough because some of them are hoarders."

"Sounds like you have your hands full."

"Yeah, keeps me busy. We have 10 full-time housing staff and 6 part-timers. There's also a program to help people quit smoking called Breathe Easy, but I don't run that."

I tried to maintain a confident smile. Learning that there were over a hundred housing clients made me concerned since I knew nothing about housing. As Donald knew all the staff, I asked him when would be a good time for our first team meeting.

"Just the accountant, me, and you work in the office. The other staff work outside with clients. The only day when all the full-timers could come in is Tuesday."

"Okay, let the staff know I want to hold a meeting on Tuesday, at 9 a.m. sharp. Tell them to allow at least an hour. Ask the part-timers to try and make it to the meeting." I was pleased to have remembered the part-time staff.

"The part-timers won't come unless you pay them."

"Tell them if they come, they can have it as flex time — time off."

"The union won't like that."

*Damn. I had forgotten about the union.* "See what you can do."

I wasn't keen to incur any extra costs until I'd found out how the finances were. The missing AGM report would have shown that.

"Who looks after the books here?"

"Trevor does," he said, pointing toward the hall.

After two right turns and a left, Donald led me to the other side of the rabbit warren and knocked on Trevor's door. His windowless office was tiny but immaculate. Everything on the desk was neatly in place. A smartly-dressed young man in his mid-twenties gave a shy smile as he stood up to shake my hand.

"Trevor, I'm Rodney, the new ED. I understand you keep track of our finances."

"That's me."

"Nice to meet you. Everything going okay with the organization financially?"

The smile drained from his face. "Okay in some areas but not so good in others."

"Well, Trevor, it's important that I know." I asked him to put together a mini report on what was and wasn't working and email it to me by the following day.

He relaxed, nodded, and agreed. "Would you like me to set up your email?"

"Thanks, that would be great."

I returned to my office and continued to dump excess files. Trevor arrived to set up my email.

"So, you look after the computers and office emails?"

He nodded.

"Were you the one that sent me the email inviting me to apply for the ED position?"

"Yeah, the interim manager who dropped by to sign cheques told me to send out a mass email to all the local nonprofits — over 20 of them."

I stared at him in disbelief. "But it was addressed to me personally."

"Yeah, he said try to make them look personal." Trevor ran his fingers deftly over my keyboard. "There you go. Email's all set up. Your computer's a bit of a dinosaur but might be okay for a while."

Feeling much less special to learn I was one of "over 20" people emailed for the job, I sat staring at my computer screen for a while, then found an ancient vacuum cleaner in the hall closet, and busied myself running it over the office floor.

Reflecting on my first day, I'd learned about the organization's history, purged the electronic and physical files, met two helpful colleagues, set up a staff meeting, and vacuumed the office. There was a wee concern about the organization's finances that I would learn more about the following day. I felt a truck rumble by and looked up. The lack of windows conjured up a trapped feeling.

## Meeting the Board of Directors   Unwelcome News

Four days into the job, I had met a few staff and was about to meet the board of directors — six volunteers who were my new bosses. Donald primed me on my duties for board meetings: I needed to make a big pot of coffee, buy milk, fill a large pitcher with water, lay out paper plates and cups, and order two large pizzas for the meeting at 7 p.m. It felt like I'd become a restaurant server.

After discovering we had no brochure, I decided to create one. To promote the organization, I needed something concrete, showing who we were and what we did, to leave in people's hands. I felt good about remedying this deficit and hoped the board would approve.

On the first Monday of October, 2004, at 6.45 p.m., I set up the long imitation-oak table and aligned the mismatched chairs. One of the three overhead fluorescent tubes was malfunctioning and casting an irritating flickering light onto the windowless 12- by 16-foot room, creating a surreal effect — an omen of things to come.

A few minutes prior to the start of the meeting, the board members began to arrive and chat among themselves. They occasionally gave a curious glance in my direction. I would have preferred to introduce myself as they came in but thought better of it. It was their territory.

At 7 p.m., Ada, the president, pulled a gavel from her bag and rapped on the table. "Good evening and welcome, everybody. I'd like to call this meeting to order and start by introducing Rodney Baker, our new executive director."

Usually I went by Rod but opted for Rodney to sound more professional.

"Finally," said the white-haired lady across from me, smiling in my direction.

Others murmured their approval. I gave a brief smile and nodded while trying to gauge the measure of the six strangers looking at me. A couple of them seemed familiar from my job interview, but I couldn't recall their names.

At Ada's prompting, we introduced ourselves. I listed my academic credentials and past work experiences: businessman, counselling instructor, and executive director at a small mental health nonprofit. I left out rag baler, deckhand, and boatbuilder.

The board members were all volunteers from the local community: Ada, the president, had led the hiring committee. She had been a geologist in Romania but retrained as an accountant when she migrated to Canada. Her ex had bipolar disorder, and she was on the board because she believed in helping people with mental illness. White-haired Joan was a retired bookkeeper whose daughter had schizophrenia; she was our treasurer. Dennis was a balding schoolteacher who fiddled with the buttons on his blazer as he waited to introduce himself. Delphi had a flamboyant manner and gave lots of detail about her part-time work as an actress while she attended art college. Grey-haired Bertha was our secretary and taught business courses at college; she tugged at the sleeve of her black pantsuit as she waited for Delphi to finish talking. The last to introduce himself was Peter, a soft-spoken fortyish guy with a glass eye, who was the past president.

After the introductions, I jumped in and explained my plans. "I want to get to know the staff, try to clean up the backlog of reports and work resulting from not having an ED for six months, and meet and greet key people from Fraser Health, our main funder, and United Way who provided us with $27,000 a year."

Nods of agreement circulated the table. To demonstrate my respect for the board members, I asked them to share their opinions regarding areas I should focus on first.

"How do you plan to raise funds for the clients' Christmas party? Have you thought of a location yet?" Delphi asked in a loud voice.

"I didn't realize we were going to have a party. Why do we need to raise funds?"

"Providing presents and Christmas dinner for all our clients costs money, and Fraser Health doesn't pay for parties."

I nodded sagely. *Maybe I should have known that.*

Dennis wondered if we could order a generic cola with the pizza next time. "Some places include it in the price."

"Good idea. I'll check it out."

Bertha recommended that we adopt tighter purchasing procedures with two people's signatures for each item purchased. I thought this would have been the treasurer's concern, not the secretary's. I promised to check into it, but it sounded like unnecessary paperwork.

Peter spoke in a quiet voice. "The AGM is coming up in a month. You need to book a hall, let all the stakeholders know, mail out invitations to our branch members, find a guest speaker, prepare your AGM report, decide what food to supply, write a program to hand out, and provide an agenda for Ada to run the meeting."

"Thanks, Peter. That certainly sounds like a lot to organize. I'll start working on it right away." The heaviness of all these responsibilities was settling on my shoulders. My breathing became more rapid. I was glad there was only one more person to speak.

Ada chimed in with a final response. "You need to find ways of raising money right away."

"Why is that?"

"Two years ago, in 2002, we lost $60,000 in annual funding when the provincial government changed the gaming regulations, and the bingo revenue became unavailable to us. We had money in the bank which allowed us to keep operating, but it's gone now, so we may not be able to pay your salary." She glanced at me, the coffeepot, then back to me.

I was stunned and looked around the table. Six averted faces were caught in the fluorescent flickers. *Was this a joke?*

No one laughed.

No one spoke.

The flickering light tube started to hum in harmonic waves, filling up the stark silence of the room.

"Maybe we should pass the pizzas around," Bertha said, "before they get cold."

I dry-swallowed a couple of times. I had left a job with secure funding, for a longer commute to an office with no windows and an organization that wasn't sure they could pay me. The joy of getting this job whistled out of me like a passing train.

"Why wasn't this mentioned during my job interview?" I asked, regaining my voice and staring at Ada. "You were part of the hiring committee."

"We thought if you knew, you probably wouldn't have taken the job," she replied, meeting my gaze. Her large brown eyes had a twinkle even as she gave this preposterous answer.

I love simple truths. I can understand them. Ada's statement bristled with clarity. I should have walked out of the room right then and there, but my body was frozen in bewilderment at the unexpected news.

The rest of the meeting slid by as though I were watching a movie — one of those avant-garde French films composed of disconnected strands, where you can't figure out what's going on and that ends with no denouement.

Bertha suggested that one of the pizzas be vegetarian for the next meeting. Delphi, the actress, after staring at the brochure for some minutes, caught my eye and started an impassioned discourse about incorrect comma placement. She reminded me that the quarterly newsletter was overdue.

"Who writes the newsletter?"

"You do. Better make sure you get the punctuation right."

Ada passed the pizza around while the board members made suggestions for the upcoming AGM.

"You should get a good speaker, Rodney. More people will come," Joan said, nodding.

"Let's not have Kool-Aid like last time," Dennis said. "It feels cheap."

Faking attention to the meeting, I scrawled a few notes on my pad. "Board's ideas — what needs doing." But my original keen interest in the meeting had been hollowed out by Ada's funding-deficit announcement.

The remaining agenda items ground by in slow motion. Mouths opened and closed without my hearing the words. I startled as Ada rapped the gavel and pronounced the meeting closed. The group stood up and bid one another goodnight. My throat had tightened up. My goodbyes came out as a whisper. Moving with heavy limbs, I started to clear away some of the coffee cups. Dennis waited till we were alone, then let me know that the association owed him a thousand dollars for a funding proposal he'd written but not tendered. He'd missed the deadline but said it could be used for other projects. He needed the money right away to get his car fixed.

"Why did you wait till the meeting was over to tell me about this?"

"The other board members don't know."

"Why is that?"

He gave a wan smile. "I was told it wasn't necessary."

Swallowing my outrage, I promised to get back to him. Delphi and Dennis seemed particularly unhelpful. I wished they weren't on the board. As for Ada, the president, at least she was there for the right reason.

During the 30-kilometre drive home, I was in a state of disbelief as oncoming lights flashed by me on the freeway. I didn't have to stay at this place. I could try to get my previous job back or the teaching job I'd had before that. No wonder Alice had gone on sick leave; she'd witnessed the lifeblood draining out of the organization.

As I walked through the door of my house, Anna said, "Hi. I've saved you some dinner. How did the meeting go?"

The fresh aroma of good food cheered me up. I was a few forkfuls into my meal before I managed to answer. "Some of the board members are nice, others not so helpful." I searched for the right words to tell her the bad news. I ate in silence, hoping the pasta marinara would fill the empty feeling inside. Swallowing the last mouthful, I took a sip of wine and blurted out, "They said there might be some problems paying me."

Her eyes popped wide open. "What? Baker, surely you have it wrong? They've only just hired you." For important conversations, she called me by my last name.

"No, the president told me right to my face. I can't believe it. Hiring me, then telling me they may not be able to pay my wages. I think I'll try and get one of my old jobs back." Like most people, I wanted to be able to buy food and pay the mortgage.

I put my plate in the dishwasher and joined Anna in the TV room. I liked to relax after dinner and turn off by watching a movie or catching up with the news. Far from relaxing, I was aghast to learn from CNN that although Iraq had been invaded on the premise of destroying the weapons of mass destruction, American forces had been unable to find any. Incredibly, a whole country had been bombed back to the stone age on a false premise. After the devastating news of a pointless war, and hearing that my new employer was running out of money, I was happy to leave the day behind and retire to the comfort of my bed.

Arriving at the office the next day, I phoned my previous employer and spoke to the president. "John, how are things?"

"Good, Rodney, good. How are things with you?"

"My new job isn't what I thought it would be. Did you hire anybody to replace me yet?"

"Sorry to hear that. Our new executive director started yesterday. We hired the woman you recommended."

I thanked John and asked him to let me know if she didn't work out. I got a similar response from my previous part-time teaching job at the Counsellor Training Institute. "There are no openings at present."

"Thanks. Keep me posted if something comes up."

I poured myself a coffee, walked outside to the parking lot, and lit a cigarette. I'd quit but kept an emergency pack in the glove compartment. Leaning against my car, I sipped, puffed, and gazed at the distant mountains. Their snowy peaks glistened like white diamonds in the morning sunshine — beautiful and inspiring, unlike my situation. I beat myself up for jumping into the job without checking it out more thoroughly. *What the hell should I do now?*

I gritted my teeth and decided to give it my best shot until the money ran out, then wash my hands of the place and walk away. If I could pull the place out of the dumpster, it might bring me some recognition. If not, at least I would have tried. I'd started a boat repair business and made it work. Maybe I could do the same here.

Stomping out the smoke and tossing the coffee dregs across the parking lot, I took a deep breath of fresh air and strode back into the office.

Now to deal with Dennis: I pulled out the lone copy of our bylaws, thumbed through the 23-page document, and found the Director Protocols:

A Director who has a direct or indirect personal or financial interest in a proposed or existing contract or transaction of the Association shall disclose fully and promptly the nature and extent of his interest to all Directors.

I phoned Dennis and informed him that he wouldn't be receiving $1000 for his proposal, because, by his own admission, the other board members had not been informed, which was against the organization's bylaws. As recourse, I mentioned that he could take it up with the board if he wished.

He complained it was unfair and banged the phone down. Later in the day, I received an email from him letting me know he was resigning his position as a board member and informing me he was considering legal action.

Donald had explained that our Simon Fraser Branch of CMHA was one of 20 branches in British Columbia. I assumed they wouldn't want one of their branches ceasing operations due to lack of funds. It suddenly felt good to be part of the CMHA family. I phoned the head office of CMHA for British Columbia and ask to speak to Bev Gutray, the CEO, but the receptionist said she was unavailable.

"I'm Rod, Rodney Baker, the new executive director at the Simon

Fraser Branch."

"Hi, Rodney. Welcome aboard. How are things working out for you there?"

"Well, that's why I'm phoning. The board of directors just informed me that there won't be enough money to pay my salary." I paused. No response. "I'm thinking we are going to need financial support until I can sort things out." More silence. This time, I waited.

"I see. Thanks for your call, Rodney. I will discuss this with Bev, and someone will get back to you."

Two days later, a seasoned head-office emissary, wearing a black pantsuit and her white hair tied in a bun, walked into my office.

"Rodney, I'm Hilda. Pleased to meet you." She smiled and shook my hand — it was cold. "Welcome to the CMHA family. Now, getting right to the point regarding your request for fiscal support, each branch is on its own financially. There are no subsidies from head office."

Dismayed to have my request for help tossed aside in the first few seconds, I tried to appear nonplussed, held her gaze, and chewed my lip as I thought.

"Wouldn't it be bad news for the CMHA brand if a branch went broke? All our clients would experience a change of workers, and a competing nonprofit would pick up the contracts."

"You're right, it wouldn't be good, Rodney. But your branch operates under a charter agreement with CMHA BC, which has no provision for subsidising failing branches. There are certain protocols you must abide by in order to use the name."

"Like a franchise agreement?"

"We like to think of it as a supportive CMHA family."

"But *not* financially supportive."

"Right. As a matter of fact, your branch owes us $657 in membership arrears."

"Membership arrears?"

She explained that our branch, like all branches, paid to use the nationally recognised CMHA name and logo and that the Simon Fraser Branch hadn't paid a cent for three years.

It was official: I had climbed aboard a sinking ship with no coastguard in sight and nothing to bail with except my wits. Even if I had enough wits, I didn't have a vision of how to keep this nonprofit above water.

Whereas government agencies are started, funded, and run by political will, nonprofits are created by inspired citizens trying to make a positive difference in society and must find funding to keep their vision afloat. The Canadian Mental Health Association was started in 1918 by two men who were shocked by the abysmal treatment of people with mental illness. Eighty-four years later, their idea of helping improve the lives of people with mental illness had spread to 120 branches across Canada.

Funding to support nonprofits comes from donations from sympathetic citizens, well-written grant proposals, contracts to provide services to government agencies, or running their own enterprises. If there is no driving force to organise funding, rudderless nonprofits drift onto the rocks and founder.

While I scratched my head for ideas to raise money, I looked for ways to save money. For some strange reason, we had four phone numbers. I cancelled three; it only saved $125 a month, but it was a start. It appeared the staff had free coffee. There is nothing free in the world. Maybe eliminating this would help the staff realize we were on shaky financial ground and encourage everyone to pull together to preserve our organization. This was a miscalculation on my part; I came to realize the staff members were focused on the clients' well-being, not the fiscal well-being of the organization they worked for.

While saving money at work was one thing on my mind, on a personal level, I was looking for ways to save time on my longer daily commute. On my fifth day at my new location and second route experiment, I found myself in the centre of New Westminster stuck in traffic. I fumed, cussed, became resigned, and laid my arms on the wheel as I watched pedestrians on the sidewalk — the only movement on Columbia Street.

I was adjacent to the Salvation Army thrift store. Remaining stationary through three green lights, I noticed satisfied shoppers with armfuls of paid-for merchandise exiting from the front door. Obviously, there were helpful citizens delivering multiple donations through a back door.

The simplicity of these revolving-money doors grabbed me and lifted me up. I could create a thrift store. Exciting ideas blazed through my head: I could look for good-hearted volunteers with a knowledge of retail sales. Maybe I could get our clients, like Jim, to volunteer — pitch the idea that we needed their help. A new twist in the relationship with our clients — more *reciprocal*. We could increase volunteer positions, not just as receptionists but in new areas: clothes sorter, cashier, shelf stocker, and greeter. The idea flamed upward, unrestricted by facts, spurred on by need. Our current location had a large room with a street entrance that would be perfect. The idea had three important elements: no cost for workers, product, or premises. If I could get the staff enthused, maybe they would encourage our clients to volunteer.

After twenty minutes, the traffic unclogged. I surged forward, inspired by a vision of smiling customers spending money in the brand-new Simon Fraser thrift store.

## Meeting the Staff

A week after having met the board of directors, I sat down with the 12 full-time staff members for our first meeting. I'd brought a dozen donuts to make a good impression. I was excited to meet my fellow workers and wanted to forge a bond so we could start moving forward as a team. I planned to let them all speak first so they felt listened to right from the beginning.

As I settled into my seat at the head of the table, the suspicious faces of the eight women and four men made me feel like an unwanted interloper. They'd been operating without an ED for six months, and now some new guy, hired by the volunteer board of directors, was going to parachute in and tell them what to do. A caretaker manager from a local college had been dropping by once a week to sign cheques but not to run meetings or direct staff.

"Good morning, everybody. Nice to meet you all, most of you for the first time." My big smile was met with impassive, wait-and-see expressions. "Maybe we could go around the room and introduce ourselves. Explain what you do, how long you've worked here, and what motivates you to do this kind of work?"

This get-to-know-you icebreaker was meant to be easy. I wanted to hear from and connect with each team member. After that, I planned to go around the table and ask what they expected of an ED, which would lead into my saying what I expected from them. From my past experience of running groups, I knew that giving each individual a turn to speak worked well — instead of just the gregarious talkers dominating the meeting.

The woman to my left started the ball rolling. She was about 30 and looked sharp in a pink shirt and black bell-bottomed pants. "Hi, I'm Paige, I'm a SIL worker."

"Paige, I haven't heard that term before. Could you explain what it means, please?"

The whole team exchanged shocked looks. The board of directors had hired a new boss who didn't know what programs the organization ran.

"SIL stands for Semi-Independent Living. We support clients with mental illness to live in their own apartments and help them become involved in the community. I've worked here for four years, and it's because I like to help people with mental illness."

"Thanks, Paige." I nodded, smiled, and wrote her name down on the blank sheet of paper so I could remember who she was.

Seated next to Paige, Sandra, an attractive brunette, smiled shyly as she gave a similar story.

As Deirdre, a middle-aged staff member, started to speak, she choked up and started sobbing. "I'm sorry. I'm sorry!" She stood up and left the room in a rush.

"Deidre's been having a tough time lately. Her relationship is going south," Sandra explained.

"We shouldn't be discussing Deidre's private life in public," Paige said.

"If she's not doing well, Rodney needs to know. She shouldn't be seeing clients if she's like this," said a thirtyish woman with pink lipstick and auburn hair. "I'm Robbie by the way," she said, flashing me a smile.

Other women dove in and gave their opinion, or used the disruption to chit-chat. Trevor, Donald, and the two male SIL workers, one around 40 in a denim shirt, the other older, remained silent.

"I'm just gonna see her out to the parking lot," Paige said.

My ideas for a convivial meet and greet had skidded sideways.

"Okay, I'm sorry to see that Deidre is not feeling like sharing today. I'll check in with her later. Let's continue, please." This pulled us back in the right direction, but it wasn't the smooth first meeting I had envisioned.

After the introductions, I asked them what they expected of an executive director.

"Someone who listens to us."

"Someone who's inclusive."

"Someone who's fair."

"We need to know what's going on. Not like Alice who kept everything to herself," Robbie said, sticking her chin out.

"Are you a hands-on type of ED?" asked Paige, who had rejoined us. "Or someone that comes up with ideas and expects everyone else to do the work?"

"Good question. I certainly consider myself a hands-on ED. As far as those with concerns about whether I will keep you informed, respect you, and listen to you, my hope is that we respect and listen to each other and will work together as a team."

"How long have you worked in mental health?" Robbie asked.

"Almost two years at a small nonprofit providing day programs."

"No housing?"

"No. Before that, I taught counselling skills for a year, and prior to that, I was in business."

"What kind of business?" Robbie persisted.

"I had a marine repair company." I noted the baffled looks around the table. "After dealing with boat owners for many years, I became interested in the mental health field."

Only Donald smiled.

"I earned a master's degree in counselling, became certified in psychosocial rehabilitation, and joined this organization hoping we can all work together helping people with mental illness to have better lives." I caught a flicker of relieved looks. "What I expect from everyone here is simply that you give your best efforts to clients, work as a supportive team, and let me know if there are any problems." I paused and looked them all in the eye. "Any questions?"

No one said anything. I took this as acquiescence. So as not to seem too tough at the first meeting, I avoided mentioning the end of free coffee. I didn't want to spook them with bad financial news in case they started looking for other work. Lacking funding was bad enough, but without skilled staff, there would be no organization.

The long spell without leadership had encouraged an autonomous streak. Not good for team unity or uniform service delivery. One staff member had been bringing home baking to her client's apartment twice a week. When the replacement worker didn't bring cookies, the client got upset and complained to her caseworker at Fraser Health, our funder. The caseworker phoned me and asked why our staff member was baking *for* our client instead of baking *with* her.

Remembering board member Delphi's question, I asked the staff how they thought we could raise money for the clients' Christmas party.

"Christmas is a busy time for us with families," said Lisa, a diminutive, raven-haired woman. "We don't have a lot of time for volunteer activities."

"Will we be getting our usual Christmas bonuses?" asked Stephanie, a tall brunette with a self-righteous tone.

I looked toward Trevor, our accountant. His face was impassive, but his eyes connected with mine.

"I need to make sure we have enough money to operate before we pay out any bonuses," I said, nodding. "So, nobody answered me about how to raise money for the Christmas party."

People tapped pens and avoided eye contact.

"I'm new here, so whatever you could come up with would be really helpful," I said with a hopeful smile, which elicited a sea of blank faces.

Undiscouraged, I informed them of my bold new brainwave of starting a thrift store to improve our finances.

"We tried that before. It didn't work," Lisa declared, shaking her head. "Besides, who would run it?"

My money-making brainwave had been blown out of the sky at first dawn. I soldiered on.

"I was thinking of volunteers from the community and some of our clients. I noticed we have volunteers at the front desk." No one picked up on this idea. I decided to wrap up the meeting while my tone was still upbeat.

"Well, great to meet you all. I'm looking forward to working together. Let's start off by meeting once a week — same day, same time."

"We haven't had a meeting for eight months and have been doing just fine," Robbie said.

"We'll try meeting weekly to start. See how it works out," I said with a wrap-up smile.

As the staff filed out, I heard some petulant comments about my decision for once-a-week staff meetings being a waste of time. On the positive side, there were no donuts left. I'd bring more next week.

As the organization was running out of money, I wondered if we should be fundraising for a party. On the other hand, I didn't want to make big changes and appear like a control freak or scare them about the lack of funding over which they had no control. Maybe as just a token of the funding shortage, I would mention at the next meeting that the free coffee would now be 50 cents a cup.

## Stuck on the Monitor

Days flew by as I tried to understand the daily complexities of everything the Simon Fraser Branch did, while trying to cut costs and provide hopeful leadership.

I grabbed ten minutes to christen a new folder on my now spacious monitor. Seeing the words written on the screen gave legs to my hopes.

Thrift Store – stuff to do

1) Get staff support for the thrift store
2) Dump the junk in the far room, make space for store
3) Paint the interior white
4) Look for a safe and store shelving on Craigslist
5) Get clothing racks
6) Find or build shelves

I was excited as the words flew onto the list. This first step of concrete action made the store seem possible! I planned to bring my tools from home and start building the shelves in between answering the phone, learning about my job, and attending meetings.

Number seven remained blank. I struggled to find the right words because I had no clue how to do it. Building the store was easy, but how I would ensure the constant flow of three essential elements — donations, volunteers, and customers — remained unknown.

*Write something!*

7) Get stuff to sell, volunteers to sell it, and customers to buy it.

Seeing it written was reassuring — like it could happen.

"'Build it, and they will come,'" I muttered under my breath. Fitting that the saying came from the movie *Field of Dreams*.

My decision to start a thrift store to help offset our funding deficit was presented to the board as a *fait accompli*. There was silence after this announcement. They probably realized the fiscal predicament they had put me in and didn't warrant a debate.

I was anxious to get started on the store but soon discovered my life as executive director was packed with meetings: I met bimonthly with Fraser Health to discuss our youth housing program, monthly with the New Westminster Homelessness Coalition and our board of directors, and weekly with our staff. Every four months, I attended a two-day meeting with the 19 other CMHA branches in BC. Less onerous was my attendance at the annual United Way meeting.

With all that talking, as well as my daily duties, it was tough to find time to create the store. Some people seemed to prefer talking to action.

My announcement at the following staff meeting that, as we were heading for an annual loss, coffee would now be 50 cents a cup brought scalding howls of protest.

"We've always had free coffee," complained Stephanie, of the Christmas bonus enquiry, with a look of genuine anguish.

"We need to watch our costs. Our clients don't get free coffee, and most of them don't work. You guys get a salary, so fifty cents a cup is reasonable." I shrugged my shoulder and raised my hands. "It costs six times that at Starbucks. I see four of you with a Starbucks cup as we sit here." It was a logical but unpopular argument. The anti-pay-for-coffee muttering continued.

"Rodney's right," said Kevin, the younger male SIL worker. He rarely spoke, and his complexion went a deep red. "If our organization's short of money, it seems stupid to spend it on free coffee. We workers shouldn't need charity."

This silenced the free-coffee supporters but drew angry looks.

Kevin had made a rare connection between the ability to pay staff wages and the financial health of the organization.

"So, as I mentioned last week, I'm gonna try and make money by opening a thrift store. Maybe you could start asking your clients about volunteering."

The soft sipping of Starbucks or last free office coffee was the only response.

The clients we received in our transition houses from Riverview [Psychiatric] Hospital had been looked after medically but not been given the opportunity to make personal choices for their everyday lives. Our work with clients, including the 90 living in their own apartments, was to form trusting relationships with them and encourage them to interact with their community. *Socialization* was the broad term used in our contract with Fraser Health, which meant helping clients to become involved in volunteering, working, attending social groups, church — any positive activity with other people. Nobody's mental health ever improved sitting alone in a room taking medication. I figured working in the thrift store, interacting with volunteers and customers, could form a valuable part of that socialization.

"What *exactly* would our clients be doing?" asked Lisa, who, as shop steward, always questioned possible changes.

"Sorting the donations and stocking the shelves." I'd never run a thrift store, but it sounded reasonable.

"There aren't any donations or shelves. What kind of sorting will they be doing?"

"I'll be putting up some shelves soon. Volunteers will sort out the good stuff from the bad and arrange...like all the teddy bears together and all the electric razors together. You know, stuff like that."

"Putting the teddy bears next to razors?" Lisa said. Titters rippled around the room. "But seriously, Rodney, we are supposed to help our clients, not them help us."

"Good point, Lisa. But I think we *would* be helping them. It's hard to feel valuable if you are always getting help and never giving it. I'm sure you go home at night happy you've made a positive difference in someone's life."

She narrowed her eyes and pursed her lips but said nothing.

"Will they get paid?" asked Robbie, a single mom, always on the side of the less fortunate. "We don't want our clients being used for slave labour."

"They should qualify for the government program that pays people with a mental health diagnosis $100 for 10 hours of volunteering a month," Paige piped up.

I wasn't aware of this program. What great news. This muted further argument. Poverty was a big challenge for our clients, along with lack of self-esteem and loneliness. My hope was that the thrift store could help improve all three.

Two days after starting on the job, I had received Trevor's financial report by email. It seemed our clients weren't the only ones for whom poverty was a challenge. We were heading for a $26,000 deficit at the end of the funding cycle in May, which meant we had six months before we started slipping into debt. I needed to get that thrift store off the monitor and into action.

## The AGM   The Fundraiser   Christmas Dinner

After two weeks, I'd found my way around the office, met all the staff, and decided it was time to visit all of our physical locations. Donald took me on a tour. We stopped by the two five-bedroom transition houses we ran in New Westminster, called Bluebird and Barnabas House. They looked like any other house in the neighbourhood — two storey, cedar siding with front and backyards. They provided our clients with a secure living space in the community. Each house had a manager who supported the clients to learn life skills: cooking, cleaning, gardening, engaging in social activities, and making autonomous decisions about their lives.

The other transition house we ran was in Maple Ridge, 30 kilometres from our office. It was called St. John's, after the church that we rented the house from. As with our homes in New Westminster, our clients were encouraged to learn daily life skills so they could transition to living in their own apartments. Some people made the transition; others found the challenge of managing on their own too daunting. For instance, at St. John's House, Dan, in his late 60s, was cooking dinner one evening, left the stove on, and burnt the potatoes black. Another resident called the fire department because he thought the house was on fire. There were no staff after 5 p.m., so we scheduled a second resident to watch Dan when it was his turn to cook.

A few clients had substance or alcohol problems. If they relapsed more than once, they were asked to leave. Our staff didn't have the training to deal with clients who had mental illness and addiction challenges.

Donald introduced me to Barney, a guy in his late 50s, who was the Community Residential Program Coordinator for Fraser Health in Maple Ridge. He smiled and shook my hand with enthusiasm. "Great to meet you, Rodney. Let me say, first off, that our top priority here is the clients' well-being."

"That's my focus too. I hope we can meet all your expectations for St. John's House."

He winked, stuck his hand into the pocket of his green Harris Tweed jacket, and handed me his business card. "Well, that would be an improvement on the last ED, Rodney. Phone me if you have any concerns."

I was unused to such candour but appreciated it. "Thanks, I'm sure we can figure out any problems." I issued smooth assurances without knowing what kind of problems might come up.

"I like your attitude," he said with a smile. "Here's something for you to think about —opening a satellite house." With an excited glint in his eye, he explained he'd got the idea from a project he'd recently seen in Victoria.

"You open another house nearby the current one and have the same house manager run both houses. That way, Fraser Health gets more bang for our buck, and the clients learn a little more independence because the worker is there only half the time."

I could hear the sound of new dollars clinking into the kitty. Fraser Health paid us 10 percent of any programs for administration. "Sounds great. I guess if we're serving nine clients instead of four, you would be giving us more funding?"

"Yes, probably another $8-10,000 a year, plus the rent for the house of course."

I was excited at the possibility of increased funding. Somehow, I was going to make the satellite house happen. We looked each other in the eye and had a long, firm handshake that said more than our conversation.

Over time, Barney became someone I could trust, an ally in a world where ego or politics sometimes got in the way of serving clients. Barney was a grassroots guy. If a client needed to relocate, he showed up with his pickup truck and a team of helpers from his office to assist with the move.

With only a week to go, organizing the AGM was the next challenge. By hunting down advice from staff, gathering information from previous reports, and a little guesswork, I concocted a report for the whole year, in spite of only having been there a month. The AGM was the first public test of my executive directorship. Buoyed by creative guesswork mixed with doses of apprehension, my emotions ebbed and flowed as we neared the big day. I rented the slightly musty, high-ceilinged Ukrainian church hall, arranged for free coffee, and convinced Bev Gutray, CEO of Canadian Mental Health Association in BC, to speak about mental health issues. I phoned the few Fraser Health staff I'd met and invited them.

The big colour printer in my office ran hot as I printed off meeting programs, new brochures, AGM reports, and membership cards for sale at the door: $20 for staff, board members, and the public; $5 for unwaged people. Only paid-up members could vote. Staff had been encouraged to get their clients out to the meeting.

The AGM was the official way of reporting on our activities and progress throughout the year. The number of people attending reflected how well the Simon Fraser Branch was valued by the community: The more folks who showed up, the more relevant we felt. In order to boost attendance, food was usually served at these events. Knowing this was expected, I began to feel queasy about not providing snacks.

Fifteen minutes before the meeting started, the few people milling around the hall made a forlorn gathering. Just as we began, I breathed a sigh of relief as another twenty or so people filtered in.

*Thank God!*

Most were clients and a few other folks curious to see whom the board of directors had hired to be the new executive director. Even with the increased swell of attendees, our meeting was still dwarfed by the cavernous hall.

Ada, our president, welcomed everyone and proceeded with the normal, mundane business of an AGM. Sounding more enthused, she launched into an upbeat introduction of me. "I'm pleased to introduce Rodney Baker, our new executive director. He has a master's degree in counselling and has worked in both business and nonprofit sectors."

This news produced curious looks and scattered applause, which echoed around the giant building like rain pattering on glass. Most EDs working in mental health were women who had spent their careers in the field.

I stood up, welcomed the attendees to the AGM, and thanked them for coming.

"I plan to make this CMHA branch grow and prosper by giving excellent service to clients and hope we can all work together to make that happen." I noticed people's attention straying toward the kitchen where mouth-watering aromas were wafting across the air toward our small group. The church people were making perogies for their own event the following day.

"Please help yourself to coffee. Unfortunately, due to financial challenges, we were only able to arrange for the smell of food."

Donald laughed out loud, but most people just looked puzzled or disappointed. I continued in an upbeat voice. "However, we'll soon be starting a thrift store to help shore up our finances and will need volunteers to work in the store. Please come and see me after if you are interested in helping." I beamed at my audience, trying to reach into their hearts, but instead of reciprocal enthusiasm, my announcement was received by blank stares. Maybe I should have told them there was no food after announcing plans for a thrift store.

Our treasurer read the budget report for the year, which mentioned a small loss of $800.

"Are there any questions?" Ada asked.

There was no requirement to forecast the current year's finances, so the organization slipped unchallenged toward a $26,000 deficit. The savoury aromas from the kitchen were distracting.

To wrap up the evening, our guest speaker, Bev Gutray, talked about the devastating effect stigma had on the lives of people living with mental illness. "We need to change our language to put the person first: a person with schizophrenia rather than a schizophrenic." She stressed that none of us want to be defined by our illnesses. "It's more important that we are human beings than that we are sick."

We all nodded and agreed. She was preaching to the converted but got so enthused that she went 10 minutes over her allotted time. People shifted in their seats and looked toward the door. As Bev wrapped up, I thanked her and asked for a motion to close the 2004 AGM. Five previously dormant hands shot up, and the meeting was adjourned.

I smiled, mingled, thanked everyone for coming, and hoped some of them would volunteer to help in the store. None did.

Six weeks later, we held the Christmas dinner fundraiser at the Moonraker, a local pub. As usual, the fundraising event was discussed in depth at our weekly staff meetings. Should we include beer or a glass of wine with the pizza? One faction was dead set against the ticket including alcohol. They claimed as a mental health organization, we shouldn't be promoting the consumption of alcoholic beverages.

"Lots of our clients will attend, and booze adversely affects psychiatric medication," Robbie argued.

Others thought we were being paternalistic toward clients by deciding what was best for them. We compromised, and the ticket read "Good for a small pizza and a beverage," which allowed people to choose a soft drink, beer, or wine.

Friends, board members, and relatives were encouraged to attend. It was a hard sell getting people to come and spend money around Christmas time. To maximize the evening's economic success, we arranged a 50/50 draw and money-raising games that some of the regular pub patrons good-heartedly took part in. Attendance was boosted by Jill, an ally I'd made at the Homelessness Coalition meetings. She was a tall, straight-talking redhead who managed multiple programs at Fraserside, a large local nonprofit agency. I confided in Jill my fears about low attendance, and the sweet lady brought six people to the event! Despite the pizza arriving way after we'd drunk our beer, everything else went fine, and we raised $318, close to the $350 we figured it would cost to provide Christmas dinner for our 100 clients. There were no reports of alcohol adversely affecting any clients, although some of the staff appeared bleary-eyed the next morning.

With funding in place, I decided to host the clients' Christmas dinner at the Ukrainian church. It was big, cheap, and had cooking facilities. Our weekly staff meetings became dedicated to discussing, or sometimes vigorously debating, how much food to buy, who would buy it, cook it, serve it, and clean up afterwards. Never having been in charge of cooking dinner for 100 people before, I listened a lot and volunteered to cook a turkey at home. I was out of my depth in such an unfamiliar venture. Maybe Anna would help.

One evening, I casually mentioned, "We're cooking dinner for 100 clients in a couple of weeks." She was clicking on the remote, looking for a show. "Did you ever cook Christmas dinner for a lot of people before?"

"Huh?" She glanced toward me.

"We're cooking Christmas dinner for 100 people in a couple of weeks. I was wondering if you felt like giving us a hand?"

She looked at me with big eyes as though I were crazy. "Why are you cooking dinner for 100 people?"

"I told you. It's the clients' Christmas party."

"What clients?"

"The people with mental illness that use our services. I wondered if you wanted to help?"

"I don't think so."

"Why not? You're a great cook."

"I've never been around people with mental illness. I wouldn't know what to say," she said, shaking her head.

"You wouldn't have to say anything. Just help in the kitchen."

"Who else will be there?"

"The staff will be helping. It'll be fun. One of them speaks Italian. You're a great cook. I'd love to have you there, especially as I don't know what I'm doing." Gradually, I won her over.

The big day arrived, and we pulled into the Ukrainian church parking lot at 8 a.m., our vehicles loaded with turkeys and vegetables. We hauled boxes and bags of food through the rain that seemed to accompany any big Vancouver winter event, and assembled under the front porch. Who had the key to get in? This small detail had been overlooked. Robbie remembered where the warden lived and drove off on a mission to retrieve the key.

"Have we forgotten anything else?" I asked as we stood stomping our feet to keep warm.

"Pepper!" Agnes said.

Anna drove off to buy pepper. Robbie returned, unlocked the door, and we surged into the kitchen, a little late, a little panicked.

This time, *we* would be making the delicious smells in the kitchen. Everything except the turkeys was prepared fresh in the kitchen for dinner at noon. It was really lunch, but Christmas dinner sounded more traditional.

Of the seven turkeys, three were cooked at our transition houses while three staff members and I each cooked one at home. Thirteen of us working together in the kitchen was a chaotic yet bonding experience as we switched from being mental health workers to chefs cooking for a hungry crowd.

Robbie took care of making three gallons of gravy. "The gravy's mine. Nobody lay a finger on it."

Paige made a giant pot of stuffing, stirring vigorously as she repeated, "Hubble bubble, toil and trouble."

The three house managers prepared two giant pots of peas and carrots.

Rick, Kevin, Donald, and Trevor were a four-man team peeling 150 potatoes. "Where's the big pot I saw?" Rick yelled.

"Robbie stole it for her gravy," Kevin said.

After the stuffing was made, Paige wore a Santa hat, sang Jingle Bells, and floated round assisting wherever needed. I carved the seven turkeys to ensure they were completely cooked and avoid any salmonella stomach drama. One bird had suspect red tinges on the flesh, so I stuck it in the microwave for an additional 20 minutes. I found a bag of neck and giblets in another but, upon sampling the meat, found it tasted okay. Anna supervised my supervising, while tasting the gravy, and lined up serving dishes.

As we prepared the meal, we could hear the hum of people arriving and sitting at the 12 tables we had set up.

Noon approached, and we ferried all the food to warmers on the serving tables in the hall. Paige announced to everyone sitting patiently at the tables that dinner was served. A long line of hungry people carrying plates surged toward us. I was on potato duty. Anna stood beside me ladling out the gravy. Many wanted individual service:

"No potatoes. I'm diabetic. Can I have more peas instead?"

"Will there be seconds?"

"Can I take some back for Bob? He couldn't make it."

"A bit more turkey please."

"Thanks. No peas. This looks great."

Someone brought a boom box, and as we served the long line of smiling people, the sonorous strains of "Silent Night" wafted through the hall. The familiar tune made me look up from serving. This was Christmas for these folks. Everybody was happy, laughing, and sitting down to eat. A wave of cool prickles washed over my skin. It didn't show because of the steam from the food warmers. I wiped my eyes. No one noticed.

As the line of hungry folks finally petered out, we served ourselves and sat down to enjoy our meal with our guests. I found it hard to relax and eat after the frenzied activity in the kitchen. I chatted with people at my table and picked at my food while scanning around the hall. We had done it! Over a hundred people were eating, chatting, and enjoying a festive meal.

To finish off, there was self-serve dessert: Jello, cookies, and coffee.

We had been blessed with 25 presents gifted to us by Dawn Black, a local politician. After people finished eating, I announced that anyone with a green masking tape "X" stuck under their chairs qualified for a surprise. Everybody immediately stood up and flipped their chairs over. Whoops of joy came from happy "X" owners. Paige pranced into the room dressed as Santa to a big applause. I think she enjoyed dressing up and handing out the presents as much as the happy recipients.

To round off the meal and gifts, schoolteacher Marcia, a helpful new board member, had arranged for kids from her class to sing carols. We all sat entranced as young children raised their beautiful high voices to sing "Away in a Manger," "The First Noel," "Silent Night," and all the timeless Christmas carols. It transported me back to my nine-year-old self singing the same songs in the school choir. A warm flush ran through my body. I took a deep breath. *Why so emotional?*

Once the carols were over, we doled out Styrofoam containers of leftovers, and people made for the door. The hall emptied, and we trooped into the kitchen and started doing the dishes.

"Whoopee," Paige yelled, "We did it! Three cheers for us." She hip-hipped, and we hoorayed. We filled the dishwasher and did the rest of the plates by forming a chain of washers, dryers, and stackers. We sang carols as we worked. Nothing had gone wrong, and all our clients had enjoyed a traditional Christmas meal. I gave Anna a hug as we finished and bid goodbye to our fellow chefs.

The last big event of the year was leaving us with good memories and tired bodies. I was happy and relieved. With one company Christmas under my belt, next year would be less worry.

With the three big events wrapped up, I could finally focus on finding a residence to fulfill Barney's satellite house idea and my pet project, the thrift store, but not both at once. Fraser Health funding to run the new house was more certain than my iffy shop.

## Launching the Satellite House

I kept an eye on Craigslist for houses to rent in Maple Ridge, visited a few, and after three weeks searching found one that appeared suitable. I put some money into the owner's hand to hold it for a week and explained I needed approval from Fraser Health. He seemed hesitant but was more assured when I pointed out that regular government rent money was more certain than dealing with private renters.

It had been six weeks since Barney floated his idea of another house. I phoned to tell him the good news. "Barney, I've put a deposit on the rental of a five-bedroom house, just down the road from St. John's. You want to meet me there and check it out?"

"What? Are you kidding me, Rodney?"

"No, Barney, I'm not kidding. Can you see it today or tomorrow?"

"Well, you certainly moved fast on that. I'll meet you tomorrow. This is terrific."

We met at the address on River Road. The house had a pink exterior with three bedrooms upstairs and two downstairs. The front yard had a lawn and a driveway leading to a garage. Behind the house was a veggie garden and a picket fence.

"It's perfect, Rodney, and we're in luck. Riverview Hospital is downsizing. I can probably get five beds, five armoires, and a coffee table for free. I'll put a hold on them." He suggested Donald and I could pick up the rest of the stuff at Ikea and send him the bill. "This is exciting, Rodney. I can't believe it's happening so fast."

Trusting Barney's promise but asking him to send an email to confirm our agreement, I secured a two-year lease with the house owner. A week later, Donald and I hired a large Budget rent-a-truck and backed it into the loading dock at the giant, brick-built psychiatric hospital. The large armoires were super heavy and seemed to have absorbed the weighty atmosphere of Riverview. After loading each one onto the dolly, Donald pushed and I pulled it up the ramp onto the truck. After loading five of them, our muscles were aching. The beds were light and easy by comparison.

The next stop was Ikea. We each grabbed a large cart and rolled around the giant furniture store, loading up on bedding, pillows, night tables, plates, cutlery, and anything else that jumped out at us as we strolled through acres of housewares. We were not homemakers, just two guys guessing what five people living in an unfurnished house might need. After trying to instill a culture of austerity in the office, it felt strange to be on a shopping spree filling up our buggies with new housewares. I would pay with my own credit card. I had Barney's word that Fraser Health would pay.

"Should we get white sheets and pillowcases, or yellow?" Donald asked.

"I dunno." I chuckled. "You're the housing manager. You decide."

Each new section we passed had things we hadn't thought of.

"Hey, maybe we should get bedside lamps," I suggested. "They might want to read at night."

"Yeah, you're right — maybe white to match the sheets? But how can we fit five in the cart?"

"I can push this cart and pull one behind with the lamps in. Listen, we've gotta get out of here. We're getting too much stuff. Barney will have a fit paying for all this," I said, laughing and waving my hand toward the overfull shopping carts.

I was getting overwhelmed from strolling through the endless shopping aisles and headed for the checkout, pulling and pushing full carts with Donald following in case anything fell off.

*Moving Furniture into Riverside House*

We loaded the goods from Ikea into the truck and at around 2 p.m. arrived at the house to find Erin, our house manager, waiting for us. Not only was she excellent with clients, but she was young and fit — a big help for the moving project. Her eyes bugged out when she saw the loaded truck, but being shy, she said nothing. The five beds were easy. We unloaded all the Ikea goods into the house and left the armoire monstrosities till last. They were made of inch-thick particleboard. As we were manoeuvring the last one up the carpeted stairs, Donald and Erin pushing from the bottom, and me dragging from the top, we became exhausted, got the giggles, and the whole thing started to slide back down. We dug in and caught our breath. With one last effort, we crested the stairs and shuffled the final armoire into a bedroom. I went home bone-tired at the end of *that* day.

I hoped Barney would soon find five clients to fill up the new bedrooms and start funnelling the extra admin money our way. There were some mutterings at staff meetings about running two houses not being in the job description. Apart from the extra funding the second house provided, another benefit could be that the residents of both houses could socialize — maybe all have a dinner together once a month and get together on festive occasions like Christmas. It was all an experiment. I kept my fingers crossed that we got paid for our Ikea shopping and that Fraser Health found residents for the house.

A month later, Barney had filled up the house with four men and a woman. Erin seemed to be managing the two houses, and the residents from both houses agreed to have a Christmas meal together the following year. The new house had worked out well, except Trevor had a minor complaint. "We can't keep calling it 'the new house.' It should have a name when I refer to it in the books. The other houses all have names." He was right. I phoned Erin and suggested she ask the residents of "the new house" on River Road what they would like it to be called. A week later, after much discussion at the morning meetings, a consensus had been reached. I hoped it would be "The Pink House" to match its funky colour, but they chose "Riverside."

It had been three months from meeting Barney to finding the house, renting it, setting it up as a five-bedroom house, and filling it with clients. This generated a new revenue stream of an extra $10,000 a year for administration. A big shot in the arm for our sagging finances. Finally, I could get on with creating the thrift store.

## Shaping the Store

The Thrift Store to-do list popped up daily on my monitor but had languished as mere words. The everyday work of addressing staffing issues, issuing reports, union concerns, general safety challenges, transition house maintenance, client challenges, fiscal deficits, and attending multiple meetings was punctuated by large annual events like the AGM, fundraisers, and the clients' Christmas dinner.

The untouched list had mocked me, made me feel incompetent. But with no more interruptions, I was excited to finally start on my store.

Kevin helped me load up my utility trailer with broken furniture and other junk from the room we planned to use and haul it to the dump. The intended space was in the corner of our building with sidewalk out front and windows looking onto the street. The room measured 25 by 14 feet. One door opened onto the street and another into our offices.

I brought white coveralls and slipped back and forth between my office duties and painting the store. Each time the phone rang, I slipped the roller into a plastic bag so the paint wouldn't dry. After three days of intermittent painting, I stood back and admired a sparkling-fresh, white room, ready to be filled with donated goods, after I had found shelves to put them on.

Three weeks of daily Craigslist scanning resulted in a prize: a sturdy set of beige steel shelving — twenty-five shelves four feet long and twenty inches wide, which hooked onto metal uprights. I picked them up in my trailer, carried two at a time down from the parking lot into the room, and assembled them along one wall. It took a whole Saturday and was tricky working alone, but the transformation was exciting: Five rows of professional-looking shelving ran the whole length of the right wall as you entered from the street. It was starting to look like a real store!

I posted a notice on the outside window:

### Thrift Store Opening 10 a.m. March 5th 2005

Committing to a date provided the motivation to keep progressing down the list. I noticed the occasional passerby peeking through the window. Maybe there would be a crowd outside on the first day, or maybe no one would come.

As opening day crept closer, it was time to work another Saturday. We needed something for clothes to hang on. One sleepless night, worrying about how to display the clothes, I dreamed up a cheap clothing rack. The next day, I bought 50 feet of 1¼ inch black iron pipe, rented a pipe threader, and made three large 40-inch-high triangles to support the 20-foot-long pipe to hang clothing on running down the middle of the room. For $50 worth of pipe, the finished rack would hold 200 clothing hangers — great value for the money. It was slightly rusty and rustic. I ran an oiled rag over it, and the rust disappeared. I hoped it would appear less rustic when garnished with clothing.

As the room began to look like a store, it attracted more attention at our weekly staff meetings.

"Why is it opening on March 5?" Robbie asked.

"I just figured that fixing a date would help me make it happen."

"Do you have anything to sell yet?" Lisa asked.

"No, but I'm going to start looking today, maybe on Craigslist. If you guys have donations, please drop them off in the store."

"Are there any volunteers yet?" Paige asked.

"No, not yet. I thought you guys could interest some of your clients." I felt like a broken record, repeating the same lyrics. I hoped the lack of volunteers to run the store would garner the staff's support, but it also might appear like a disorganised venture they would rather ignore.

"Will we get first pick of the donations?" Stephanie asked.

Her question made me bristle. "What do you mean, first pick?"

"Well, if our clients need something. The donations *are* to CMHA, and we are here for our clients."

I wasn't sure we'd have enough donations and didn't want staff wandering around the store deciding what their clients would like. The idea was to make money.

"Is there a changing room to try on clothes?" Stephanie continued.

"No, it's a bare-bones shop."

The eight female staff exchanged sceptical looks. Paige took the role of enlightening me. "Rodney, most of the donations are going to be women's clothing."

"How do you know that?" More flashing eyes. I wasn't sure if they signalled sympathy or incredulity.

"Women like buying new clothes, so they have to get rid of their old ones," Robbie explained.

"Because their husbands don't provide enough closets," Lisa chimed in, giggling.

Paige explained, slowly as though dealing with a child, that if women couldn't try on the clothes to see how they looked, they wouldn't buy them.

Affirmative nods flew round the table, all focused in my direction.

"With a mirror," Lisa added.

I decided to make a simple changing room with a shower rail and curtain.

"I'm not sure I like the idea of us running a business," Stephanie said. "We're a nonprofit. Are we allowed to make money?"

"Well, making money is the point, Steph. We are heading for a deficit. If we don't have money, we can't pay anyone's wages." She pouted and stared at me, appearing not to like facts disturbing her reality.

Two weeks prior to opening day, I hauled my trailer to work and started picking up donations from people who had responded to my Craigslist ad:

New thrift store opening for mental health charity. Donations wanted.

I was surprised at some of the awful things people donated: large old plastic toys, sun-faded from many years in the backyard; broken tricycles; ancient wooden skis; and leather ski boots. I smiled, said thanks, and loaded the junk into my trailer with the good stuff. I hadn't figured out how to say no yet. It soon dawned on me that it was easier for people to donate junk than pay to get it hauled away. I learned to be more cautious in my questions to potential donors before arriving at their houses.

By the end of February, I'd made a changing room with a shower curtain and started to fill the shelves with donated goods. A few packages were dropped off outside the thrift store door. Some were washed clothes, folded and carefully wrapped; others were threadbare garments that nobody in their right mind would buy. I decided to rent an industrial garbage container for all the unsellable items. Bin rentals cost 45 dollars a month, a cost I hadn't figured on. I hoped other unplanned-for costs wouldn't jeopardize any profits.

## The Un-grand Opening

As March 5 grew close, advice-givers suggested I have a grand opening with pizza, coffee, and music.

"You should put ads in newspapers, post flyers around town, provide free food, and get a local celebrity on-site to attract customers," Paige said.

"Get the press in to take pictures of the opening," Robbie suggested.

I smiled and thanked people for their ideas. I didn't want a lot of hoopla on opening day. For one thing, hoopla meant organizing. I already felt depleted from my daily work *and* setting up the retail space. As I'd been the sole promoter, builder, and stocker of the thrift store, inviting a lot of strangers to celebrate the launch of an idea built on the shaky foundations of hope, need, and guesswork seemed too risky. I wanted the store to slip quietly into being, except for the sound of money clinking or, better still, fluttering into the cash box.

To keep it simple and save labour, I decided all the clothing would have fixed prices and installed two handwritten signs at either end of the clothing rack:

**Coats, $4; Jackets, $4; Pants, $3; Shirts & Blouses, $2.50; Hats, Socks, & Underwear $1.**

I'd price the other items by guesswork as we went along.

The newly installed metal shelves groaned under the weight of donated gems: books, toys, tools, china knick-knacks, jewellery, cutlery, paintings, vases, plastic flowers, small appliances, a wooden stepladder, Christmas decorations — a grand potpourri waiting to be snapped up by keen shoppers.

At 9:30 a.m., March 5, half an hour before the store was set to open, I carried the calculator from my office to my new workstation in the thrift store: a donated mahogany desk, with veneer peeling off the legs, that I'd commandeered into service and positioned by the front door. This allowed me to greet people as they came in, charge them for the goods on their way out, and watch for shoplifters.

Responding to my request, the staff had brought in lots of plastic grocery bags which were stuffed into the top left-hand drawer of my sales desk. I'd printed off fifty new CMHA brochures to slip in the bag with each purchase. The thrift store would be our first interface with the surrounding community. Our work wasn't visible to the public because it took place mostly behind closed doors. For the first time, members of the surrounding community could see pictures of our transition houses and read about the services we provided in the brochure. Next year, I planned to print invitations to our AGM and distribute them to customers three weeks ahead of the event. I was excited about the store's three-prong prospects of making money, creating a venue where our clients could have meaningful work, and letting the public know about the services we provided.

At 9:45, I was thrilled to see a lineup of people had gathered outside. The big moment had arrived. I drew back the window blinds and turned on the lights. New white paint made the interior sparkle, but the store had a musty relics-of-basement odour. To remedy this, I plugged in two lavender-scented electric deodorisers at either end of the store. Instead of masking the smell, they merely added a sickly-sweet floral odour to the already nauseous mix, which made me dry heave. I grabbed a donated fan from the shelf, plugged it in, and went to open the outside door to let in some fresh air. The first person in line, an older woman wearing a pink beret and red shoes, tried to push her way in.

"Good morning, madam. Thanks for coming. We're not open for another fifteen minutes." I tried to sound firm.

"Can't you let us in? It's freezing out here," she said loudly.

She was right; I felt a cold wind whip across my face through the part-open door.

A customer behind her yelled, "Hey, there's a fire in your store."

I pushed the door closed and looked behind me. The electrical cord of the fan was burning. I dashed back inside and yanked the cable out of the wall socket. Hot melted plastic stuck to my hands. I grabbed a pair of underpants off the shelf and tried to wipe off the stinging plastic. More melted goo stuck to my shoes as I stamped on globs of burning plastic. Holy shit! After all my hours of careful preparation, the store almost burned down on opening day.

Turning back, I saw the line of customers surging through the unlocked door. The acrid blue smoke from the burned electrical cable blended with the sickly lavender and old-basement odours to form a noxious melange. A few customers made choking sounds. The flickering fluorescent lights gave the smoky, coughing-customer scene a jerky, 1930s movie look.

To relieve the customers' distress, I raced to the front door, swung it back and forth to waft fresh air into the store, and left it wedged open. Frigid air was sucked into the store, taking the temperature to a new low but doing little to dissipate the stagnant blue fumes. I leaned against the clothing rack and picked bits of congealed plastic off my shoes. Thankfully, there were no members of the press or local dignitaries to witness this debacle.

"I have asthma," an older lady wheezed. "I can't breathe."

I grabbed her arm, whisked her into my office, and sat her down. "Hang on, madam, I'll get you a glass of water." I grabbed Robbie in the hallway. "There's an old lady in my office coughing. Can you give her some water? Make sure she's okay? Got to get back to the store." Robbie looked at me wide-eyed but did my bidding.

Pulling a serving tray off the shelf, I stood by the door and started fanning the smoke toward the street.

Paige walked into the store and grimaced. "Rodney, what is that awful stink?"

"A fan caught fire."

"It smells like a whore's armpit."

"A smoking hot armpit?"

Wide-eyed, she scanned all the coughing customers in the flickering blue haze, then looked back at me. Her face crinkled. Her laughter was infectious, and I allowed myself a chuckle.

"Can I get some service please? If you can stop chatting with that young woman, I'd like to buy these items." It was Pink Beret. She had an armful of clothes and was standing by the front desk, looking miffed. I walked over, sat down, and turned the calculator on, nervous about serving my first-ever customer.

"How much for this shirt?"

"They're all $2.50, madam, like the sign says."

"But this one has a button missing."

I looked her in the eye and smiled. "You are right, but it's still $2.50." If customers learned that prices were negotiable, it would establish an annoying norm.

She stared at me. I raised my eyebrows and met her gaze. Neither of us blinked.

"I'll probably be coming here quite a bit. I live close by."

"Good to know," I said, giving my best smile. As she was first in line, I figured she was a regular customer at thrift stores. "We'll be happy to have your support. We also accept donations if you have anything you don't need." Better to appear upbeat than defensive.

"Well, I might consider coming again if you give me a deal on this shirt and get rid of this awful smell."

"Okay, with this particular item, the deal is you get 15 buttons for $2.50, a great bargain, plus we throw in a free shirt. And by your next visit, you have my personal assurance the smell will be gone." I raised my eyebrows, gave her another smile, and started clicking on the calculator. I didn't want to be railroaded by my first-ever customer. Her lips twitched to almost a smile.

"That will be thirty-three dollars and fifty cents, madam."

She took her time counting out the money while fixing me with a penetrating stare to see if there was a possibility of negotiation, saw there wasn't, and paid in full.

"Thanks for coming in today. My name is Rodney. Hope to see you again." I popped the bill and a brochure into her bag, smiled, and turned to the next customer.

After two hours of customer service, my energy flagged. The constant chit-chat, confirming prices, smiling, tap-tapping the adding machine, and explaining why the store smelled funny was tiring. During a small break between customers, I nipped outside and added a closing time to my makeshift sign, which now read,

**Thrift Store - Open 10 a.m. to 2 p.m. Weekdays.**

Paige came to visit me again at noon. A big smile spread across her face. "Ooh, Rodney, look at all the people in the store. This is fun. I'll give you a break so you can eat lunch. I'm gonna see if any of my clients want to volunteer here."

Good old Paige, this was what I'd hoped for — getting enthusiastic, asking her clients to help out. Paige was a clothes junkie and made her own garments. She was the first person to express excitement about the thrift store and involve her clients. I hoped her enthusiasm would ripple outward and inspire other staff members.

As I walked through the store to leave for my lunch break, I got a rude shock. After only two hours, we'd sold half the stock. If people kept buying at this rate, the shelves would be empty by closing time. Maybe the prices were too low. My three major fears were that no one would volunteer to run the store, no customers would come, or that we'd run out of donations. The last fear was already coming true on my first day. I poured myself a coffee and tossed two quarters into the empty tin en route to my office. Opening my container of tuna-celery sandwiches, I grabbed the phone and munched as I phoned people to find more donations.

"Daph, it's Rod. Remember you said you had some donations for the new store I was starting? Could I drop by on my way home from work and pick them up? We opened today and are running out of stuff already."

Daphne was a fellow Brit from Brighton, England, close to my hometown. She congratulated me on the store's success and promised to have donations ready to pick up on my way home. I arranged for another pickup from a buddy who'd let me know he had items left over from a garage sale. I let out a long sigh of relief.

I finished my sandwich, brushed the crumbs off the desk, and had a quick scan through Craigslist for more donation leads. Returning to the store, I noticed Paige assisting customers. "That looks great on you! It's your style, really you."

I had no idea about anyone's style and realised how inadequate my knowledge of clothes shopping was. I had to focus hard just to operate the adding machine, especially if people insisted on chatting to me at the same time.

"Paige, you're doing great. Thanks so much!"

"Rodney, I'm having fun. I'm gonna bring my two o'clock client in here. She'd love it."

"You can't. I just wrote on the sign outside that we close at two o'clock."

"Can you change it to 2:30, just for today?"

I handed her the felt pen to change the time — anything to get clients helping in the store.

Each day the following week, Paige brought two clients into the store to help. They caught her fun spirit for sorting and displaying clothing.

"We need a better place to sort the clothing, Rodney. What about the little empty room next to Trevor's?"

"Sure. I'll throw up one of those collapsible tables to sort stuff on."

"What are we gonna do with all the garbage we're getting? Some of the stuff is disgusting."

"I've already ordered an industrial garbage container for Friday. We'll put it in the parking lot out back."

At 2:30, two customers remained in the store. I tried to politely hustle them out. I really wanted to total up the first day's take. "Hi, ladies, just to let you know, we are closing now. Please bring your purchases to the front desk." I mimicked similar announcements I heard in stores.

"I've never seen a clothing rack like this one," the last customer said, looking me in the eye. She was in her late 40s with greying hair and green eyes.

"Yeah, I made it myself," I said in what I hoped was a finish-the-day tone.

"I meant that the clothes are all higgledy-piggledy on it."

"What do you mean?"

"Well, the pants, shirts, and jackets are all mixed up together. The sizes aren't in order either."

"Yeah, I never thought about that. I was just happy to get them on the rack."

The green eyes stared at me, apparently trying to figure out how I could *not* have thought of that. "I'm Sharon," she said, holding out her hand.

"I'm Rodney."

"I could come in tomorrow and sort out your clothing rack if you want."

"Sort out the rack?"

The green eyes fluttered, and she sighed. "Put all the pants together, all the shirts together, and sort the clothing by size, so people can find what they want. Chuck out all the yucky items that no one's gonna buy."

I thought I *had* chucked out the yucky items. *Who is this woman?* I wasn't expecting to find volunteers on the first day, and she seemed critical of my efforts.

"Can I think about it and let you know?"

"What's to think about, Rodney? It's free help to make this place better."

I laughed. "Yeah, you're right, Sharon. That would be great. Thanks so much. I'll have more donations tomorrow."

"Okay, I'll go through them and make sure you don't put any more crap out."

*Crap? She could have been nicer.* "Okay, sounds good."

"You're welcome. See you tomorrow."

I had just welcomed a complete stranger into the store to help. It felt weird, and unexpected, but good to get help, mixed with mild shame about crap on the rack. She was very forthright about what was wrong. Maybe that was okay. *Should I have set up an interview first? It's only a clothes rack. What can go wrong?*

I started counting the money in the cash box — one hundred, two hundred, and counting. I couldn't believe it, $234.48 for half a day. Wow, that was a lot of money. Thank you, traffic jam outside the Salvation Army thrift store, for giving me the idea. It was working. The damned store was working!

I put the money in an envelope, proudly walked into Trevor's office, and handed it to him.

"See that, Trev? $234.48 from 10 till 2:30. Not bad, huh?"

Trevor smiled, opened the envelope, and totalled the money with accounting precision, even sorting the bills so they were all the same way up.

"You're a $1.34 high, but that's surprisingly good, Rodney. Excellent." Trevor was rarely surprised.

I walked out of his office elated. I couldn't wait to tell Anna.

As I walked into the kitchen that evening, Anna was speaking Italian on the phone as she stirred the risotto. I gave her a hug, opened a beer, and pulled up a stool to the kitchen island. When she hung up, I blurted out, "We made $233 at the thrift store today."

She smiled. "Bravo, Baker! That's good, really good. It's going to work then?"

"Yeah, it felt good to see lots of people in the store spending money. We almost ran out of stuff. I picked up donations on the way home."

"That's great. I'll sort through my stuff and see if I have anything to donate."

Nine a.m., the following day, saw me hauling a trunk load of new donations from the parking lot to the store. With nervous energy, I tossed donations onto the shelves before customers arrived. I couldn't face people coming to an empty store. They might never come back. I heard a rap on the window and saw Sharon motioning me to unlock the door. She was wearing a green leather coat she'd bought yesterday from the store.

"You're early," I said, letting her in.

"Well, you said yesterday you had more donations coming. If you open at ten and you want your donations sorted and put on the rack, I'm not early." She shrugged as though it was obvious.

"Thanks, Sharon. I really appreciate your help. How often can you come?"

"Let's try a couple of days a week. I'm on disability, but I don't want to sit at home doing nothing."

"Okay, sounds good. Just to let you know, I hope to get some of our clients with mental illness to work in the store."

"No worries, my sister had schizophrenia, and I've suffered from depression, so I know about mental illness," she said, catching my eye. She sorted through Daphne's clothing donations as we chatted. Her hands were quick. She seemed to figure in a flash where everything should go.

"What was your work before you went on disability?"

Sharon squinted at me with her cool green eyes and then carried on sorting. After a couple of minutes, she said, "I worked in logging camps up north."

"Really?" I'd visited logging camps when I worked on tugboats. They were isolated, rough places. "Not many women in logging camps!"

"Exactly. I was the only one. Had lots of guys interested in me."

"I bet."

"Sometimes, I used to charge 'em. You know, the good-looking ones, if there wasn't enough work in the kitchen."

"Charge them for food?"

"No, the food was free," she said, chuckling.

I wasn't sure how to respond. "So, I guess those days are over?" I stammered.

"Hell, that was 20 years ago, before I got arthritis. I'd have to pay *them* now," she said, throwing her head back and laughing.

I chuckled, but not too hard. "Are you okay to carry on here for a bit? I've gotta couple of things to do in the office."

I closed my office door, lowered myself into the beat-up leather chair, and checked my emails while contemplating my new quirky helper. I liked Sharon. She had a take-no-prisoners, can-do attitude. There was something in those green eyes that was feisty yet forgiving. She had a crooked grin. Maybe she was BSing me about the logging camp guys, just testing my mettle. Either way, I decided it was information I wouldn't share with others at the store. I needed to interview all future volunteers, so I wrote down an outline for questions and filed it under Thrift Store.

## Organic Growth

The store flourished like an unpredictable beanstalk. I was the gardener adding water, pruning unruly shoots, and admiring new growth. July 5, four months after opening, I had ten volunteers: six of our clients, two customers who morphed into helpers, and two from Craigslist ads. We boasted a $75 Craigslist cash register and a safe to keep the revenue in. The store was open from 10 till 4, five days a week, and had earnings of $40 to $80 a day.

While growth was positive, it also brought unexpected challenges. One warm Monday morning in July, I pulled into our parking lot behind the office to find the dumpster lid pried open and all the donations we had thrown away strewn around the parking lot. It had rained overnight, and an odour of wet, sun-warmed old clothing greeted me as I jumped out of the car. The unexpected mess slapped me in the face.

"What the fuck?" I blurted out. It smelled bad and looked even worse. I picked up the sodden refuse piece by piece, held it out in front of me so it wouldn't drip on my clothes, and carried it to the bin: old sweaters, socks, shoes, overcoats, underwear, plastic toys, books, and broken plates. I wished my gardening gloves were handy.

With the garbage back in the bin, I stared at the broken five-dollar lock. This wasn't the work of racoons. Somebody had forced the lock, opened the lid, and chucked the discarded donations all over the lot, hoping to find something useful. I'd heard about dumpster divers in downtown Vancouver, but here in sleepy New Westminster? It was bad enough they broke the lock. Why did they have to spread the damned stuff all over the parking lot?

I washed my hands with extra soap and fumed about having to deal with such a mess. Then the phone started its incessant daily bleating. Hell, it was only ten to nine; the office wasn't even open yet.

I shook my hands dry and grabbed the receiver. "Rodney speaking."

"Hi this is Melvin, the building owner. Is Alice there?"

"No, she doesn't work here anymore. I'm the new ED."

"Maybe someone should have told me that. I'm the landlord. I've had a complaint from the renter in the business above you. He said there was garbage from your dumpster all over the parking lot when he tried to park on Sunday."

"Yeah, sorry about that. I just found it and cleaned it all up. I don't know what happened."

"Well, you better fix that problem so it doesn't happen again. Make sure you sweep the parking lot clean. Apparently, there was broken pottery everywhere. I don't want people phoning me about getting flat tires."

"Right, I'll do that now."

Robbie drove up as I was sweeping the lot. "Hey, Rodney, got a promotion?"

"Yeah, sweeping the parking lot is a step up from chairing team meetings for you guys."

She giggled. We shared a dry English humour.

At noon, I bought a large $16 lock, secured the dumpster lid in place, and gave Sharon the new key.

*Break through that!*

Three Mondays later, my $16 lock was gone, the dumpster lid thrown open, and the lot littered with garbage again.

This was becoming personal. I was angry at having to waste my time on this disgusting cleanup, tempered with a tinge of "poor me" because my thrift store initiative was biting me back. The building owner phoned and gave me hell again. I picked up the big items by hand, swept the lot clean, and ignored comments from the staff as they drove up to park. After telling the clerk at the hardware store about my problem, I returned with ten feet of chain, a larger, $25 lock, and another new key for Sharon. Wrapped in chains, it looked like we were protecting valuable goods instead of guarding dumped donations.

Stung by the unfairness of it all, especially as I had to clean it up, I complained to anyone who would listen. The owner of the Sandwich Shop, a block up the street, was fair game as I bought lunch on Friday. "I'm going crazy. Some bastards have been breaking into the dumpster and throwing the stuff all over the parking lot."

"Ha, we often see guys from the local crack house walking by carrying clothes and stuff. We wondered where they got the stuff from."

"Where do they live?"

"Up the road and left on Sapper Street. The house with the blue door and a broken fence."

Finally, I knew who the culprits were: people with addiction issues looking for free stuff to use or sell. I tried an appeal to fairness and stuck a sign on the side of the dumpster.

**Lid open 12-4 Fridays. Help Yourself.**

I peeked around the corner a few times on Fridays but never saw anybody. Maybe they were taking stuff when I wasn't watching or had taken pity on me and quit.

Either way, the chain worked. Each Monday, as I drove into the pristine parking lot, I heaved a sigh of relief. Victory! It felt like a good start to the week.

Eight weeks later, I arrived at a freshly littered parking lot. My chains were in tatters. They had used bolt cutters. To make matters worse, some idiot had dumped household trash on top of the existing pile. I was seething mad. Okay, dumpster divers, *this* was war! No more Mr. 12-to-4-help-yourself nice guy. I jammed all the junk into six garbage bags, spun my wheels out of the parking lot, and deposited them on the doorstep of their house on Sapper Street, arranging them so the bags would fall inward as the door opened.

*Garbage strewn over the parking lot*

Zooming through town to the hardware store, I bought 25 feet of high-tensile steel chain and a huge black industrial strength $40 padlock. I phoned a mobile welding company and got the guy to weld four large steel lugs around the top of the bin. Wrapping the chain over the lid four times and looping it through the lugs, I held it all together with my new giant lock. It looked impressive, like Fort Knox. Bolt cutters wouldn't work on this. They'd need an oxyacetylene cutting torch to get into the bin now. I hoped it was the final new key for Sharon. It looked mega secure.

A passerby quipped, "Hey, is that where you keep all the store profits?"

The dumpster-diving problem never raised its ugly head again. Either they couldn't crack my new system, or they disliked garbage on their doorstep. After four months, the game was over. Rodney four, garbage spreaders three.

Most of our clients were uncertain about the new venture of working in the store, but as their skills grew, so did their confidence. They took ownership of their jobs and thus pride in the store. Sometimes, I wandered through to see how things were going, chatted, and thanked them for volunteering. It helped me get to know our volunteers and made a pleasant distraction from sitting in my windowless office stressing about money, writing mostly unsuccessful funding proposals, and responding to the ever-ringing phone.

Volunteer David was in his early 40s with curly brown hair. He helped carry donations from the back room and put them on the shelves. He liked talking with me about trips he had made, especially camping. I liked camping, and we often exchanged stories. One day, the person running the till didn't show up.

"Hey, David, looks like I have to run the till for a while. Want to sit with me and learn how?"

"No thanks," he said, looking away.

"Okay, no worries, but I think you could do it. It's pretty easy. It adds up the amount by itself."

"I've never done it before."

"Yeah, I hear you. It worried me too because I'd never done it before. But I gave it a shot, and it was okay." One of our regular lady customers, a grandmotherly type with coiffed blue hair and clutching a Whole Foods bag, overheard our conversation.

"I'm going to buy this jacket for four dollars. Would you like to help me by ringing it in?" she said with a warm smile.

"Okay. I'll try," David said but avoided looking at her. He rang in the four dollars. She smiled and asked him for a bag.

"They are in the top left-hand drawer, David." He selected the right-sized bag, folded the jacket, and placed it inside.

"Thanks for your help," she said.

David smiled as she left.

"That was great, David. You got it right the first time. If I sit beside you, maybe you could do just a couple more."

"Do I have to say anything?"

"No, just thank you."

When you live alone and have little interaction with the world, small talk can pose a problem. I sat with him for the next two customers, then heard my office phone chiming.

"David, I'll be back in a few minutes." I returned to see him ringing in the next customer's purchases and putting them in a bag. I shook his hand and congratulated him.

He grinned and looked away. "Maybe I'll do it for another half hour."

"Great! That's really helpful. Thanks so much."

"What if the items are not priced, like pots and pans?"

"Great question! Just make up a price. They are all donated items anyway, so whatever you charge, we still make money."

The following Wednesday, I was building a bookcase — a step up from having books in cardboard boxes on the floor. David had volunteered to do one hour on the till every Wednesday. I heard my phone ringing, set down my tools, and scooted back to my office. It was Agnes letting me know the fridge had quit at Saint Barnabas House and that the food was going off. I phoned around to find a repair guy who could come that day. After six calls, I found one.

After a fuzzy moment staring at the phone, I remembered what I was doing, walked back to the thrift store, and stood looking at the half-built bookshelves. Where had I left my drill and screw gun? I looked and looked.

"David, did you see where I put my drill and screw gun?"

"I sold them."

"You sold them? You are kidding, right?"

"No, they were sitting on the shelf, and a guy came in and said how much. I just guessed at a price, like you said, and sold them for five bucks each."

Prior to pursuing a career in mental health, I'd been a tradesman for 25 years. My tools were extensions of my hands; they'd helped bring creations in my head to life and become a part of my building persona. I'd bought these two power tools when I finished my apprenticeship as part of my rite of passage to becoming a journeyman.

"They were still plugged in. Didn't the guy notice?"

"I dunno. He just brought them to the front desk and asked how much."

"Did you recognise the customer?"

"Yeah, it's that tall Scottish guy who comes in every Wednesday."

"Actually, David, those tools weren't for sale. They were mine, and I'd like to get them back. If that guy comes in again, could you come and get me? I would like to talk to him."

"Sorry, I didn't know."

"It's okay, no worries. You didn't mean to." I was devastated at the loss of my precious tools and mad at the Scotsman. I'm sure he knew they weren't for sale and took advantage of David's inexperience.

Although upset at the loss, after a while I could see the warped humour of my precious tools being sold for five bucks each. Luckily, next week, the Scotsman returned to the store, I explained the mistake and offered him double what he paid, and he accepted. By not losing my cool, David continued as cashier, the customer continued to shop, and I got my equipment back.

The day I regained my electric drill and screw gun, I finished off the bookshelf — the final work the store needed — and repatriated my tools back home for good.

Arriving home to the smell of tasty food, I greeted Anna in the kitchen as she was ladling broth into the risotto.

"You're late."

"Yeah, I stayed to finish building a bookshelf for the store. We get lots of books donated and had nowhere to put them."

"That sounds like a big improvement."

"I've been meaning to do it for a while. Funny thing, last week, one of the volunteers sold my drill and screw gun by mistake."

"They sold your tools?" she said, looking incredulous, as she spooned the risotto into neat mounds on our plates. "You never said anything. Were you mad?"

"At the time, yes, but I got them back. We're all learning as we go. I kind of pop in and out of the store when I get time."

"You should have someone looking after everything, a store manager."

"Yeah, you're right." Her comments floated into my must-do-sometime box, alongside the tangle of many other good ideas with missing legs.

## Losses and Gains   New Hope   More Losses

Miraculously, a couple of weeks after Anna pointed out the obvious to me, one of our regular customers, Paula, a rotund lady in her fifties, who had a penchant for heavy jewellery and ponchos, asked if she could be the manager. She mentioned she could bring a friend who could help her. Paula's friend, Vera, was a charming First Nations lady with big eyes and a friendly smile.

Great! My magical store was running itself — a self-perpetuating entity. A manager and helper had just popped up out of the blue. Paula said that she and Vera would come in on the three days when Sharon wasn't there. That meant there would be responsible people running the store five days a week. Less stress for me.

Three months later, Vera walked into my office half an hour before the store opened.

"Wow, you're a keener coming in early, Vera."

Vera stared at me with wide-open eyes. Her mouth opened and closed several times. She swallowed and stared at me then looked away.

"What's the matter?"

She cast her eyes down and clutched her hands together.

"I can see you're upset. Just take your time. Have a seat. I'm listening."

She sat down heavily, took a deep breath, and pursed her lips. "Rodney, I don't know how to say this. It's Paula. She's stealing from the store." Vera's hands began to shake, and a couple of tears rolled down her cheeks. "I've seen her stealing two or three times. She also goes through the pockets of all the donated clothes. Last week, she found $50 in a donated jacket and kept it." The words tumbled out. "I've been to her apartment and seen things she stole there: two vases. I'm sorry to tell you this, but it's been eating me up inside." She heaved a sigh of relief, and the tears flowed down her cheeks.

Women crying in front of me does something weird to my stomach. I stepped forward and laid a hand on her shoulder. "Hey, thanks so much for telling me. It took courage. I can see it put you in a very difficult situation, especially as she's your friend."

"That's the thing, Rodney. She's *not* my friend. I live in the same apartment block, and we've had coffee twice, but to tell the truth, I don't really like her. She's very bossy. She talked me into coming to the store. I didn't want to come. But now I really like it." She took another deep breath. "It's not right, though. I just wanted to tell you. I'm going home now. I don't want to work with her anymore."

"Yeah, I understand. Thanks so much for telling me. Looks like I will have to get rid of her. Of course, I won't mention your name."

I felt my bile rising up to my throat. Paula, the manager, was stealing from the store! Worse, if Vera had seen her, others may have too, which could create an atmosphere of unease. I decided to put things on hold, wait till Sharon came in, and discuss it with my wise, no-nonsense, thrift-store helper.

The following day, I called Sharon into my office and closed the door. "Vera came to me yesterday and told me Paula was stealing."

"Ha! That bitch. I knew it! The first day she was here, I thought I saw her putting something in her pocket and questioned her. She got angry and stopped working on the days I was in the store."

"Oh, I thought you guys had worked it out that way for efficiency."

"No, she knew I was suspicious. I struggled with telling you because I wasn't a hundred percent sure and couldn't prove anything. What are ya gonna do, Rodney?" Sharon asked, fixing me with one of her take-no-prisoners looks.

"She's gotta go, I guess."

"You guess?" she said, cocking her head to one side.

I laughed. "It's okay for you. I'm the one that has to tell her. If I fire her, are you going to find me another manager?"

"Yes, Rodney. I will. There's a volunteer fair being held next week at the Royal City Centre Mall. Give me some brochures, and I'll go there. See if I can find someone."

When I'd been in business, I hated firing people. It was the worst part of my job. The first guy I fired started crying and said, "What am I gonna tell my wife?" I couldn't handle it and hired him back. Two months later, I fired him again.

I didn't know what to say to Paula. I couldn't tell her Vera had seen her stealing. I worried over this for three days while surviving dirty looks from Sharon.

"The volunteer fair is coming up tomorrow, Rodney. My part of the bargain was to go find you a new manager. Yours was to fire Paula."

She was right. Roused by Sharon's call to action, I asked Paula to come to my office. My heart was thumping. I was apprehensive about telling someone they were no longer wanted — especially a volunteer.

She arrived a few minutes later. "What's up, boss?" she said in a cheery tone.

I swallowed. "I'm sorry to inform you that your services are no longer required by this organization."

Her back stiffened, and she stared me in the eye. "What? Why? What the fuck is going on? Pardon my French! But I'm busting my ass here for no pay, and you're firing me? You can't do that!"

"Well, I appreciate the help you have given the store. However, this will be your last day. Again, thanks for your service."

"Why? Can you just tell me why? You can't just kick me out for no reason. I'm not going. I'm gonna go into the store now and tell all the customers that you are firing me for no reason."

I wavered but carried on in a louder voice. "Obviously, I have my reasons. If you think about it, maybe you can guess, but I'm not going to discuss it any further. If you go into the store and tell the customers, I will tell them why I'm asking you to leave. Thanks again for your service." I opened the door and gestured for her to leave while trying to look resolute.

"Well, fuck you and your flea-bitten store," she yelled, stormed out, and slammed the door so hard a picture fell off the wall and broke. Luckily, it was from the thrift store.

I sat down until my breathing returned to normal and phoned Sharon. "I just fired Paula. She's gone."

"Ha, good for you. You sound shook up. Let's see what I can rustle up tomorrow."

Sharon was a great rustler. Three days later, there was a knock on my door, and a woman with short red hair and a brisk manner walked into my office.

"Hi, I'm Sandy. I met a lady called Sharon at a volunteer fair. She said you need a thrift-store manager."

"Yes, Sandy, we certainly do." We shook hands, and I offered her a seat.

"What can you tell me about this job?"

I explained that the thrift store helped fund the organization, the staff were volunteers, and some had mental illness.

"We've been open less than a year. It's working well, except that we need a new manager. Perhaps you could tell me a bit about yourself."

"I recently retired from the Royal Bank, and I'm looking for something to do."

"I guess you're probably pretty trustworthy with money?"

She laughed. "With other people's money. Not so great with my own. What do you need me to do exactly?"

I explained that Sharon looked after the centre clothing rack and the volunteer scheduling and that as manager she could organize putting the donations on the shelves, help train volunteers, and price items.

"I don't know much about running a thrift store."

I looked her in the eye. "Me neither." We both chuckled.

"How do you price the donations?"

I explained that as we were on the edge of town, I didn't want people to make the trip for nothing, so I priced things pretty low. That way, shoppers felt good about walking out with a deal and didn't have to look at the same items on the shelves week after week.

She nodded in agreement.

I had a reassuring feeling about Sandy. She seemed honest and competent. I suggested she come in for a few days and see if she liked running the store.

"Okay, I'll try a couple of days next week and see how it goes."

Every time someone volunteered to help run the store, I felt grateful to my core; it validated my belief that people were good at heart and cared about one another.

Sandy got started, took over, and never mentioned the couple-of-days trial period. The shelves became more organized, she found a charity that bought unwanted clothing donations by the pound, and our volunteers became better trained. After eight months, I started paying her $10 an hour for a 10-hour week, although she worked much more. The store had never run so well, and I wanted to reward her valiant efforts with something other than my frequent thanks. I felt guilty about all the time she was putting in. After her first year in the store, net revenues rose by 30 percent. Occasionally, she came into my office frowning and biting her lip as she confessed her unease.

"I have no experience working with people who have mental illness. Maybe I'm making mistakes. I just told one client how to improve the way she was dusting, and she burst into tears."

"Sandy, you're patient and coming from a good place in your heart. In my opinion, that's all you need."

"It doesn't always work."

"Yeah, I understand it's not easy." I nodded and gave a sympathetic smile. She was still frowning, looking worried. "Look, do you have something that *always* works with your husband?"

She shot me a rueful look and laughed. "No, of course not. But that's because I think he suffers from hearing problems."

"Hearing, or listening?"

We both laughed.

"You're doing your best. That's all you can do. Remember, it's difficult for the clients too. It might be the first work experience for some of them."

"Yeah, some of them for sure. On the reward side, I can see them growing in confidence and feeling good about themselves," she said with a smile. "Come to think of it, we should start having thank you parties to let them know how much we appreciate them."

I agreed and suggested we could buy some treats or invite them to have lunch out.

The number of clients working in our store steadily grew, as did volunteers from the public. I tried to have two people per three-hour shift, which meant four people a day, twenty people a week. There was a good mix of clients, high school kids looking for volunteer experience, and local citizens just wanting to help. Sharon still arranged the volunteer scheduling, but as the volunteer numbers grew, she trained others to look after the clothing rack. When phoning volunteers for shifts, she often spent extra time listening to their troubles. Thanks to Sandy and Sharon's caring help, and the increased number of volunteers, the operation had really improved. As business grew, we needed more space. Someone donated five long, shallow iron baskets. I fastened them to the top of my sturdy iron clothing rack to create another 40 square feet of display space. The store was always brimming with goods, with more in the storage room waiting to replace the sold items.

*Full shelves in the thrift store*

By the second year of operations, the store had made a net profit of $21,000. Combined with the $8,000 from running the satellite house, we had made up some of the $26,000 annual shortfall resulting from the loss of bingo funding. While the store was running smoothly, we always needed more help. Attracting new volunteers was paramount. People came and went as their life circumstance changed. I advertised on Craigslist and put posters in apartment block elevators.

Interviewing new applicants made me aware that we were attracting a gold mine of talent, and I sometimes talked them into using their skills in other positions. We recruited two board members this way and one grant writer.

Many of the volunteers were very competent with their use of computers, which gave me an idea of how to address a real concern of mine: As our culture embraced the computer age, everything was becoming *online*. Lack of computer skills was further marginalizing our clients. As we had willing free talent and space, I started the Computer Training Program, where anyone — clients and volunteers — could learn to use the computer with our competent trainers. This became a popular program and stayed in place for the duration of my tenure. While it didn't generate any revenue, it helped many people learn or improve their skills and gain confidence in navigating the computer world. I advertised this service in the newsletter, and clients from other nonprofits started to show up. Many of the volunteer trainers were new immigrants, and one-on-one conversation helped improve their English skills.

I encouraged one volunteer to write about her experience for the newsletter; I wanted to reflect a variety of voices, plus a positive review might encourage clients to take advantage of the program or others to volunteer. I was touched by what she wrote:

As a newcomer to this country, I learned that Canadians volunteer. I live close by and interviewed for the thrift store to practice my English and learn about Canadian life. I was also asked to teach people with mental illness how to use a computer.

I learned that I like teaching and not to be scared of people with mental illness. When my first student couldn't understand my explanation, maybe because of my Romanian accent, she would reach for my hand and look at me with laughing eyes. She would twist her lips and pull a face, and we would start giggling.

I tried laughing about mistakes with other students, and it worked. Having fun while helping is my reward. I'm so happy I volunteered.

***Laughing and learning computer skills***

While the thrift store was helping financially, I was always on the alert for new sources of revenue. My efforts at writing grant proposals had met with little success. On one occasion, I spent about 36 hours writing a proposal to Fraser Health to run another transition house. It was turned down. Disappointed at the wasted hours, I asked Jill Bloom, the director of mental health from Fraserside, another local nonprofit, how they wrote proposals. She explained that they had a three-person team for writing large proposals and that much of the proposal wording was reused from prior bids and tweaked to fit new circumstances. She also shared it was safer for proposal evaluators to award contracts to previously successful applicants. Having none of these components helped me realize I was an amateur at this complex skill.

However, an opportunity to increase revenue came up that I felt we had a better shot at getting: Bev Gutray, the head of CMHA in Vancouver, had negotiated funding from BC Housing for a Homeless Outreach Program. Bev was a great negotiator and very savvy politically. Homelessness was a concern of mine. In a wealthy society like ours, it seemed inhuman to have people living on the streets — demeaning for the homeless and the non-homeless who walked past them every day looking the other way. Many street people had mental health challenges, which was another reason to be involved. Plus, more programs meant more administration money. As we were barely scraping by, I was always interested in new sources of revenue to guard against future financial shocks.

I phoned Bev to enquire about our branch being considered for this program. I wasn't her favourite ED: I was new to CMHA, newish to mental health, and had sometimes protested at the bureaucratic requirements imposed on our branch by the CMHA head office. I'm sure from her perspective of trying to keep 20 branches in line, she would have preferred to reward more compliant EDs than me. She asked me how things were going in New Westminster.

"No big problems here," I told her. "The thrift store is going well. We have 12 clients working in the store and have finally paid you guys our branch membership fees." In the silence that followed, I could imagine her evaluating my positive tone.

"Good. So, what can I do for you today, Rodney?"

"I heard you are offering some branches the opportunity to start a Homeless Outreach Program. I would very much like for our branch to be part of that."

A long pause followed.

"I see. Why do you think your branch should qualify?" she said in a slow, deliberate voice.

I piled on the reasons. "The outreach worker would have to be very skilled to get people off the street and into housing. From 20 years of running my own business, I'm used to hiring people who get results." I explained that the outreach worker would be exposed to people in dire human conditions, which may negatively affect their well-being, and that as a clinical counsellor, I could offer monthly supervision to help them cope. I waited to let my words sink in and perhaps receive a positive comment. No comment came.

"We're in the mental health business, right, Bev? I believe it's important to ensure my workers are looked after." I paused to let that sink in. "One last thing. We get lots of donations for our thrift store — microwaves, kettles, crockery, and bedding — that we could donate to people moving off the street into housing."

More silence.

"I don't know any other branch that has those assets, Bev. So, I hope you will consider us favourably." I waited through another long pause.

"Write me a proposal, Rodney, and I'll look it over."

Excited at the opportunity, I sat in my pink-walled office, spurred my ancient computer into action, and spent the latter part of the morning crafting a sparkling-bright Outreach Proposal. I got Trevor to proofread it and emailed it to Bev the same day.

Feeling satisfied about my prompt response to Bev's request, I sat back in my beat-up office chair and relaxed, but not for long. I realized it was 1:30. I'd got caught up in the proposal and forgotten about my next meeting. I just had time to make the two o'clock annual United Way meeting in Burnaby. United Way collected donations throughout the Lower Mainland and distributed them to nonprofit organizations.

Scooting down Canada Way, I turned right and hunted for

parking — tough to find as the meetings were well attended. I liked the annual visit here. I didn't have to speak, and they provided coffee and biscuits as we listened to updates about United Way's past accomplishments and future plans — free food and free money.

The wonderful thing about United Way funding was that the $27,000 annual gift to us was "discretionary funding" and could be spent however we wanted, which in our case was for administration. It wasn't tied to providing programs, like Fraser Health's funding. I was into my third chocolate-chip cookie when the president's smooth presentation got my attention.

"We are pleased to announce a new initiative, 'Success By 6,' a broad range of programs investing in children aged zero to six years old."

What a great idea. Spending money on kids would have mega benefits to society as a whole.

"Unfortunately, to finance this initiative, funding for most mental health programs will have to be cut."

"What?" I choked on my cookie and started coughing.

Leticia from Point Grey Family Place patted me on the back. "Take a deep breath."

"I need medicinal brandy rather than deep breaths. It sounds like we just lost our bloody funding."

"Yeah, I think that was a surprise to us all."

I could see from United Way's perspective: the visuals of young children evoked more donor empathy than adults with mental illness. Kids are cute and, of course, deserving. Early investments in their future made sense. However, the multiple mental illnesses that people suffer from last from early adulthood for the rest of their lives and profoundly compromise their ability for social inclusion. Mental illness has far less donor appeal than young kids or breast cancer — it is not visible, is often regarded with fear, and is an often-neglected cause.

I no longer owed United Way my allegiance and left the meeting early. Pushing through the double glass doors, I strode to my car, slammed the door shut, and put my head in my hands. Each time I plugged a money gap, another funding chasm opened ahead of me. *Take deep breaths, exhale slowly.*

I reached home, headed for the fridge, and opened a beer. I saw Anna was sitting on the lawn having a cigarette. "Hey, give me a few puffs, will ya. I had a rough day."

"Thought you'd quit. What happened?"

"We are going to lose the United Way funding of $27,000 a year."

"Why would they do that?"

"Because United Way is going to focus on supporting kids and end funding for mental health organizations like ours."

"Finish the cigarette," she said, giving me a compassionate glance.

I went back to the fridge, opened another beer, sank onto the sofa, turned on the TV, and vegged out while Anna cooked. The quiz game *Jeopardy* was on. I knew some of the answers, but I wasn't playing. One category was on the origin of sayings.

"Where does the saying 'Go big or go home' derive from?"

I'd heard people use that phrase, so it drew my curiosity.

"What is a California surfer term?"

"That is the correct answer." Alex Trebek smiled.

Ha, yes. I imagined surfers lying on their boards, scanning the horizon for the big one. It had a good ring to it. "Go big or go home." I said it a couple of times. Yes! It smacked of courage, of bravado. I should do the same. Take a risk. Go big or go home.

"Dinner's ready," Anna yelled. I walked into the kitchen, grabbed another beer, and sat down to eat.

"That's the third beer you've had in an hour."

I smiled at Anna. "Yeah. Go big or go home!"

"Are you talking about drinking beer?"

"No, work! That's what I'm gonna do at work. Break the lease and move the store and office to a bigger, better location close to the town centre. Maybe we can make up the $27,000 United Way loss by relocating." I laughed. "Go big or go home!"

## Searching for a New Location

When exciting ideas grab me, they fill my spirit, lift me up, and drive me forward. I'd been fired up opening the thrift store, starting a new transition house, and coordinationg a homeless outreach service. Now my latest brainwave of deciding to move to a better location consumed my mind with enthusiastic energy.

I needed that spark: Bringing big new ideas to fruition was like climbing a steep mountain with weak legs and a heavy pack. Steep because I didn't know what I was doing, weak legs because I was largely doing it alone, and the heavy pack because I was already scrambling to fit in my current workload. I often woke up around 3 a.m. and worried how I would cope.

No problem, I would wrap myself around the challenge of finding a new location and just go faster, like a circus performer with multiple plates spinning. I could zoom out to Maple Ridge, attend a client intake meeting, check on a plumbing problem at St. John's House, race back to New Westminster for our bimonthly Youth Housing meeting, spend an hour writing the newsletter, sort out a staff schedule problem, fix a broken shelf in the thrift store while thanking the volunteers for their time, and pick up calls forwarded to my cell phone. Running orange lights and cramming everything in felt busy, lively, and productive.

One duty I never rushed was interviewing volunteers. I decided from the get-go that this would be my responsibility. I wanted to know who was coming into our midst. If we inducted a predator or thief, like the previous manager, the blame would be mine. It was also a way of grounding me and of keeping in touch with the people we served.

The first morning after deciding we were moving, I had an

interview with a client sent by Agnes, the silver-haired woman who ran Barnabas House. She'd suggested he might volunteer at the thrift store. She called him Big John. When interviewing potential volunteers, I asked about their lives to help me understand who they were and what motivated them to work in the store.

I was writing the newsletter while waiting for the interview. As usual, my office door was open. The room darkened slightly, and I glanced up to see John's big frame filling the space.

"Come in, John. Thanks for dropping by." I shook his big bear-paw hand and motioned him to sit down. He was about 50 and wore older-style twill pants with suspenders. He sat down slowly and stared at the wall behind me.

"Agnes said you might be interested in volunteering for the thrift store."

"Yeah," he said, nodding.

"Great! Perhaps you could tell me a bit about yourself."

"About myself?" He looked wary.

"Yeah, you know, about your life," I said with a smile.

John's eyes flickered toward mine then back at the wall.

"Did you grow up around here?"

"I grew up in Marpole by the Fraser River."

I nodded. "Did you like living there?"

"Yeah. Me and my brother, we went fishing off the log booms." A smile crossed his face.

"For Springs?" I wanted to keep him talking.

"Yeah, and Coho."

"Did you use salmon eggs?"

"Yeah, and sometimes a Tom Mac for casting, but eggs were good. Then, when I got older, I liked chemistry and got into university. My dad was pleased." He looked at me then down to the floor. "Then things went wrong."

"Went wrong?" I asked in a soft voice.

"Yeah." He grimaced and gave a sigh. "I was walking through the halls at UBC one day when I realized I was getting messages from the fluorescent lights above me. I had to jump from light to light so I didn't miss a message." He looked up from the floor to see how I reacted.

I nodded. "Okay. Were the messages important?"

A wisp of a smile crossed his face. "Yeah, really important. We were going to be invaded by aliens, and I was the only one that knew."

"Wow, what did you do?"

"I phoned all my friends and told them. I had about 50 friends then — not now." He explained that the good news was he was in charge of the allied troops. "About that time, my professor started speaking gibberish. I couldn't understand him and stopped going to classes. I stayed up all night drinking Coke and smoking cigarettes while I planned the defence of earth. I thought I had special gifts and didn't need sleep." He took a deep breath and looked at me.

I nodded.

"Then one day, the police came and took me to St. Paul's Hospital."

"I see. How was that?"

"I didn't like the other patients."

"You didn't like them?"

"No." He chuckled. "They stayed up all night, smoked, and drank Coke. Until I met them, I thought I was special, but all the other people with bipolar disorder did the same thing. That's when I stopped doing it."

"You didn't want to be like them."

"Right, but it didn't help me get better." He continued on without emotion, as though speaking about someone else. His friends and family stopped speaking to him, and psychiatric experts took over control of his life: He had to take medication that made him put on weight, made his mouth dry, and his head was fuzzy till late afternoon. "If I didn't take the meds, I would be 'noncompliant' and cut off from benefits."

"Did the meds help?"

"They stopped my mind racing, but I had to quit university — my mind was too slow. There was no graduation ceremony and no job."

"Sorry to hear that, John. Sounds like you had lots of challenges."

I was moved by his story. Mental illness wasn't a lifestyle choice: The onset of bipolar disorder and schizophrenia strikes people in early adulthood, usually between 18-24 years old. The majority spend the rest of their lives struggling to cope with symptoms, medication side effects, low self-esteem, stigma, poverty, and loneliness. As working at the store had the potential to address some of these issues, I said yes to most applicants — to see if it worked for them.

"Okay, John. Thanks for sharing. How is life treating you these days?"

"Pretty good. I've learned to ask for help with my moods. I tell people around me to watch how I dress. If my shoelaces are undone and my shirt's buttoned unevenly, it's a sign I'm heading for a manic high, so I up the meds. My sister still speaks to me, and I made friends at Barnabas House. I enjoy living there. I like cooking. Agnes is nice. She said I might like working at the store."

"Do you think you would like it?"

"I dunno. Maybe."

"Ha, you're right, John. It's hard to know if we would like something until we try it."

"Do you like your job, Rodney?"

I smiled. "Some days I do, and other days — well, I dunno." We both chuckled.

I suggested he talk to Sharon so that she would slot him in a volunteer time. "If you like it, fine, if not, you tried." I explained that without volunteers, the thrift store couldn't operate, and this organization would run out of money.

"Thanks for coming in, John."

"Thank you, Rodney." John gave a hint of a smile, stood up, and lumbered out.

I appreciated John's courage and volunteer spirit: He would try working with the public in an unfamiliar environment and role with people he didn't know.

Sometimes, at the end of a long, tiring day when it felt like little had been accomplished, I found myself sitting stationary in a long line of freeway traffic. Negative thoughts streamed into my mind. *I gotta get a different job. The drive is too long. I'm wasting my life stuck in traffic.* Then I reminded myself I owned a car and a house, had a job, and had someone who loved me waiting at home. Comforts that few of our clients with serious and persistent mental illness would ever enjoy. These thoughts always dissipated the self-pity.

The first day of my big decision to move the office and store flashed by without my taking any action. The fire in my belly simmered down a bit. The initial step, finding a new location in town suitable for our office and thrift store, was daunting. The day after my brainwave inspired by three beers and a TV show, it sounded less wonderful and more half-baked. Never mind. Nothing ventured, nothing gained. I worried a lot about the consequences of breaking a ten-year lease registered with the land office. *Why on earth did the former ED do that for this crap location?*

The next morning, sitting at my desk, fifty-cent coffee in hand, I deleted my iconic "Thrift store – stuff to do" file and changed it to "Moving – stuff to do."

1) Find a new location
2) Tell the landlord
3) Tell the staff
4) Locate a mover
5) Organize the move

I scanned the yellow pages for a real estate agent that specialized in office rentals. One ad suggested, "Let us do the work for you." Yes, what a wonderful idea, someone else doing the work. I rested my hand on the phone. Did I really want to do this? The phone rang, sending a tingle up my arm. "CMHA, Rodney speaking."

"Good morning. It's Bev Gutray." *What? She usually gets her second-in-command to phone.*

"I just wanted to let you know in person that I liked your Homeless Outreach proposal and we're offering your branch a year's funding — see how you make out."

Bev shot up in my rating. "Wow, that's great, Bev. Thanks so much."

"Training will start in one month at the downtown office."

"Training?"

"Yes, the six EDs whose proposals were accepted will all get outreach training."

"I was planning to be on holiday at that time."

"The training is mandatory. We've got Judy Graves doing it. She pioneered fast-tracking homeless people in the Downtown Eastside. You need to be there." Bev's tone signalled this was non-negotiable.

I was thrilled we'd got the contract. It meant another $9,000 a year for administration. But for the past couple of months, imagining myself going on vacation was all that pulled me through the heavy workload. I'd take a couple of weeks off after the training.

*With the outreach money coming in, do we still need to move to a better location?* I drained my coffee and considered smoking a cigarette in the parking lot to help me decide. I reached for the phone, but pulled back and stuffed my hands in my pockets. Moving was a big thing, was a lot of work, and would affect everyone in the organization — *if* I could get out of the lease.

After glaring at the phone for some minutes and chewing my lip, I looked around my dismal, windowless pink walls and phoned the real estate company. Let them give me some options, then I would decide.

The first salesman I spoke to was a cold shower.

"You want a street-level space that would accommodate an office and a retail store close to the centre of town for $1500 a month? Ha, that's pretty unlikely." His mocking tone got my back up.

"Well, it could be an older space. We could paint it. Just keep your eyes open. Tell prospective landlords they'd be helping the cause of mental health," I added, hoping to arouse the Good

Samaritan in him or the property owners.

"Mental health? If there's gonna be crazy people in the building, I'd have to warn my clients."

*Prejudiced asshole.* "I don't think your company is going to work out for us," I said and banged the phone down.

Other companies I phoned were equally unenthusiastic. I was adamant about having the store and the office in the same building. I liked to stroll through the store, chat with volunteer staff, as well as support Sandy and Sharon with any problems that arose.

So as not to become despondent, I limited myself to phoning two real estate companies a week. My spirits lifted with each call and fell with each negative result. I was starting to feel gloomy about this new direction when an unexpected opportunity caught me unaware and changed my focus.

## The Beginning of a Funny Idea

After my ninth disappointing call to a real estate office, I hung up the phone and busied myself with writing the newsletter to take my mind off the lack of positive results. I tried to fill the newsletter with upbeat accounts of clients' accomplishments, uplifting world events, and research articles such as how to keep a positive attitude. Regarding my dismal results at moving, I needed that advice myself.

"Hi, are you Rodney?" I turned to see a man in his 40s wearing a dark suit standing in the doorway.

"Yes, that's me. How can I help you?"

He surged toward me with an outstretched hand. "Hi, I'm Darcy. Darcy James. It's more like how I can help you," he said with a mega-friendly smile.

I stood up and shook his hand. "And how can you help me, Darcy?"

"I can make you some money."

*That* got my attention. His face was glowing, like a preacher with a vision.

"I have this idea of teaching people with mental illness to be stand-up comics."

*What? That sounds crazy!* I shuffled some papers on my desk and glanced up at him. "And then what?"

"After they're all trained, we get a big location downtown, like the Hotel Vancouver, and put on a graduation gala and dinner. We get a lot of sponsors, the food donated, have art donations for an auction run by celebrities, a silent auction as well, and charge $150 a ticket. Your organization will get all the revenue, minus costs."

Words flew from his mouth like a California wildfire consuming any resistance in its path. He spoke rapidly, smiled a lot, and fixed me with an intense stare.

I swallowed and looked away. "I see, and what role do I or this organization have to play in this...idea?"

"You supply the people with mental illness who wanna be stand-up comics and the venue for training. It would be called Comedy Courage."

Despite his bubbling enthusiasm, it seemed like an unlikely idea.

"Why would people with mental illness want to be stand-up comics?"

"I have a mental illness, and I'm a stand-up comic. It gives me confidence." Darcy bristled with confidence — enough for two or three people.

"Why did you pick us? We're just a small nonprofit."

"I talked to the executive director at the Vancouver branch of CMHA, but he wasn't interested. They're supporting The Courage to Come Back, another fundraiser for mental illness." For the first time, his mood damped down. His lips pursed. He looked crestfallen. "They didn't want me to use the word *courage* — said it would be confusing to have two events with similar names. I'm not changing the name. It's my idea. Comedy Courage tells it all. It takes guts to get up on stage and joke about mental illness."

"People are going to joke about mental illness?" *Would this be politically correct?*

"Yeah, that's the point. Educate people about living with mental illness through humour."

I hadn't noticed anything funny about mental illness, but his energized enthusiasm was infectious; I didn't want to be another spoiler that turned him down. Also, *if* we did make money, it would help offset the United Way loss.

"What do you say, Rodney? Do you want to make some money and have fun doing it?" His face lit up again with an infectious smile.

"Look, Darcy. I don't really understand the concept or how you're going to pull it off. Sounds like a huge amount of work. But at this point, I am open to it."

He grasped my shoulder with a firm hand and shook me back and forth.

"Thank you! Thank you! You won't be sorry. We're gonna get people laughing and giving from the heart."

Unnerved by the physical contact, I stepped back and changed the subject. "Do you have a team working with you?"

"My partner George helps me. We're just lining up a comedic trainer. Now I've got a nonprofit to work with, I can start lining up sponsors." The fiery glint was back in his eyes. Whatever mental illness he had, it didn't appear to be general anxiety disorder.

Pulling out a manila envelope from a battered black briefcase, he said, "I've got an agreement for you to sign, Rodney." He pursed his lips and tried to contain a triumphant smile.

The one-page agreement was simple and stated that either side could withdraw from the agreement at any time and all costs would be paid from the money received by the gala event. We both signed, and I ran off a copy for Darcy.

"I'm gonna keep all my Skytrain and bus tickets costs. That's how I get around. I don't have a car."

*A promoter without a car?* "Okay, fine. What needs to happen first?"

"You need to line up ten people with mental illness who wanna be comics."

"Okay, send me all the details by email, and I'll make a handout that my staff can pass out to our clients."

"Right away, Rodney. As soon as I get home. Now, can you show me the room where the comics will be doing their training."

I led him into the boardroom.

"There's no windows!" He swallowed, and the smile left his face.

I explained it was the only room big enough that was available. "You guys will have to brighten it up with sunny laughter." I smiled and patted him on the back. *I can do physical too.* "Darcy, great to meet you, but I have to get back to work. I'll start recruiting people and let you know."

Another smile flashed across his face. He pumped my hand as though inflating a bicycle tire and whirled out of the office, leaving a faint vapour trail of Brut aftershave.

I grabbed a coffee, sat down, and took a few deep breaths. What had I just agreed to? The whole episode seemed bizarre. Darcy bubbled over with such positive energy I found it difficult to say no. Well, it wouldn't cost us any money, and it was at least four months away. I'd started the thrift store to improve our finances, but it had generated other benefits. Maybe this would too.

I decided not to mention Comedy Courage to Anna just yet. It sounded too weird. I could imagine her looking at me with her big eyes and saying, "An unknown guy walked into your office and wants to train your clients to tell jokes about mental illness in public to raise money — and you said yes?"

It might be a hard sell to the staff. Darcy's dynamic personality had won me over, but I couldn't replicate his enthusiastic energy. It had rocked me off centre. I couldn't remember what I'd been doing before he walked in.

My gaze fell on my computer screen. That was it. I was writing the newsletter to distract myself from getting another negative response in my quest to find new premises. With my three-week holiday coming up, starting an outreach program, and now a three-month commitment to provide a room for training comics, my fire-in-the-belly plans to move were being downgraded to gonna-move-sometime musings.

The first Tuesday after Darcy's visit, I brought up the topic of Comedy Courage at the staff meeting.

"What's so funny about having a mental illness?" Robbie asked. "Why on earth would anyone with mental illness want to get on a stage and make fun of themselves?" She pursed her lips, looked around the table, and got some nods. "I can't believe you'd want to expose our clients to that."

Stephanie chimed in. "Yes, sounds weird to me too. People already face stigma. Why would they want to joke about their illness in front of strangers?" Others nodded. I felt discouraged by their disapproving stares. Getting the bone between her teeth, Stephanie continued, "It seems that in the two years that you've been here, Rodney, it's all about making money. First you start a store and get our clients working there as slave labour, then you want them to get on a stage and make fun of themselves just to earn CMHA a few dollars."

*That stings — maybe some truth to it.* "You're right about the money, Stephanie. I'm trying to keep this organization afloat so it can continue to pay our wages and serve our clients, but you're wrong about slaves. Slaves don't have a choice, whereas our clients do. They volunteer because they like it, and most get $100 a month. I'm sure you feel rewarded at the end of the day because you've helped somebody. These are opportunities for our clients to feel rewarded by working in the store and helping us." I paused to let this sink in. "In our psychosocial rehabilitation (PSR) model of helping, we're supposed to encourage clients to take risks and try new things. This Darcy guy has a mental illness and said being a stand-up comic helped his confidence. So, instead of *us* making decisions about what is good for our clients, why don't we present them with the opportunity and let *them* decide for themselves?"

PSR was a positive approach that I really believed in: It encouraged mental health workers to consider clients as people with possibilities rather than patients with problems. This mindset helped me decide to give the Comedy Courage a try. The premise was that if we believed in our clients, it would be contagious, and it would help them believe in themselves.

To boost staff understanding of this approach, I ran an eight-week course from a PSR textbook. I also showed a video by Patricia Deegan, who at age 17 was diagnosed with schizophrenia and depression.

"I woke up, had breakfast, smoked, and watched TV till lunch. I watched TV after lunch, smoked, had a nap, had supper, watched TV, smoked a few more cigarettes, and went to bed around 7 p.m." She explained she was depressed because the doctor said she would never get better. "Every day for two years, my Irish grandma asked me if I'd go grocery shopping with her. I knew I could say no and it was okay. She didn't try to guilt me into it. One day, I said, 'Yes, but I'm not pushing the cart.' My recovery started on that day." She explained her grandma wasn't a psychologist but had hope, empathy, caring, and patience.

Patricia resumed high school and finished grade 12. She attended university, earned a doctorate in psychology, and became a leading mental health advocate in the USA.

When staff members were having a challenging time with clients, I reminded them about Patricia's grandma and the need to keep providing opportunities. I added that clients who decided to be a stand-up comic were definitely becoming engaged in life — courageously engaged!

As the dissent was quashed, or at least quietened, I passed out the info sheets for their clients.

Free training to be a stand-up comic & educate people about mental illness. Contact Rodney.

Beneath these words, I'd included a stick figure standing on the stage speaking to a packed audience of laughing people. I let staff know that Jill Bloom from Fraserside and Dave Brown from Lookout Emergency Aid were also being contacted to see if any of their clients were interested.

"It would be nice if our own clients accepted this opportunity to support us, but I will accept all comers." I hoped this might create a competitive spirit.

Over a period of two weeks, I got responses from ten interested clients. Seven from our branch of CMHA and three from Jill's and Dave's organizations. Amazing! My own doubts and the staff misgivings proved wrong — so far.

I began to receive multiple burst-of-victory phone calls from Darcy about the new heights he had reached in finding sponsors and donors.

"Rodney, I've got the Hotel Vancouver to hold the event for us free of charge."

"That sounds great, Darcy!"

"Rodney, I've got the *Surrey Leader* and *Westender* newspapers to give us a free ad campaign."

"Well, that sounds wonderful. Well done, Darcy!"

"I've found a comedic coach who will train our clients for ten bucks an hour and will wait to get paid from the profits."

"That's good, Darcy. Well done!"

"I've got..." and "That's great!" phone calls became a weekly feature of my interactions with Darcy. It didn't matter if I was busy or not; he gushed reports onto me like a waterfall overflowing a bucket. I learned to give accolades as I did paperwork.

One month after meeting Darcy, the would-be comedians assembled in the boardroom for their first training session. Still uncertain about the idea, I met the five women and five men who had volunteered.

"I'm glad you have all taken advantage of this opportunity to get free professional training to be stand-up comics. I'm sure it will be a great experience for you all." I thanked them for their time and courage and hoped they would find it a wonderful experience. They smiled and looked pleased at my encouragement.

"Hey, maybe I'll even drop in sometimes and hear the jokes. Sometimes, I need cheering up."

My doubts about the program were left unstated. I gave the would-be comedians two thumbs-up, smiled, and walked slowly back to my office. Unlike Darcy, I was not a hoopla guy, and I worried that with all the sponsors he was getting, if the event crashed or the comics jammed out at the last minute, it would generate a negative image of people with mental illness. It might also have a bad impact on our clients, if they had tried their best and failed. I kept my fingers crossed and continued my support.

Two months into the training, Darcy phoned in a panic, his perennially effervescent mood punctured.

"One of the comics, Jackie, didn't show up today. I heard she might have quit. If she bails, others might get the idea that quitting is okay. It could be like the first leak in the dam. We need to plug it, Rodney."

Darcy had a point. Jackie was a tall, good-natured mother of two lovely teenagers in her late forties. She had a zany sense of humour, excellent for Comedy Courage, but sometimes suffered from debilitating depression. I decided to phone and discuss her decision.

"Jackie, I was just chatting with Darcy. He was concerned that you'd missed the last training session."

"Yeah, I'm thinking of quitting. The trainer is driving me nuts. She squashes the individuality of the comics. I can't take it anymore." This sounded serious — a valid gripe. Jackie explained that one trainee, Sammy, wanted to go onstage in a straightjacket to show as well as tell how restricting mental illness was. "Kim said it was a dumb idea and that he couldn't wear it."

"Yeah, that does sound a bit harsh, but please don't quit, Jackie. You'll be missed if you leave. I heard some of your jokes. They were really funny."

"I would be missed?"

"Of course. You are a valuable part of the team."

"I've never heard of anyone missing me before."

I pointed out that we had agreed on a deal: We would give the training, and she'd agreed to do the show. Not holding people accountable because they have a mental illness could be considered condescending.

"How about I talk to the trainer, see if I can get her to loosen up a bit, and you try coming back onto the team for the next session. We had a deal, right?"

"Rodney, I didn't expect to be missed. I'll try coming back next week — see how it goes."

I thanked her and told her to check in with me to see if the situation had improved.

*Have I done the right thing? What if she just said yes to please me and can't cope with the stress of the big night?*

I approached the trainer before the next session started. She was in her 20s and kept looking at her shoes during our meeting.

"Kim, thanks for coming on board and training our comics. I'm sure it must be a challenge. However, I was concerned that one of the comics might be quitting."

She bit her lip and avoided eye contact. "Yeah, me too. I've never trained people with mental illness before. Actually, I've never trained anyone."

"I guess it's a fine line. Letting each person be creative but making sure they're funny."

She looked relieved. "Exactly, exactly. That's what I'm trying to do."

"Maybe with Jackie and some of the others, you could cut them a bit of slack — see how it works out?"

"Sure, I can try. It upset me that she didn't show up for training."

I wrapped up by telling her the team of comics seemed to be coming along well and that I enjoyed hearing gusts of laughter coming through the walls every training day.

A smile lit up her face as we left the room. Maybe surviving a tricky discussion with the executive director 40 years her senior, and receiving praise, was an encouraging outcome.

Jackie came back and stayed the course. I checked in with her a couple of times. She said she wasn't *completely* happy but that things had improved enough to stay.

Over the three months of training, I noticed subtle changes in the participants: They smiled more, walked taller, and seemed imbued with a quiet sense of purpose. Maybe the weekly exercise of bringing their diagnosis out of the shadows into the daylight and laughing about it as a group gave them power over the illness rather than it having power over them. Laughing about problems can diminish them. The camaraderie of working for a cause bigger than themselves seemed to have helped them feel more valued, more confident, and less alone.

I lost my ambivalence about Comedy Courage. Even if the gala night failed, positive gains for the comics had been achieved.

On the eve of the gala, I became less casual about failure. Giant butterflies started flapping around my stomach. It was the highest profile public event our organization had ever held and the only one I hadn't handcrafted myself. What if the donated food was crap, no one bid in the two auctions, Darcy talked too much, one of the comics had a meltdown, or the $150-a-plate guests didn't think the jokes were funny?

*Courageous Comics on Gala Night*

    The ballroom was buzzing with expectant voices. Members of the audience strolled around looking at the items for auction or sat chatting at tables. Darcy, dressed in his familiar black suit, was flitting between the comics, the guests, Joey Thompson of *The Province* newspaper who would run the auctions, and John Daly of Global News who was hosting the evening.

    Darcy had allotted me six tickets: I gave two to Bev Gutray, used two myself, and gave two to Jackie's kids. We all sat at the same table. I tried to relax, sip beer, and make small talk with the three adults and Jackie's children. I wanted them to experience their mother shining in the spotlight rather than her depressed side they sometimes saw at home.

    John Daly picked up the mic, and the audience hushed. "Welcome, everybody, to what is going to be a fabulous evening here at the gorgeous Hotel Vancouver ballroom with our courageous comics." He hoped we'd enjoy each other's company, the food, the auctions, and the wonderful comedians. "And now, ladies and gentlemen, please give a big hand to Rodney Baker, the executive director of Canadian Mental Health Association - Simon Fraser Branch, the beneficiary of this evening's fundraising gala."

I walked onstage and looked down at 150 people applauding. Nerve-wracking. I hoped the large crowd wouldn't spook our comics. Grasping the microphone with a sweaty hand, I kept my speech short. "Welcome, everybody! Thank you for coming to help break the stigma of mental illness by believing that our stand-up comics can deliver a great evening of entertainment." I commended John and Joey for donating their valuable time and the donors for their auction contributions. I thanked the comedy trainer and, pointing toward Darcy, congratulated him for putting it all together. He beamed from ear to ear, flushed a proud red, and bowed so deeply I thought he was going to fall over.

"And last but not least, I would like to recognize and thank our ten courageous comics. Please give them a huge hand!" The crowd's enthusiasm erupted in clapping and whistles.

As the first comic went onstage, I stopped breathing. It was Imran. He took two medications, one for schizophrenia and the other to stop the side effect of his eyes rolling upward. In his excitement about performing, he had forgotten the second medication. He had cheat cards to help him.

He blurted a few words out, "Hi, my name is," his eyes rolled up; he forced them back down and peered at the card, "Imran Ali." He smiled at the success of completing the sentence. The audience tittered.

"I suffer from," eyes rolled up, he pulled them back down to the card, "schizophrenia and gender dysmorphia. But it's okay." He gave a brief smirk. "If I don't like the dress I'm wearing," he forced his eyes back down to read, "I can hallucinate a different one." He gave a small victory smile each time he managed to read a card.

People loved it. They thought he was faking only being able to remember three or four words without looking at the card. He wasn't.

Next up was Leone, tall, in her 60s, and smartly coiffed for the show. "Hi, I'm Leone, and I'm a member of Jill Bloom's Friendship House. I used to love going there. We did lots of activities, painting, bingo, and quiz games, but lately, due to Fraser Health budget cutbacks, we can't have friends anymore, only…acquaintances."

Her grave sincerity brought peals of laughter

Lyle was in his late thirties, soft-spoken, with wispy red hair. He talked about how religion had helped him. "I like all the inspiring stories. Like when God told Abraham to throw his only son on the burning bush. As Abraham approached the fire, God said, 'Hey, just kidding, Abe.' It was then I realized that God had a sense of humour."

Enthusiastic applause burst from the audience.

"Back in those days, a lot of interesting stuff happened — the talking snake in the Garden of Eden, Adam eating the apple, Noah and the flood, manna from heaven. I think it was Abraham who said to God, 'Hey, there's a lot going on down here, maybe we should write a book about it.'"

Anna, raised Catholic, was in hysterics. Bev and her friend were enjoying the jokes. Jackie's kids were chuckling but looked nervous as their mother stepped onstage.

She wore a well-tailored red suit and her blonde hair in a bouncy ponytail. She looked beautiful and oozed playful confidence. She talked about the many diagnoses she'd received from different psychiatrists and rattled off a list of eight disorders like an auctioneer. "How could my diagnosis change with each different psychiatrist? Hey, maybe they were the ones making me sick!

"The last psychiatrist thought he was a straight talker, said I'd faked all the previous mental illnesses just for attention. Hell, if that's all I wanted, I could walk down Columbia Street naked and get a lot more attention than I got from all those shrinks." The audience tittered. "The most intriguing diagnosis was bipolar disorder, not otherwise specified. I see some of you folks laughing out there about the 'not otherwise specified disorder,' we know who we are, don't we? All you folks secretly smiling, well, the secret's out. Like me, you're unspecified."

The audience rippled with nervous laughter.

"Anyway, this shrink said because I had trouble walking over bridges meant I had an anxiety disorder and the best way to cure it was something called exposure therapy, which means...they make you walk over a frigging *bridge*." She waited for the laughter to die down. "Really? Who thinks this shit up? Anyway, he accompanied me over the bridge, and when we got to the middle, I threw him over. Just for attention!"

The jokes rolled on. I had another beer, breathed, and relaxed. The comics were genuinely funny, many better than professional comedians. The food was delicious — Anna approved of the quality. John Daly hosted the evening smoothly, and Joey Thompson did a great job of the auction.

Darcy had done it — pulled the whole thing off just like he said he would when he had burst into my office five months ago, spouting hot enthusiasm for fantastic Comedy Courage plans. Well done, Darcy James! You made your vision come true exactly as promised and raised a net sum of $14,540.

But also important, maybe more important, for one evening, due to their own hard work and courage, 10 volunteer comics' lives had been lifted into the limelight of celebrated centre-stage performers receiving well-earned applause from a receptive audience. A brief window of respite from their everyday lives. As Jackie said later,

"From that day on, things were different. I realized I could do stuff. I could help others. I could shine."

The local paper reported on the successful event and took a shot of Kim, Darcy, and me holding a giant cheque for the money raised. Some of the comics went on to perform in comedy gigs around New Westminster. The money earned was used to pay down the Bluebird House mortgage. Real estate was a bankable asset. If there were further financial crises ahead, we could borrow against the mostly paid-off house.

## Outreach

I pulled off the Lions Gate Bridge onto Pender Street toward the CMHA head office for our first Outreach training session. I liked the sound of "Outreach." It had a positive ring to it, an action word — someone cared, was trying to help homeless people. But how do you help someone living on the street? Employers don't hire people without an address. Without paid work, how can a person get an address? If they've lived on the street for a long time, how would they suddenly acquire the skills to live in housing?

Much of the public assumes that homeless people are lazy, whereas in reality, being homeless can be a lot of work: Having no income and nowhere to live creates the daily challenge of finding food, shelter, and, if you are addicted, drugs. A hit of crystal meth can work instead of food — lifts you up and decreases your hunger for a couple of days. Each night, you need to find somewhere to sleep where your meagre possessions won't disappear by morning. If you are cold, hungry, wet, and haven't slept, it's hard to make healthy life decisions, even if you're not addicted and don't have bedbugs, scabies, lice, AIDs, or Hepatitis B or C.

I found parking and joined executive directors from six branches, or their lieutenants, in the CMHA headquarters conference room. I'd always been confused about how to help panhandlers. Sometimes I'd given them money, but I wondered if it went for drugs instead of food, so I looked forward to learning more about their world. It felt ironic that while we waited to learn about homelessness, we sat around a long oak table in plush chairs with two walls of glass overlooking the city, snacked on fruit and bran muffins, and helped ourselves to coffee.

Excitement hung in the air as our group waited for our trainer, Judy Graves, to arrive. We were going to get insider knowledge from the top outreach worker in the Downtown East-side on how to get people off the streets and into housing. I also sensed apprehension: Could our well-dressed, well-fed group, who lived in comfy homes and worked in warm offices, learn skills to administer a program that encountered homeless people on the sidewalk and helped them find housing? Up to this point, our branch's clients had been carefully vetted by the public health provider, Fraser Health, to ensure they were a good fit for our housing programs. Now, any person sleeping rough would be a potential client needing our help, an increased responsibility and role for our organization.

None of us had been street people. All ears were intent on absorbing every detail to get a gut feel for the job. In just a few days, we would be hiring outreach workers. Bev Gutray, the head of CMHA in BC, joined us for the presentation. Having CMHA branches start a Homeless Outreach program was her initiative: She found the funding from BC Housing, located Judy Graves to train us, and helped roll out the program.

As we sat chatting in the meeting room, Judy Graves breezed through the door. She wore jeans, runners, and a Gore-Tex jacket. Her face had a warm look, street weathered but alight with mission. Her voice was soft, firm, honest — touched you straight inside. I understood why street people trusted her. After introducing ourselves, Judy started right in.

"You want to work with homeless people? Get them into housing? Show respect. No one will go anywhere with you if you don't respect them."

We all nodded. That made sense. Did we know *how* to respect street people?

"I find the best time to reach people is in the morning, while they're sleeping, before they get busy with their day. I approach slowly, nudge a foot gently with my foot. Don't lean over them." She shook her head. "Too threatening. As they wake up, I say, 'Hi, wanna smoke?' That gets their attention right away."

I smiled. Judy did her own thing. Smoking was no longer PC. But of course, on the street, maybe not being PC doesn't matter. I decided not to share this aspect of greeting potential homeless clients with the staff, especially Robbie, who started our smoking cessation program. From a harm reduction viewpoint, I reasoned that living on the street is more dangerous to health than smoking.

"I wait nearby till they've finished the smoke, then approach again and offer to buy them breakfast. I don't get many refusals."

We got it. Make friends. Give smokes and food. Who would refuse a free breakfast? We hung on every word. I worried about getting carried away with the story and then forgetting what she said, so I jotted down a few notes. *Was cigarette and breakfast money included in the funding? Ask later.*

"Eating breakfast, getting some protein inside 'em, helps 'em think better."

We all nodded. That made sense. "Then I ask, 'Would you like to sleep inside tonight? Get a place?' After buying breakfast and handing out smokes, they get that I'm for real. Some say yes; some say no. After sleeping rough in the rain for a couple of weeks, most people start to say yes."

"What happens then?" asked Katy from the North Vancouver branch, a mother of two young kids.

"I take them to find a room, then go to social assistance to get the money."

"What kind of room?" Bev asked. "Where do you take them?"

"An SRO downtown. Not great, but inside and dry. You need an address to get support money or a job. When I started, it used to take forever, and some folks would get fed up with all the paperwork and

BS questions. They'd just walk out in the middle of it all."

"What's an SRO," Bev asked.

"Single Room Occupancy," Judy said. "One-room accommodation. Usually pretty crappy but out of the rain and cold — better than nothing."

"Do you work alone?" I asked, wondering if I'd need two workers.

"I usually work with a buddy." She nodded. "Especially in the beginning when it took longer to get the payment. Once we arrived in the ministry office, I kept my hand on the person's arm throughout the process — to reassure them, keep 'em calm and in touch. If I needed to fill in paperwork, my partner rested his hand on their arm. Most of these folks were not used to filling in forms or an office environment. It freaked them out."

I could imagine! The street meets bureaucracy. Bureaucracy wins by death from a thousand questions.

Judy started to smile. We felt good information was coming. Like the people she served on the street, we began to trust her. "As I'd woken these folks up and got them breakfast early, we arrived before the ministry offices were open, so I got them to open earlier."

She said it in one casual sentence, as though ministry offices often switched their opening times to accommodate clients. She continued on in her earnest, look-you-in-the-eyes way and explained that it used to take forever to get the money for housing but she spoke to the mayor and a few other people and got things fast-tracked so she got the money the same day.

Okay, now our group became mesmerised. She'd got the Ministry of Social Assistance offices to open early? Procured the money in one day?

Usually, *people* don't change government systems. *Government systems* change people.

"Now that outreach is being spread through the Lower Mainland, I've asked the minister in charge to make sure all the social assistance offices in your regions use the fast-track-to-housing program."

Holy shit! How could one person get this to happen? She must have made friends in high places. Street smart *and* politically smart — a remarkable combination. Most people I knew in mental health often bitched about *the system*. This simple, unpretentious woman *changed* the system — made it work for the people.

I felt a sudden sense of chagrin. Judy's accomplishments belittled my own helping efforts. One of the reasons I'd gone into mental health was to help make a positive difference for people diagnosed with mental illness. Schizophrenia or bipolar disorders aren't lifestyle choices. I always reminded myself, "There, but for the grace of God, go I." Not that I was religious, but invoking God made it seem more profound. Compared to Judy, my days at work often seemed steeped in trivia, finding items for the newsletter, proofreading a new brochure, giving a presentation to a Rotary Club to rustle up money to buy refurbished computers for the staff, writing grant proposals, and losing time sitting around in meetings. This person, Judy Graves, was making a real and immediate improvement in the lives of homeless people by helping them get inside out of the cold and rain.

Inspired by Judy, I became determined to find a great outreach worker and support her or him to make a real difference in the world. Maybe I'd go with them sometimes. Hell, maybe I should be an outreach worker myself, stop sitting at a desk all day, worrying how to make everything work — go into the streets and find people housing. But at close to 60 years of age, I was probably too old to change jobs. *Who would hire me? Could I hire myself then quit my role as ED?*

Bev's voice pulled me back to the room. "Okay, people, we're going to have a little break now. Help yourself to coffee and muffins, have a chat about what you've heard from Judy, and we'll come back to our meeting in 15 minutes."

Grabbing a coffee and raisin-bran muffin, I walked to the window and stared at the forest of high-rises. Green slivers of Stanley Park peeked through behind the tall office towers. Being the only male and older than everyone else, I didn't usually fare well in CMHA free-range chat sessions.

A window full of giant buildings, booming new construction, and bustling streets spoke of a vibrant, wealthy city. I grew up in a village. No one slept outside at night there. What was it about cities that caused people to sleep on the streets? Why were so many homeless?

"Nice view," Judy said, approaching me from behind.

Perhaps her radar for lost men had homed in on me. "Yeah," I said, trying to think of more to say.

"How do you think the talk is going so far?"

"Good." *Am I a monosyllabic moron?* I swallowed. "Uh, I'm getting a feel for what you do. It'll be helpful for hiring someone — you know — an outreach worker."

Bev's voice reached through the room. "Okay, people, let's come back to the table. We'll break for lunch in half an hour."

I returned to my seat and looked around the room. The 12-storey view, free coffee, and lunch was light-years away from my noisy, windowless, 50-cent coffee, ground-level office below the New Westminster cemetery.

Bev's commanding voice whisked me back to the meeting. "I'm finding this all very interesting," she said, looking in Judy's direction and smiling. "Perhaps before we go on, now would be a good time for any questions."

My colleagues had intelligent, well-thought-out questions. I wrote down lots of notes from Judy's answers. The more I understood the job, the better chance I had of hiring an effective outreach worker. This pilot program was only for a year, but if I made a success of it, I hoped it would continue.

A day later, I was back in my office scanning my notes and trying to formulate an ad for someone to fill the outreach position. After fussing, fuming, and reducing, I came up with,

Wanted, outreach worker, must have experience with homeless people.

I placed ads in the *Vancouver Sun* and Craigslist.

From my newly acquired knowledge of outreach, I formulated 10 pertinent questions with a possible score of 10 for each one. I didn't want to be caught empty-handed when besieged by applicants for the job. Whoever got the highest marks would get the job. Simple! I had scheduled the outreach interviews for Wednesday mornings, which were usually free. Wednesday mornings were also when the Comedy Courage training was taking place in the boardroom next to my office.

The first candidate arrived, a 39-year-old woman in a black business suit and a crisp manner accompanied by a perfect resume retrieved from a black leather briefcase. As I interviewed her, gusts of laughter ricocheted around the adjoining room as the Comedy Courage crew practiced their jokes. Miss Perfect Resume looked alarmed.

"Where's that, that laughter coming from?"

"We're training people to be stand-up comics," I explained.

Her jaw tightened. "Stand-up comics?"

"Yeah, some of our clients are learning to tell jokes. It's okay. Laughter is good for you, isn't it?" I said, smiling. She looked dubious — as though I shouldn't be enjoying it.

"It's not at all appropriate when I'm trying to answer questions."

She had a point. Gales of laughter had seemed strange to me too at first, but I decided that it was liberating and livened up the day. Maybe it wasn't fair on her. Then I reasoned if she couldn't deal with harmless laughter, how would she cope finding housing for street-hardened homeless people, many of whom were addicts and may have an array of illnesses or mental health issues? She got a miserable 45 out of 100 on my score sheet. After interviewing three more applicants, I was getting disappointed; none of them seemed right. The highest mark was 54, not great out of 100. This was going to be tougher than I thought.

On the third week of my search, I received a resume in WordPerfect and couldn't open it. I replied asking if she could send it in Word. I almost didn't bother. No one used WordPerfect anymore. About three days later, I got her resume back in Word. She wasn't in a rush. The result wasn't great; it had a couple of spelling mistakes and wasn't well laid out. I felt a tad sorry for her and sent her a couple of resume examples with the personal info blanked out and wrote, "This is what you're competing with."

The next day, Heather phoned. "Hi, I applied for the outreach job, but I can't change my resume. There's a glitch in my computer."

"Your resume is important. Just trying to let you know what you are up against." Silence on both ends of the phone.

"Couldn't you give a single mother a chance?"

She caught me off guard. Saying "No" sounded harsh. "Okay, come in tomorrow around ten." My father had died young, and Mom had raised my three younger siblings on her own. Her emotional and financial challenges had left a soft spot in my heart.

The following morning, I was scrambling to finish a funding proposal, and the outreach interview had slipped my mind. Leaving my office to pick up some computer paper, I glimpsed a woman sitting down in reception. She was gaunt-looking, with unruly red hair and baggy green shorts.

I walked back to my office and picked up the phone. "Jim, is that woman here for the outreach position?"

"Yes. She's here a little early."

*Bad resume — unusual interview clothes.* "Okay, send her in to me in five minutes." I went to my computer, printed off the sheet marked Outreach Questions, and picked up my pen.

"Heather, how are you doing today?"

"Good, thanks. And you?"

*No sense of nerves there.* "Fine, thanks. Can you tell me why you applied for this job?"

"I believe in helping people who are homeless. If we can offer assistance to get them off the street, it's the first step to rebuilding their lives," she said calmly. "People don't want to be homeless, but they need help navigating the system to get housing."

I perked up and marked down "10."

Heather sounded like Judy Graves. She answered each question in a thoughtful manner. Her clear blue eyes shone into mine. She spoke with the quiet confidence of someone who knew the street. The clarity of each answer struck my mind like truth gongs. My hopes skyrocketed. I wrote "10" for each answer. Finally, I had found someone. I felt like hugging her. She was going to make the Outreach Program work. Instead of saying, "We will be in touch with you shortly and let you know," I blurted out, "Heather, I liked your answers. If you were offered the job, when could you start?"

"My former employer, The Health Contact Centre, was closed down due to lack of funding, so I could start anytime."

"Okay, sounds good. Why don't we say you can start in two weeks? I'll be in touch about where you are going to work and how to set things up."

"Great! Thanks." An elated, single-mother-found-work smile crossed her lips.

"You're welcome. I'm looking forward to working with you."

We shook hands, and I followed her out of my office, planning to get a coffee. Stephanie was in the hallway. It was a small office and not much happened in private.

"I hear you're advertising for outreach workers."

"Yeah, that's right."

"You're supposed to list any new position internally first. You should know that. Union policy."

"There's no one qualified. It's an outreach position, not a housing position."

"You still need to post it." A wisp of a smile touched her face as she tossed her head and walked away.

I swallowed my frustration. This job sometimes felt like I was a policeman trying to direct traffic in a straightjacket: Any new initiative I proposed needed to align with union protocols, comply with our eight-page CMHA franchise agreement, be approved by the board of directors, and, in reality, be accepted by the staff.

Copying and pasting the outreach job description, I added, "Must apply within five days," found two thumbtacks, and posted it on the staff notice board. Stephanie was right, but it never occurred to me that any staff would be interested.

Providing services for homeless people was a new direction for us. At our weekly staff meeting, the news that we were starting an outreach program provided much fodder to chew on.

"Do street people have to be mentally ill before we can find them housing?" Stephanie asked.

"I don't think we'd want to ask them, do you?" I replied.

"Well, I've been looking in our constitution, and it says our purpose is to 'help people with a psychiatric disability.' Are we allowed to help people if they are homeless but don't have a mental illness?"

"Well, as Bev Gutray, head of CMHA in British Columbia, has found training and funding for the program, I'm pretty sure it's okay."

"I saw the posting for an outreach worker," Robbie said. "It gave only five days to respond. What's the rush?"

"I want to get going with the program and didn't think anybody here would be interested. You have to have experience."

"I've volunteered with homeless people in Maple Ridge," Robbie said, sticking her chin out. "I'm thinking of applying."

"It's a full-time job. You'd have to give up running your smoking cessation program."

Robbie frowned. She was a passionate anti-smoker and had found federal funding to run a successful program for our clients who wanted to kick the tobacco habit.

"What kind of safeguards will there be in place for workers?"

Stephanie asked.

"Safeguards?"

"Yeah, so you know they made it home each night after working on the streets all day."

"Good point. I'm going to work on outreach safety aspects after this meeting."

Stephanie was right. I'd been treating the position like any other staff job, but it wasn't. I researched "outreach worker safety protocols" on the web. Reams of information came up, and I synthesized the protocols from different organizations. Two hours later, I had a five-page working outline on safety procedures, which I emailed to Heather, Judy Graves, and Bev Gutray for their comments. Outreach protocols were far more complex than I had imagined:

3.1 Outreach workers will report to their supervisor at the beginning of their shift and at the end of their shift. If report is done by phone, outreach worker will detail what they are wearing and their vehicle specifics (make, model, colour, and license plate).

3.2 Outreach workers will phone supervisor or a designated check-in person every 2 hrs if they're working in the field; supervisor will log the time and location of calls.

Five pages of protocols was a lot to swallow, a lot to follow. As the outreach program supervisor, it was a big increase of responsibility for me. Never mind — I believed in this program and was excited to be part of helping homeless people find accommodation.

No staff applied for the job, and Heather started working for us. After a couple of months working in New Westminster, Heather found the local welfare office was not fast-tracking her clients and asked if she could try working in Maple Ridge. She had grown up there and wanted to make a difference in her own community. I agreed but was hesitant. It was too far to trek from Maple Ridge to New Westminster every day, so she would have to keep her client files at home, plus I'd envisioned monitoring her progress with frequent meetings.

However, she was doing a good job, and I agreed to her new location. Things went smoothly in Maple Ridge. I was in daily touch with her by phone, and she mostly managed to make it to our weekly team meetings. After nine months of Heather being employed with us, I received phone calls from other nonprofits, the police, and a social worker telling me what a great job she was doing. This was remarkable. Kudos to Heather. I'd never experienced that before.

After eleven months of operations, all the agencies with outreach workers funded by BC Housing were asked to meet at a hotel in Surrey for a kind of pep talk and exchange of views. I was curious about the meeting but unhappy about spending half a day away while things piled up on my desk. On the plus side, they had coffee and great cookies. I pondered if it was right to spend money on cookies for forty people when street people were going hungry.

We were welcomed by Helen, the BC Housing liaison. Having worked in outreach for a while in Prince George, she had acquired some knowledge of the street. Helen thanked us for coming and recognized the stellar work the agencies were doing in the new Outreach initiative. She introduced us to William, a young man in a dark suit, who was responsible for the Outreach program budget.

William cleared his throat and wished us good morning. "From now on, we need you to keep track of the clients you have housed for a period of six months, so we can evaluate how this housing program is working." This news was received by puzzled looks and subdued muttering as people discussed this new protocol.

Heather spoke up. "How are we supposed to do that? Most street people don't have cell phones, so we can't reach them to ask questions."

This unforeseen complication caused William to look puzzled. He went into a huddle with two assistants and re-emerged after a few minutes sounding more confident.

"Okay, we understand that not everybody has phones. What you need to do in that case is get the landlord to fill in a form detailing information about the client's length of stay." William looked satisfied, nodded to Heather, and sat down. A buzz of uneasy muttering broke out among the agency workers but stopped as Judy Graves's clear voice rang out behind me.

"Most of the SROs used by our homeless clients are owned by biker gangs, or similar people, who deal in cash, don't file income tax returns, and would laugh at the idea of filling out government forms."

Government bean counters meet street-savvy soldiers. I suppressed a grin. William and colleagues looked perplexed and huddled again but failed to come up with a new plan.

"We will get back to you on that one," Helen explained.

After some more general discussion on Outreach challenges and solutions, Helen wrapped up the meeting. I grabbed a last cookie and walked out to the parking lot with Heather. We were happy to be part of the program and shared a few chuckles about the meeting. It was a great initiative of BC Housing, and it had felt good to meet workers from other agencies and have our problems listened to.

One of the biggest challenges for outreach workers was that the government allowance was not enough to house homeless people decently. This meant putting them into substandard housing, often bug-infested, run-down apartments run by slumlords, or trying to find them a roommate to share the costs. If the person had lived on the street for a long time, once in housing they needed support to learn or relearn the skills of living inside.

Heather would drop by to make sure they were doing the basics: opening mail, remembering to lock doors, taking the garbage out, cooking simple meals, etc. Families were often a source of housing or temporary couch-surfing, and Heather invested time reconnecting family members and trying to heal past conflicts. She visited clients who were in prison and helped them make housing plans for their release. People with addiction problems were assisted to find placements in recovery centres and then to find housing when they had finished the program.

After running the program for a year, we concluded from our own research that 76% of the street people we helped showed signs of having mental illness. There was a popular theory that Riverview [Psychiatric] Hospital downsizing caused an increase of street people. Many ex-Riverview clients living on the streets had paranoid schizophrenia, a disorder where the sufferer trusts no one; some Heather talked to claimed that they'd been sedated so they were less likely to cause disruptions. Although their lives on the street weren't great, many preferred that to life in the psychiatric unit. Heather's first set of Outreach business cards had "Outreach – Canadian Mental Health Association" printed on the card. When many potential street clients saw the words "mental health," they tossed the cards and left. We printed another batch with just the words "Outreach – Heather" and her cell number.

One of Heather's clients had been living in a cardboard box on the street for two years and had Hepatitis C. She found him housing and encouraged him through the painful medication regime to cure his illness. Two years after meeting Heather on the street, he was living in an apartment, had got married, had become a father, and found work.

Some clients were barely clinging to life. Occasionally, one of them would die, and I would meet and try to help Heather through her grief. She needed to talk things through — be assured she couldn't have done more — not the sort of conversation to have with your friends or partner. Her tragic stories often affected me. There were also heartwarming tales of helping people find housing and of street camaraderie: When Heather ventured into the bush looking for people living rough, street people she knew and trusted accompanied her to make sure she was safe.

After the first year of operation, BC Housing concluded our homeless outreach program was a success and continued our funding. During a homelessness marathon event in 2011, J. Peachy, an independent reporter looking at homelessness around the province, recorded an impromptu video interview of Heather at work. Utube: https://www.youtube.com/watch?v=2D0rROFUcTY

Officially a mother of six, she was a virtual mother to the many homeless people she helped find housing from 2007 until 2018 when that branch of CMHA discontinued their involvement in the Outreach program.

## **Problems at Riverside House**

As the outreach program came to be part of the fabric of our organization, Sandy and Sharon became spotters for household items that Heather's homeless people might need as she found them housing: Sheets, toasters, kettles, microwaves, plates, and cutlery were in regular demand. Some of our clients also needed similar goods when moving from one of our transition houses into their own apartments. Sharon and Sandy were proud that *their* store was able to help.

One morning in the thrift store, as I was giving Sandy a list of goods needed by one of Heather's clients, our conversation was interrupted by my office phone ringing. I sprinted the familiar route to my office and grabbed the receiver.

"Hi, it's Daren."

Daren? The name didn't ring a bell. "Your voice is familiar, but I can't recall how we know one another."

"You rented the house from me on River Road in Maple Ridge."

That was almost two years ago; no wonder I didn't recall. "Okay, right. Everything okay?"

"The lease is up in three months, and I'm putting the house up for sale. Just thought I would let you know."

Numbness spread through my body.

"Are you still there?"

"Yeah. Just a bit shocked. Didn't expect this to happen. I'd planned to renew the lease."

"Well, if I was keeping it, that would have been fine. You were good tenants. I had my doubts when you said mentally ill people would be living there, but it worked out well."

"Daren, could you think about making it four months? The people there have become kind of like a family, and it may take a while to find another house?"

Daren agreed to think about it. Deflated, I sat down heavily and stared at my swimming fish screensaver. It took a while to reinflate my spirits. I gathered myself together, called Barney's cell phone, and gave him the bad news.

"Damn, Rodney, that house was working out so well. What are you going to do?"

"Do? I only just heard about it, Barney. I'm still numb. It's a problem for both of us. You'll have to find housing for five clients if we lose that house." In the silence that followed, I heard a cigarette lighter flick. We were both quitting.

"Why don't you buy the place, Rodney?"

I snorted out loud. "Yeah, right, Barney!" Working for the government, he was clueless about funding challenges. I almost forgave him — but not quite. "Listen, my government-funded friend, I struggle daily to keep this damned place afloat. Buying real estate is currently absent from my survival plans."

"I hear ya, Rodney. But seriously, think about it. BC Housing may have money for that kind of project. Why don't you give them a try?"

I wanted sympathy, not more work. "May have money" wasn't inviting. I had always struggled to buy and pay for my own home. I didn't want to replicate that kind of challenge at work. But he had planted a seed — a pesky seed. I couldn't find the money to buy a house for the organization — too difficult. But if I could, owning real estate would mean more security for the future. We already owned Bluebird House, with a mortgage of course. In the Vancouver area, housing had always been a great investment, except for the real estate market crash of 1981, when I had been caught owning three properties and almost lost everything.

The afternoon drifted by in a slow fog. On the journey home, the jam-packed freeway couldn't drown out Daren's voice echoing in my head, "I'm putting the house up for sale." Being stuck in interminable traffic wasn't so bad. I was in limbo, out of reach, a hideout from responsibility.

Arriving home, I sat in the kitchen and watched TV with the sound off as Anna cooked.

"You okay?" she asked.

"Yeah. No."

"What kind of answer is that?" She never minced words.

"That house we rented in Maple Ridge, the owner wants to sell it."

No answer. She checked the oven and smiled at me. "Pasta al forno. Getting brown on top. Almost ready."

"Did you hear me? He's going to sell it."

"Yes, sorry to hear that. You'll think of something."

"I don't want to 'think of something.' I'm fed up with thinking of something." I was starting to sound whiny, so I shut up.

The next day at work, I told no one about the house being put on the market. Not discussing it maintained the calm, gave me some breathing space until the news sunk in. By afternoon, saying nothing became uncomfortable. I called Donald, the housing manager, into my office at the end of the day.

"Hey, what's up?" he said in his usual upbeat tone.

"The owner is putting Riverside House on the market."

Donald's brow creased, and he lowered himself into a chair. "No!"

"Yeah." I took a deep breath. "He told me he wouldn't be renewing the lease. We've got three months, maybe four."

I outlined three possibilities. "We could hope the new owners want to rent it to us — a long shot. We could look for a new house to rent in the same vicinity or try to buy it." Saying "try to buy it" sounded good, like it could happen — a possibility.

"Buy it?" Donald said in a squeaky voice as he flashed me a confused look.

"Barney thinks BC Housing might help. In the meantime, you check around for suitable rental houses, and I'll see about raising funds." It was encouraging to make positive plans, but I needed to digest the idea and took no immediate action. After years of running my own business, I still felt awkward going cap in hand and asking for handouts.

After a week of beating myself up for doing nothing, I decided to drive out to Maple Ridge and tell the residents that the house was going on the market. I phoned Erin, the worker who managed Riverside House, to let her know I was coming and why. She was shocked into silence then whispered, "No, Rodney. Surely not?" The line went dead.

Pulling into the driveway, I turned the motor off and stared at the house. Memories flooded through my mind: the elation we had felt at finding it, Barney's enthusiastic support, the busy day we'd picked up all the housewares and packed everything from the truck to the house. The satellite house idea worked, and the extra funds it had brought in helped us stay afloat — shocking that it might all collapse. I took a big breath and walked through the door to tell the residents that their home was going up for sale.

The familiar smell of cabbage, potatoes, and coffee greeted me as Erin opened the door. Her smeared mascara and averted eyes set the tone for the meeting. She gave me a quick, unexpected hug then left to call the residents, Ted, Billy, John, Wally, and Sarah. They walked into the living room one by one, said "Hello," and sat in the worn but comfy donated armchairs.

I smiled. "How's everyone doing today?"

"Fine."

"Good."

"Okay."

They didn't seem curious about why I was there. They were old hands at having things dropped on them. When you had a serious and persistent mental illness, people often told you what to do and where to go. The blitz of instructions tended to erode self-esteem, the first casualty of having a psychiatric diagnosis. Other people, experts, psychiatrists told you what was best. However, our focus was to encourage them to figure out their own paths through life and support them to get there. But here I was, about to tell them that the lives they had been building in this house would probably be uprooted.

I cleared my throat and tried to smile. "Two years ago, we started this house, and you all moved in. How's it working out for you?" Silence. They were expecting more, the other shoe to drop. I made eye contact around the room, sat back in my chair, and waited.

"I like having the cat," said Sarah, who was in her 60s and wore a red poncho. "She's cuddly, and she's got diabetes like me." Two others nodded.

"I like feeding the cat," Wally said. "He's got a little pink tongue."

"Yeah, good for you guys having a cat. The other houses are jealous," I said, nodding. The conversation stopped. "Anything else that you like, folks?"

"I like the washing line you put up, Rodney," Ted said, shaking his mop of unruly grey hair up and down. "It's fun putting the clothes on the line and watching them flap dry."

"Sometimes they blow off in the wind," said Billy, who wore bright red shirts and, at 31, was the youngest of the residents. "I like the dryer better."

"I like my bedroom," said Jim, the oldest resident at 67. "It's quiet, and no one bothers me."

I was glad they were speaking up, joining in. It would help me put a positive spin on the situation.

"I'm glad the house is working out for you guys. As you know, this was a new house for CMHA. With Barney's help, we rented it and you all moved in." Silence. I glanced at Erin. She looked away. I swallowed. "So, I talked to the owner a couple days ago about renewing the lease, but he has decided to sell the house."

More silence — a deeper, profound silence with a dark centre. Sarah picked up the Siamese cat that sat beside her rocker and started stroking her. Everyone stared at me with worried eyes.

"Are we gonna have to move, Rodney?" Jim asked from the far corner of the room. He had been an electrical engineer before becoming ill and rarely spoke.

"Good question. The truth is I don't know. We might try to buy the house. If any of you have rich relatives, let me know." Blank stares informed me that my attempt to lighten the mood had bombed. "If we can't buy it, the new owner may rent it to us like the current owner does. If neither of those things work out, we'll try to find a new house to rent for you."

The faces in the room reflected the subdued mood.

"The fact that you are all living here is proof we made it work once, and we'll do our best to make it work again."

"Should I tell my brother's wife we are moving?" Jim asked. "She usually sends me a Christmas card. I keep them on my dresser all year."

I suggested he wait until we knew what was happening.

"When will we know what's happening?" Billy asked in a louder voice.

"Good question, Billy. I don't know. I just dropped by to tell you that if you see a For Sale sign going up on the house, not to worry because we are trying our best to keep this place for you. If not, we'll try to rent somewhere just as nice."

"It's the best place I've lived in," Billy said as he looked at the cat.

"Yeah, it's good here. Erin's nice," Wally agreed.

"What will happen to the cat?" Sarah asked.

"Hopefully, he'll be able to remain with you," I said with a smile and a nod.

"It's a she." There was a hint of distrust in Sarah's eyes. If I didn't even know the cat's gender, how could I be trusted to secure their future home?

"As soon as we know what's happening, we'll let you know." I stood up, smiled at everyone, gave the cat a stroke, and left.

On the way back to the office, I drove much slower than usual, kept to the speed limit. I didn't want to get anywhere fast. I didn't want to get anywhere at all. I drove past the turnoff to the office and carried on to North Vancouver and home. Anna wasn't home. I distracted myself by reading a back issue of *The Economist*.

The following Tuesday at our team meeting, I brought up the topic of Riverside House being for sale. When I mentioned the possibility of buying it, Stephanie asked how we could do that when I was always saying we were short of money.

"Obviously, we don't have the money. I would have to raise it."

Robbie cautioned me. "I think it's a good idea, but check with the municipality first. I live in Maple Ridge, and there is a bylaw that prevents more than three unrelated people from living in a single-residence dwelling."

"But we are already doing that at Riverside House."

"I know that. Either they are turning a blind eye, or they don't know. But you don't want to buy the house and find you can't use it."

Robbie had a great point. Maybe no one bothered about enforcing the bylaws, but I decided to meet with the mayor of Maple Ridge and see if it would be a problem. I had once visited the mayor of Burnaby to ask about some funding, but he had hustled me out of the office and harangued me: "All you nonprofits are the same — always asking for money."

This made me apprehensive about asking a favour of another mayor, but circumstances propelled me forward. Buying the house was a long shot, but if we could pull it off, the last thing we needed was a measly bylaw blocking us from using it.

I combined my trip to Maple Ridge with several other tasks and left visiting the mayor till last, a personal trait, putting off worrisome tasks. I found parking and sat in the foyer outside the mayor's office, twiddling my thumbs. What if the guy was a nitpicker and stopped us using the house right now because we weren't in compliance with the bylaw?

A burly guy in his 50s burst into the foyer. "Must be Rod Baker. Come on in. I'm Gordie," he said, shaking my hand and smiling. "Grab a seat. What can I help you with?"

I handed him a brochure and gave my spiel about who I was and that we ran two transition houses for people with mental illness in his municipality. Before I could ask him about the bylaw, he asked me for advice about a young man who phoned him every day and complained. "First, I thought it was a prank, but he's been doing it for four months. He must have a mental illness, don't ya think?"

"Well, hard to say really. Only psychiatrists can diagnose mental illness."

"I'm sure the poor fella's crazy. You're in the mental health business. What should I do?"

*What a question! We're getting way off topic.* "You could try being honest. Tell him that phoning every day doesn't work for your busy schedule and maybe he could just phone once a week."

Mayor Gordon seemed to like that idea. Having earned brownie points, I brought up the bylaw regarding nonfamily members living together, let him know we were already breaking that bylaw, and if we managed to buy the house, could we continue to house five unrelated people?

"Ha, we've got biker gangs, crack houses, grow-ops, and hookers all operating out of residential homes," he said, shaking his head. "If you buy the house, it won't be a problem to keep running it just like it is."

"Good to know. That's a weight off my chest. It will be a stretch raising the money to buy it, so if we do, I don't want things going sideways because of that bylaw."

"Look, I'm a businessman really," he explained. "This is my first stint at being mayor, but you seem like you're doing good work for us. Don't quote me on ignoring the bylaw, but you have my word."

The mayor stood up. I guessed the interview was over, so I stood up too. He squinted at the brochure I'd given him.

"Is it you we have to thank for Heather, the outreach worker?"

"Yeah, she works for us."

"I heard great reports about her. She's doing a damn fine job," he said with a smile. "Hey, you want another house? Maybe you could put some of Heather's homeless people in this one." He retrieved a set of keys from his drawer and tossed them through the air. I caught them with one hand — a good omen.

"We own it, but we're not using it. Squatters have taken it over as a crack house. I send the cops round once in a while to clean 'em out. It needs a bit of fixing, but you can use it rent-free for a few years. The address is on the round disk."

I was in shock. The sudden offer of a free house "for a few years" seemed amazing. I swallowed. "Okay, thanks a lot, Gordie. I'll take a look — let you know if we can use it."

He strolled toward me and shook my hand.

I left his office walking on air: no problems with the bylaw, admiration for Heather, and the possibility of a new house. Incredible! Could I handle another house? *Charge ahead. See what happens.*

I sat in my car and phoned Barney. "Guess what just happened? The mayor gave me keys to another house — said we could use it for free. Want to go check it out?"

"Wow, you're kicking big-time housing butt, Rodney. I'd love to take a look, but in a week's time. I'm up to my asshole in alligators here." Barney's response about being busy reminded me I was supposed to be back for an intake meeting for a new resident coming into Bluebird House.

I phoned Donald. "Hey, I'm running a little late. Go straight to Bluebird. I'll see you there." I hurried back to the meeting, but my mind was on the incredible offer of a free house. Due to our busy schedules, it turned out to be a week before Donald and I got to see it.

The "For Sale" sign posted on the front lawn of Riverside House was a worry for the residents, but I had talked the owner into holding off selling while I tried to raise funds. A spark of hope was that BC Housing said they may be interested in partially funding purchasing the house. I had completed some lengthy paperwork for them and paid for the house surveys they requested. I don't mesh naturally with bureaucracy but, with the occasional muttered swearword, had persevered. The bottom line was they would lend us $280,000. We had to keep the house in perpetuity for housing mental health clients, and in ten years' time, they would forgive the loan. The Toronto Dominion bank would lend us $50,000 on a mortgage. Barney got Fraser Health to kick in $10,000, and I had drummed up $5000 by giving mental health presentations at Lions and Rotary clubs, which all added up to a total of $345,000. The price agreed upon with the owner was $355,000. We were $10,000 short.

While patiently dealing with paper pushers working at glacial speed, I had been giving the owner positive hang-tight messages. "Things are looking good. I'm getting the money together."

Three weeks past the original three-month deadline, the owner got fed up. "You either get the money in a week, or our deal is off."

I had agreed to pay the asking price and not dicker if he waited four months for me to raise the funds. As a last resort, I considered using my personal $10,000 line of credit to seal the deal but decided against it in case I had problems getting the money back. Because of my concerns about CMHA finances, I had already decided not to put myself on the pension scheme because it would cost the organization $3,000 a year — a decision I later regretted.

That week while rollerblading around Stanley Park, I fell and broke my right wrist. The bone came through my skin. I took my blades off and phoned Anna. After some miscued directions to my location, she finally found where I was in the park and transported me to Lions Gate Hospital. When I woke up after surgery, my wrist was held in place with two iron posts screwed into the bone and a connecting bar in between. It looked awful.

Three days later, I soldiered through the third Annual General Meeting. Holding the microphone with my left hand and the notes at an odd angle in the right hand of my pinned-together wrist, I read the notes I had tapped out with my left index finger.

The AGM was well attended; forty people showed up, but the success was tempered by having to let go of the dream to buy Riverside House: I had exhausted all possibilities and was unable to find the last $10,000.

The whole house debacle along with breaking my wrist was depressing, especially as my car was a manual shift. The previous week when Robbie contracted the flu, I had agreed to cover for her by running a Smoking Cessation group in Coquitlam. Returning after the session in heavy traffic on Lougheed Highway, I rear-ended a brand-new BMW. The driver of the other car stared but refrained from comment when I awkwardly wrote down his particulars with my left hand while trying to hold the paper with my pinned-together right hand. I got my car towed and took a taxi home.

Feeling incompetent on many levels, the following day I rented a car and drove to Maple Ridge to meet with Daren's real estate agent, Debbie Sheppard. I sat in her office and confessed. "Debbie, I've been telling Daren all along we would buy the house. I've tried everything, but I'm $10,000 short." Exhaling a long sigh, I blinked my eyes and looked away.

Debbie had been staring at the metal contraption screwed into my right forearm. She walked around her office for a minute and stood looking out of the window. Was she pissed off? She turned to face me.

"I've been to that house, Rodney. I was impressed by what you are doing. We need organizations like yours, looking after people with mental illness. What if I threw in my commission to make up the $10,000?"

With my wrecked wrist, the car accident, and feeling defeated about buying the house, my emotions were raw. A lump formed in my throat. I started to cough, walked over to the window, and stared out. I kept swallowing. My breathing was shallow. I didn't want her to see my wet cheeks, so I took some deep breaths, wiped my eyes on my left sleeve, and turned to face her. "Debbie, that would be amazing. Thank you so much." If I'd said one more word, my voice would have cracked.

Back in my office, I said nothing to my colleagues. It might break the spell. I had never heard of a real estate agent donating her commission. I phoned Daren to let him know the deal was finally going through in a week.

"I'm not gonna wait more than a week, Rodney. You've been stringing me along. The market's on an upswing. Even in three months, the price has gone up. I could get more now."

My heart started to pound. "Daren, be fair. The price could also have gone down, but we had a deal. Please stick to the agreement we had. A week today, you'll have the money in your hand, I promise." I broke the long silence that followed by reminding Daren we'd been trustworthy renters and to rest assured that we'd pay the full amount in one week. I heard a resigned "Okay" as he hung up.

I phoned BC Housing to confirm that their funding was on track. We had reached the last week of their offer. Then to ensure the deal went through, I went to visit the Toronto Dominion Bank in person. I usually phoned, but they were always slow getting back to me, sometimes a day or even two days. This couldn't wait. Wayne, a young loans officer sporting a pink shirt and gold earring, met me.

"Wouldn't it be better if I dealt with Darlene, Wayne? She's my usual contact and knows about the deal."

"Darlene said to say hi, but she is busy and knows you need this done right away."

I signed the plethora of legal papers that no one reads but everyone signs when they get a house mortgage.

"How is the BC Housing money getting to us?" Wayne asked.

"I don't know. Don't you guys do all that stuff?" *I should have insisted on Darlene.*

"No. Usually, we collect all the funds and prepare a cheque for the agent, but I've never dealt with BC Housing before."

"Well, could you phone them and find out, please?" I hadn't foreseen these kinds of hurdles.

Wayne tapped his pencil on the desk and looked annoyed. "I wouldn't know who to talk to. Why don't you find out who you are dealing with and come back later?"

"I need this done right away. Can you hold on, please?" I phoned Donald on my cell and explained the bank needed my BC Housing contact. "It's in my phone book." I smiled at Wayne.

The large black wall clock with gold numbers on the office wall clicked as the second hand lurched its slow journey around the face. Wayne tapped his pencil and glanced at his watch.

"Got it," Donald said and relayed me the contact name and number, which I passed to Wayne.

"Do you need anything else to complete this?"

"No, we should be fine. I'll see you in a week with the documents ready."

Six days later at 4 p.m., I got a call from Wayne. "Hi, Rodney.

There's been a slight hitch with the mortgage papers. They won't be ready for tomorrow."

I was stunned and stared at the phone in disbelief.

"Are you there?" Wayne asked.

"I'm here, Wayne, but can't believe what I just heard. This deal has been months in the making. I have struggled to get the funds together to buy this house. The owner is already upset that he has had to wait this long. Not having the funds ready tomorrow could jeopardize the whole deal. All the real estate documents are dated for tomorrow. The owner expects his money tomorrow." I railed at Wayne, listed all the problems I had overcome to buy the house, explained why we were buying it, and stated how upset I was with him and the bank. It was Wayne's turn to be silent. "Are you listening, Wayne?"

"Yes, and I want to apologise profusely. I..."

"I'm not interested in apologies. That blue pencil that you like tapping so much, grab a hold of it, and write down the real estate agent's number, the house owner's number, BC Housing's number, and explain to them all why the bank is not ready for this transaction on the completion date."

"I'm sorry, Rodney. The bank doesn't make those kinds of third-party calls."

"Have the bank manager phone me right away. Then make sure *all* the papers will be ready to sign for the following day and that the other parties, the third parties as you call them, know we'll be a day late and why."

I was livid, shaking. The bank manager didn't phone, but 20 minutes later, Debbie Sheppard phoned. "Some stuttering guy just phoned from your bank apologising up the wazoo for not having the papers drawn up to buy Daren's house on the completion date. I'll change all the dates and fax you the documents to initial."

"Can you deal with the owner? He's going to be pissed off."

"Sure, don't worry. I'll calm him down."

"Debbie, you're an angel!"

One day past the deadline, the phone rang. "Rod, it's Debbie. The house sale went through. You got it." I could barely speak but croaked out my heartfelt thanks. I sat back in my chair and exhaled a long victory breath. We had done it! The residents could keep their home and their cat. Barney's crazy idea had worked. Our organization owned its second house!

I took a few breaths, composed myself, and phoned Erin. "Great news. Please tell the residents that CMHA now owns Riverside House. They don't have to leave. The cat doesn't have to leave."

There was a long silence, but we could hear each other's uneven breathing.

"Oh my god. That's the best news ever."

"Yeah, we did it. We bought the house!"

I could imagine the residents' relief as she told them that they no longer had to walk past a For Sale sign on their house — their home.

Two days later, Wayne dropped by. He carried an expensive bunch of roses in his hand, which he explained were for me as an apology for the bank being a day late in preparing the papers.

"Wayne, I appreciate the sentiment, but we are two guys doing business together. If you screw up, don't bring flowers, bring a bottle of whisky." He laid them on my desk, started to stutter, turned red, and left.

I took the flowers to Terry, our wonderful Friday receptionist. "Terry, as a small token of appreciation for all the work that you do,

I'd like you to have these flowers."

Her face flashed a big, surprised smile. "Thanks, Rodney. They are beautiful."

"You're welcome. Someone donated them to CMHA, and I thought you deserved them."

The following week, I opened an account at Vancity and started the process of switching banks. Encouraged by the recent success at buying Riverside House, I cruised into Donald's office and arranged a time for us to check out the house the mayor of Maple Ridge had "given" us.

## **Sheppard House**

"It looks like two houses," Donald said as we stepped out of my car. "There are two front doors."

I fished the keys out of my pocket and checked the address on the disc. "Yup, this is it. I guess it's a duplex. Let's try the door on the left."

I rapped loudly on the door, in case there were squatters inside. No answer. After trying four keys, one of them fit, and we walked in. I gagged on the dank smell of mildew. The roof had leaked, and winter rains had wreaked havoc on the drywall. The windows were steamy from condensation. We walked warily through the house and opened each door with caution, not knowing what to expect. We found spiders, mouse droppings, a crack pipe, and a dead robin. Scattered clothes in one bedroom and cigarette butts on a dinner plate indicated recent human occupation.

The toilet flushed, the kitchen and bathroom faucets ran, the lights worked, and the furnace clicked on when I hit the switch. Strange that there was still power. In the three bedrooms, the drywall had disintegrated and revealed the stark wooden studs like bones poking through a rotting body. Many of the remaining walls were tagged with graffiti.

The adjoining rancher was better. The roof hadn't leaked, but some walls were vandalized. The dining room window was broken. A squirrel scurried out of the living room, and we both jumped backward. Donald had been silent during the whole inspection and made a quick exit when we reached the kitchen — someone had defecated in the corner.

I closed the back door of the second house and met Donald in the backyard. "Well, I think it's fixable."

Donald looked incredulous. "Are you serious, Rodney?"

"Yeah. I'll get an electrician to look at the wiring, make sure it's safe, get a price on the drywall and roof." We both looked up toward the roof. "If the leak can be fixed without replacing the whole roof, the rest of the house won't be bad."

"I can't believe you'd try to fix that place. It's a dump — a nightmare."

"The first house I bought for myself was a bit like that," I explained, trying to help him understand. "It's mostly cosmetic. With new drywall, fresh paint, and a good cleaning, it will look great."

Donald didn't speak on the return journey. Maybe he was right and I was being too nonchalant: What if the roof cost too much, the furnace quit, the plumbing went haywire, the wiring caught fire, I couldn't get free furniture, or the squatters came back in the middle of the night when our clients were living there? Who would pay for any unexpected extra repairs? It was all a gamble. I was glad Barney was going to take a look. The decision to proceed wouldn't be on my shoulders alone.

I gave Barney the address and suggested he check it out. "You don't need the keys. I left the back door unlocked. I figured someone might kick it in if it's locked."

Two days later, I got an enthusiastic phone call.

"Rodney. I had a walk around the house the mayor gave you. I think it will work if you can get it fixed cheap, say under $10,000. Think you can do it?"

Great! Barney was hooked. "Probably. I'll get some prices."

"While you're getting prices," Barney suggested, "figure on knocking a hole in the wall from one house to the other so it's one unit. They could all eat together without running back and forth through the front doors."

"Good idea, Barney. Will do. Also, as we can probably house six clients there, that should be another $9,000 a year for administration?"

"Rodney, let's not get ahead of ourselves."

I asked him which other nonprofit organization phoned him up and offered a free house? "Normally, you'd spend way more than $10,000 a year on rent." I heard Barney's good-natured, raucous laugh.

"Ya got a point. Get me some prices."

After overcoming the challenges of renting and then buying Riverside House, I felt more confident about finding the resources to set up the mayor's free house — like I was on a winning housing roll: find 'em, fix 'em, furnish 'em, and fill 'em up with clients! Don't stress too much. Ask the universe for help and see what comes up.

If we could get this next house into operation, in less than three years, we would have increased the houses we ran in Maple Ridge from one to three. I liked the concept of running houses. It was a great way for clients to transition from institutional living where everything was done for them to learning the skills for independent living so they could move into their own apartments. It also provided the opportunity for me to meet and connect with the people who lived there. I rarely got to meet the other clients who lived in apartments unless they volunteered or came into the office.

I phoned the Maple Ridge mayor and let him know that Fraser Health would put up some money for repairs for the house he had offered us, but I also had a question for him. "As you mentioned you'd been in business before, I wondered if you had any connections that could help us with paint and drywall?"

Silence.

"So, you want a free house, free paint, and free drywall?"

"Well, yeah," I said, laughing. "Sure, if I can get it." I pointed out what awful condition the house was in and that the neighbours would be pleased to know it was because of the mayor that it was being spruced up.

"Ha, ha," Gordie guffawed. "I hear ya. You should be in politics."

"Well, I'm working in mental health. It's less crazy." He laughed out loud again. I reminded him that all our efforts went to help people like the young man who phoned him every day. "How's he doing, by the way?"

"Good, good. Got the secretary to only put his calls through on Mondays."

Two weeks later, I had an offer for the drywall we needed from the local Rona store and 10 gallons of premixed light beige paint from another store; both business owners were buddies of the mayor.

Maple Ridge seemed to be a community of caring, generous people. This inspired me to check with the local Lions Club to see if they would like someone to come and talk about mental illness at one of their weekly lunches. They'd heard of the work we were doing in their community and were happy to accept. The audience was older white males. I gave my standard presentation about the challenges facing many people with mental illness peppered with real-life examples from some of our clients.

"One of our clients, we'll call him Billy, was at his first year at university when he started hearing voices telling him that Satan had taken control of the Internet. He told his parents, his friends, and his doctor who referred him to a psychiatrist. He was diagnosed with schizophrenia. Then and there, his autonomy ended."

I looked around the room. They were all listening — some nodding. "Billy was hospitalized for observation and told to take medication that had side effects of making him gain weight, having a dry throat, and feeling fuzzy-headed." I explained that refusal to take the meds would mean he was noncompliant and wouldn't get any benefits. "When he emerged from hospital three weeks later, his mind couldn't focus, so he quit university. Most of his friends didn't return his calls, and his place in the family home was gone."

"Where did he live then?" asked one of the few women in the audience.

"He lived on the street for about six months, then our outreach worker took him to Maple Ridge Mental Health, now he lives in one of our houses." I sipped a glass of water and looked around. They were all engaged — getting the message. "No one likes mental illness. It scares people. It's not like having a heart problem when friends and relatives visit you in hospital." I saw heads nodding — sad eyes.

"Perhaps even some people here have suffered some kind of mental health problem." The audience looked around uneasily. "What we do at CMHA is provide a safe place to live and support for our clients to live as full lives as possible."

My allotted 20 minutes was up, so I closed by explaining that we were setting up a new six-resident house in Maple Ridge. "There's a company in Vancouver who refurbishes beds and mattresses and ensures they're bedbug free. Six single beds would be $1,200. Any donations you see fit to give would be used for this purpose." I thanked them, waited till the applause had finished, smiled, and left the room.

Two weeks later, I got a call from the Maple Ridge Lions Club to come and collect a cheque for $1,200.

Buoyed up by the Lions Club's friendly reception and generosity, I picked up the cheque and went on to tackle something I had been avoiding: speaking to the neighbours of the new house we were planning to start.

Feeling nervous, I knocked on each door, smiled, and explained who I was. "Your mayor has suggested we could use the duplex next to you for six people recovering from mental illness." I let them know we ran similar houses in other residential neighbourhoods with no problems and that a staff member would be there through the day.

I was pleased to find the folks in the four surrounding houses were very accepting and thanked me for letting them know. I left my business card with them and told them to phone if there were ever any problems. At least they had a number to phone, unlike when the squatters lived there.

The roofer I talked to about the giant leak scoped the job and explained because the house had shifted, there was a crack the length of the roof valley which he could fix easily for $500. "It will look like shit. There'll be a foot-wide swathe of asphalt the length of the repair."

"But it won't leak?"

"That's the point, isn't it?"

"Right, if you can start next week, you've got the job." I had learned through running my own business that you need to impose time limits on contractors. Without the roof fixed, we could do nothing.

Ads on Craigslist produced competitive bids from drywallers and painters. After the roof was fixed, the refurbishing got under way. I visited once a week to check on progress. I paid them half down with the balance on completion and kept my fingers crossed that Barney would make good on his promise of $10,000 for repairs. We would have been under budget, but somebody in Fraser Health, above Barney, decided that the house needed double-glazed windows. Once these were installed, the house was finished, and we received full payment from Fraser Health. I was relieved. We were barely scraping by with all the outflow of money for the repairs.

Six weeks before the house was finished, I let Barney know that there was an ad in the *Maple Ridge News* asking for donations of furniture. "If people respond with good-quality donations, can you throw them in the back of your pickup truck? We can store them in the garage."

"What about bedbugs, Rodney?"

"Don't worry, we'll bring our own." I heard Barney chuckle. It was a worry, but I would try to reduce the risk by examining any furniture before it was moved into the new house.

Instead of calling it "the new house," Barney and I agreed to name it "Sheppard House" to honour the role Debbie Sheppard played in helping us buy Riverside House by donating her commission. Trevor was happy the house had a name before it went on his books.

In the second week of running the furniture ad, I dropped by the house of a woman offering a gorgeous six-chair dining set and hutch in polished walnut. The donor was an elderly psychiatric nurse from Russia.

"Thanks so much for your generosity. It's an amazing set of furniture."

"Yes, it was wedding present from my parents. But now I go into home for old people." She stopped and went silent for a minute. "Only one room. I offer my kids, but they don't want. Too old fashion. Everybody like Ikea style now." Her eyes were welling up. I put my hand on her shoulder until she caught her breath. "So, these people in the house you start, they will like, yes?"

I ran my hand over the polished walnut table. "I'm sure they will love it. It's beautiful. I'm jealous!" We both laughed.

This woman had spent her life helping people with mental illness and now, as a last unselfish gesture, instead of selling it, was donating her treasured furniture to the same cause. The community of Maple Ridge had proven to be a river of generosity.

As the house neared completion, I got an unexpected message from Barney. He explained that Fraser Health would be giving us protocol instructions on how to proceed with the opening ceremony. *Opening ceremony? How to proceed? Where were Fraser Health when we were sweeping up the drywall dust or lugging furniture from the garage into the house?* They were swooping in to claim ownership of the house the mayor had provided and we had fixed. I supposed, as they had contributed $10,000, they were entitled to some favourable publicity.

"You'll be given $100 for celebratory food, and CMHA will be allowed two three-minute speeches for yourself and a resident."

"What if it were three two-minute speeches? Would that be okay?" I was irritated by the list of instructions.

"Rodney, don't be difficult. The last thing is you are to direct any questions from the press to the Fraser Health media person. Oh, and try to get as many people to the event as possible."

"*Ja, mein fuhrer*, anything else? Maybe dancing girls or a juggler for the big day?"

"Don't shoot the messenger," Barney pleaded. He explained the instructions were coming from high up. The Fraser Health bigwigs were excited about the collaboration with CMHA, the mayor, and local citizens donating building materials and furniture. "They want to encourage more of the same."

"I bet! Are they giving you a raise for this, Barney? Ten thousand dollars for four or five years' rent is pretty darn good."

The opening celebration was held one month after the first resident moved in. The house had been cleaned, finger food prepared, and, as ordered, a crowd assembled — mostly our workers, some of Barney's staff, neighbours, and a newspaper reporter. Heather had managed to gather up some of her homeless people interested in free food. All gathered at the appointed hour on the front lawn of Sheppard House.

*Sheppard House Opening Ceremony*

Two Fraser Health officials spoke about how they were thrilled that the Maple Ridge community had pulled together to make this house happen. Barney and the mayor got up and said more or less the same thing. I was getting fidgety — too many speeches.

Stepping onto the small front porch, I thanked the staff for all the preparation they had done for this event, the mayor for letting us use the house, the citizens of Maple Ridge for their support, and Fraser Health for funding the repairs. "We have called this new transition home Sheppard House in honour of Debbie Sheppard, whose large donation enabled us to buy a house on River Road. Thanks to everyone for coming here today. The final word goes to Billy, the first person to move into this house."

I shook his hand as he climbed up the front steps.

Billy was about 50 — a man from the local Stó:lō nation. He stood on the front step and stared at the crowd for a long time. People shuffled their feet, and there were a few nervous coughs. I heard someone whisper, "You can do it, Billy." A hint of a smile crossed his face, and he took a deep breath.

"When I first got sick, about thirty years ago, we didn't have places like this for people like me." He spoke slowly, with feeling, finding the right words. "I lived in kind of barracks with lots of people all sharing one toilet and one washbasin. You could only shower once a week, even in the summer." He swallowed a few times and looked down as though remembering those days. "We weren't allowed to leave except with a family member. My family never visited. My mom said she didn't want to visit because I had a mental illness. I never went outside — only once a month for fire drills. We stood on the sidewalk." He bit his bottom lip with his teeth, and his chin trembled as he tried to get the words out. We waited. He stared at his shoes then slowly back up at us. "We have really nice places now — places like this house. I have my own room. I like to watch the birds outside my window. I cut the grass once. I'm free to come and go as I want. Sometimes I help with the shopping. People are nice to me. They show me how to do things. I've learned to cook. I can make meatloaf." He nodded and smiled. "I just wanna say thanks for this house. It's great here. Thanks to everyone."

He nodded and bit his lip again. He had gone over the allotted three minutes. The people standing on the lawn had grown silent as he spoke. One person started clapping, then everybody. The applause lasted two or three minutes. Billy smiled but looked confused as the applause continued. He turned and stepped through the front door into the house — his house.

Arriving back at the office, I poured myself a coffee and relaxed into my beat-up chair. It had been five months since the mayor had tossed the keys to me. We'd found the money, the contractors, fixed the whole house, located furniture, and moved people in. Starting a new house meant more residents and increased our administration funding to help keep us afloat. But what impacted me at the end of the day were Billy's words — they reminded me why we were doing what we were doing. We had created a home, Billy's home — a good place to live for our fellow citizens who, through no fault of their own, had been dealt a mental illness card in life's lottery. According to statistics, one in five Canadians would suffer from a mental illness during their lifetime.

The phone rang, interrupting my happy moment. I tried to ignore it, but the damned thing kept chiming. I reached for it. Maybe it was something important. I recognised Jill Bloom's voice. She sounded excited. "Fraserside is putting Friendship House up for rent. I know you were looking for a place in town for your office and store. I'm sure you could get a reasonable deal on the rent."

My heart rate shot up. The allure of not spending eight hours a day in a windowless room, with the roar of trucks rumbling past our office on the edge of town, sandwiched between the cemetery and the river, captured my mind.

"Sounds great, Jill. If the rent's reasonable, tell your boss we're interested."

## Moving Obstacles

Fraser side was a large multi-purpose nonprofit service provider. Friendship House was an old three-storey residence on a cul-de-sac providing psychosocial day programs for people with a psychiatric disorder. It had a lawn out front with a picnic table and trees. In a flight of fancy, I imagined myself sitting outside having a tranquil lunch.

We could fit the thrift store into the basement and have the two upper floors as office space. All the rooms had windows. It was close to the town centre, within easy reach for our clients. We could walk to a variety of restaurants for lunch. There was no traffic in the cul-de-sac — from 100 trucks a day to zero.

As with any big decision, I needed to convince our board. Like most nonprofits, we had volunteer directors interested in helping fulfill our mission. By advertising on Craigslist or co-opting promising candidates from thrift-store volunteers, I had gradually changed the board's makeup to be more diverse and professional.

I found that the best way to bring up new projects with the board was to paint with a broad brush and stay away from details. I recalled my first board meeting when I had proudly passed around my new brochure, only to get stuck in a 10-minute discussion about comma placement.

Before buying Riverside House, I explained to our seven directors that we should try to buy the house so our clients wouldn't be turfed out of their home, and that it would be beneficial to increase our real estate holdings.

As borrowing money is a serious step, I let them know we were on track by quoting a line from our 1998 constitution and bylaws which stated one of our purposes:

To construct, provide, maintain, lease, own, and manage houses and housing projects for persons living with a psychiatric

The board approved the motion to get a mortgage

I had followed this pattern with my other big ini
thrift store, the Outreach Program, and Sheppard House. I found from experience that asking *if* we should embark on a new project or *how* best to accomplish it provided a platform for never-ending debate, often with different factions pulling for different ways to achieve the same goal.

My modus operandi was that I did the groundwork and, when everything was in place, presented it for the board to approve. I realized it was difficult for anyone to get the day-to-day pulse of the organization with one two-hour meeting a month. I encouraged board members to visit the houses we ran and to attend functions such as the Christmas party and the summer barbecue in Queens Park so they could meet the staff and better understand the organization's culture.

To get the board's approval for moving our office and store to Friendship House, I started off listing the positive benefits we would reap. "We've been offered a great location in town that I think we should take advantage of. The thrift store would do more business, and it would be easier for our clients to access."

"How can we do that? I thought we were locked into a ten-year lease," asked Joan, our treasurer, as she glanced around the table at the other directors. Joan and Ada, our past president, were the only remaining board members who had been here when the former ED had moved to this location. Ada kept quiet, but Joan continued. "Won't the landlord sue us for breach of contract?" These were the kind of details that alarmed board members — hints of public scandal, breaking the law, or unmet financial obligations. Concerned voices rumbled around the boardroom table. Breaking the rental agreement was now a new hot debate detail.

Well, of course I wouldn't break the lease without the landlord's permission," I said in a calm, reassuring tone.

"Joan's right," said Richard, our new, young president with a recently acquired law degree. "This could be a heap of trouble. But if we do get out of our lease, which I doubt we can, I want to see the lease for the new place." The other board members nodded their approval. Informed guidance from a legal expert was always welcome. Encouraged, he continued. "It might be better if I draw up any new lease agreement. That way we'll know what we are getting into."

Nods of approval circulated the table.

I was getting frustrated. The rental details were hijacking the meeting. If I could wriggle out of the lease with the landlord's approval, why not? Regarding any future leases, landlords not tenants write them. According to our constitution, the board was not supposed to get their hands into day-to-day operations. That's why they'd hired me. However, telling our keen new president that his help writing a rental agreement wasn't needed could be tricky and even endanger my good standing with the rest of the board. I'd heard stories from other CMHA branches of rogue boards who started to fight their ED — often led by one member who convinced the rest of the board that the ED was making bad choices. Occasionally, the reverse happened — an ED controlled both the board and staff, as I would one day understand. When big egos become involved in power struggles, the main focus of supporting clients becomes collateral damage.

Trying to get the conversation back on track, I spoke up. "Moving to Friendship House would be a boost for the thrift store. I'm sure operating from a more central and accessible location could raise revenues by 30-50%." I pointed out it would be easier for clients to attend the computer training program and that we could have more in-house programs by being closer to the town centre instead of being stuck on a truck route on the edge of town with no bus service.

There were approving nods. Richard's wasn't one of them.

"We could have in-house yoga sessions," I suggested. No one argues with yoga! "I'll discuss this with our landlord."

"What will you say to him?" Richard interrupted.

"I plan to tell him the truth. That United Way cut $27,000 in funding. That we lost $60,000 in funding from the government bingo gaming money, we are barely solvent, and that he'd be better off finding a renter with more secure finances."

"But we are paying the rent at present," Richard emphasized, looking around at the other members.

"True, but one more funding loss and we won't be able to pay the rent. Having the thrift store making more money in a better location will help insulate us against future financial shocks."

The rest of the board remained silent, switching their focus back and forth as we each made a point.

"Being unable to pay the rent is not a legal argument," Richard said. "It's contract law you're dealing with here!" he said, raising his voice.

"Yeah, I realize that, Richard, but the right and wrong of the law doesn't pay the rent. I owned a warehouse once, and suing tenants who are too broke to pay the rent isn't the brightest idea."

I took a breath and continued on in a slow, logical manner. "So, I'll talk to the landlord, tell him that we're barely solvent, see if he's agreeable, then get back to you at the next meeting." I flashed my best smile around the room. Some members appeared confused. Others nodded in agreement. "It's not breaking any laws to ask, Richard, and it's free!" I nodded in agreement with myself.

There was a knock at the door, and two steaming-hot large pizzas arrived. The aroma dissolved the controversy. Everyone helped themselves, and we moved on to other agenda items — the thrift store profits, the increased number of volunteers, new grant proposals I had written, and other positive topics.

But Richard and Joan were right. Getting out of a lease registered at the land office was a tricky challenge.

The next step was to bring it up at the staff meeting coming up in a few days. Having the staff on board with the move was vital. We had all bitched about our current location, but moving meant change. I brought donuts, always a good start to the meeting.

By nine o'clock, the staff were sitting chatting in the meeting room.

"Good morning, everyone, how are we all doing?" Murmured "okays" reverberated around the room except for Paige, who said nothing. Her eyes were glued on the agenda

"What's this about a possible change in office location?" Paige asked. All eyes cast down to the agenda. I had emailed it to the staff the day before, but apparently it had remained unread.

"Jill Bloom said that Friendship House would be available to rent. I thought it would be a great location for us — closer for our clients, off the truck route, six or seven restaurants within easy reach."

Only Donald, Trevor, and I worked in the office full-time. The others either worked in the five houses we ran or visited clients in their apartments. They dropped by the office to fill out their weekly client reports on the computers.

"I thought we were locked into a lease here," Robbie said. "Can you break it?"

"Well, we can try. I've discussed it with the board."

"If we move to Friendship House, where will we park?" Stephanie asked.

The sole redeeming feature of our current location was the large parking lot behind the office — staff, thrift-store customers, and visitors had all-day parking.

"It's on a cul-de-sac. Parking should be easy. There are no two-hour time limits there," I said, smiling and nodding.

"I was at Friendship House last week with a client," Stephanie said, wrinkling up her nose. "It's kind of yucky inside. I saw spiderwebs. There's peeling paint and stuff."

I reached for a donut, took a swig of coffee, and drew a deep breath. "That kind of stuff can be easily fixed. I was hoping to get off this truck route. Trevor said the diesel exhaust exacerbates his asthma." Everyone liked Trevor, especially Stephanie. They often had a tête-à-tête in his office. Resistance petered out.

"When would it happen?" Robbie asked.

"I have to talk to the owner. I will get back to you all as soon as I know. Meanwhile, keep your fingers crossed for an office in town and no trucks.

"Now, for our weekly check-in," I said. "Let's go around the room and talk about any wins or challenges that people are experiencing with clients." This was a standard meeting topic. It helped air and solve any problems with staff or clients and helped me take a general pulse on the work we were doing.

Lisa explained that a client, Mathew, had bedbugs. His psychiatrist noticed he was more anxious than usual and wanted to up his meds. Mathew didn't want his meds increased because they fogged his mind and he was worried he wouldn't be able to keep up with the community college course he was taking. "What should I do, Rodney? Anyone would be anxious if they had bedbugs. Should I tell him not to take the meds and lie to the shrink?"

"Lisa, do you know the difference between God and a psychiatrist?"

She looked puzzled and shook her head.

"God knows he's not a psychiatrist."

There were titters around the room. Psychiatrists earned $130 an hour and were at the top of the mental health food chain in charge of diagnoses and medication. Our workers were at the daily-care end and earned $25 an hour. They supplied empathy, encouragement, and practical support. Both jobs were important.

"I hear your concern, Lisa, but I can't condone going against a psychiatrist's wishes." I caught Lisa's eye and smiled.

Looking worried, Erin explained that the cat at Riverside House had partially chewed through a client's supply hose to her oxygen tank. "I noticed the client was starting to look a bit blue and checked out her breathing equipment."

This shocked me. Giving permission for the residents to have a cat seemed like a good idea at the time. As a result, a client had suffered oxygen deficiency and flammable oxygen was floating around the house.

"Good for you for noticing! Anyone got any ideas?"

Robbie suggested coating the hose with a liquid that tasted awful. "I got it from the vet to stop my dog licking a wound so it would heal."

"Good idea. Erin, get some of that liquid today and try it out. If it doesn't work, phone me right away. The cat will have to go."

Every week brought new problems to solve. It was good to get everyone involved. It let people know they weren't alone in having challenges and provided access to group wisdom for solutions.

Days after telling the staff and directors about phoning our landlord, I still hadn't made the call. I disliked being the bringer of bad news. After another morning of putting it off, I told myself to get a grip, grabbed the phone, and dialled the landlord's number.

"Melvin, it's Rodney from CMHA."

"I'm sorry, from where?"

"Canadian Mental Health Association. We rent your building on Columbia Street."

"Oh yeah, we rented it to Alice, and you took over."

I dove right in and explained my concern about our future solvency due to losing two sources of funding from the government bingo and United Way. "Any further losses," I explained, "would result in an inability to pay the rent."

"But you're government. How can you run out of money?"

"Actually, we're a nonprofit organization, and we rely on renewing our funding contracts every year."

After a long silence, Melvin explained that he was in a partnership with his two brothers and had convinced them that this building was a good investment.

"Okay, kind of like a family business and you feel responsible."

"Yeah, exactly."

"Well then, I'm talking to the right partner." I explained that since renting the building several years ago, we had lost two sources of funding and may lose further funding from Fraser Health for a youth housing program that we run. "The problem is it's tough to find kids 16-19 responsible enough to live on their own, and when we do, they soon become too old for the program. Lately, we've been having trouble finding suitable youths. The contract comes up in three months and may not be renewed." I waited. Melvin was silent.

"So, it might be good to give your brothers a heads-up. Maybe look for another renter?"

"But you can't just move!" Melvin exclaimed. "You can't break a commercial lease registered at the land office."

"Yeah, I hear you, Melvin. But in fact, as soon as we don't pay the rent, we've broken the lease. I mean, you could sue us, but if we're broke, there's no point. You'd be paying lawyer's fees as well as losing rent and no guarantee of winning."

Melvin coughed. "So, what are you suggesting, Rodney?"

"Chat to your brothers, see what they say, and get back to me. The rent is secure for another three months, plenty of time to find a new tenant, and we can look for cheaper rent. Another thing, we opened up a store here, which might be an attractive retail space for a future renter."

"You guys opened up a store? That wasn't in the lease agreement."

"Yeah, I found out just after I took over that we were going broke, so I started a thrift shop. That's how we've been able to pay the rent for the last two and a half years. Remember you phoned about the garbage in the parking lot? It was from the dumpster we use for unsellable store donations."

"I'll get back to you on this, Rodney. I need to have a serious talk with my brothers." Three days later, Melvin was on the phone with a suggestion. "I talked to my brothers. The younger one suggested as there is still five years on the lease, you should pay a year's rent as penalty."

I was speechless. "How can we pay an extra year's rent if we are already in a financial bind? Please feel free to come and look at our books, which will verify exactly what I'm saying. As a token of good will, we might be able to pay for four months and move out after three. That would give you a month's bonus if you got someone as we left."

I hung up. The fate of our all-important move hung by a thread, dependent on three brothers I'd never met.

## Moving the Office & Store    Fine-Tuning Operations

Four days later, Melvin phoned. He said the whole situation was very upsetting, but as they didn't want to go to court, they felt they had no choice other than to accept our offer.

Finally some good news! I sent an email to Melvin, outlining our agreement, and asked him to verify his decision by return email. I forwarded his email to the board of directors then phoned Jill and explained we could move into Friendship House in three months.

"Let's get together and figure out the lease," I suggested.

"Okay, Rodney. I'm free next week."

I mentioned that Richard, our president, wanted to write the lease.

Jill laughed. "I doubt if my boss would accept that."

I had Trevor send the landlord four months' rent in advance as a sweetener to cement the deal and marked, "As agreed, final rent," on the cheque. At last, we'd be moving from this unsuitable, dingy, traffic-ridden location.

When I got home that afternoon, I found Anna sitting in the garden enjoying the sun and having a glass of wine. I poured myself a glass and joined her.

"Guess what? We are moving in three months. It's all lined up, and the landlord agreed. I can't believe it!" We clinked glasses.

"Great! Good for you, Baker. I never liked that place. Do you have somewhere lined up?"

"Yeah, a three-storey house in a residential neighbourhood. It's only four blocks from the main shopping plaza."

She gave me a big-eyed look and raised her voice. "How can you run your office and store from a house?"

"It'll be fine — the thrift store in the basement and offices on the two floors above."

She said nothing but changed the subject. "One of my colleagues at the travel agency just got an iPhone. They've just come on the market and look very cool. I'm thinking of getting one. You should too."

"What's an iPhone?"

"It's a new cell phone, from Apple, the computer company."

"Mmm, I-see, iPhone. Probably just a gimmick. Let's have another glass of i-wine? I'm celebrating."


Later that week, Sharon and Sandy accompanied me to Friendship House. Jill let us in, and we walked around the large basement — the site for the new store. They were enthused about the empty room adjacent to the main area.

"Having the sorting room next to the store will be way more efficient," Sharon said. She was developing mobility problems due to poor circulation from having diabetes.

"Your clothing rack will fit right down the middle. Can we bring it here?" Sandy asked.

"Sure, I can disassemble it, throw the parts in my trailer, and rebuild it here."

They meandered around, chatting about where to put shelves, books, chinaware, paintings, and the cashier's desk. It was good to see their enthusiasm — made me feel it was the right choice.

*Goodbye to our Columbia Street Location*

They had done their best with the current location, even displaying wares outside to attract attention, but after a day on the sidewalk a few feet from heavy traffic, things often needed washing. Columbia Street had been our embryonic location. Now it was time for a more suitable venue.

I priced movers, planned how to move our phone system, and scheduled a half-price sale at the store, so we'd have less to move.

I accompanied the staff to the new location, and we walked through deciding who would have which office, where the meeting room would be, where to install the coffeepot, and where to locate the giant fax machine, which was supposed to be in a lockable room to comply with privacy rules. People seemed to be warming to the idea, smiling as we trooped around planning how to use each room. I wanted the staff to support the new location, be part of the move. We discussed paint colours.

"I think mauve for the meeting room would be cool," Stephanie suggested. The women were keen on choosing colours. The guys didn't seem to care that much. Trevor and Paige said they'd help with painting.

The three months until we moved submerged into the depths of our daily work but surfaced more urgently a week before the big day. After we held the store's half-price sale, Sandy and Sharon organized a host of volunteers and started packing the remaining goods into boxes. We closed the store three days before moving and put a sign on the door indicating our new address.

Two days before we moved, I walked into the thrift store with a pipe wrench ready to disassemble the clothing rack, but stopped in my tracks and looked around the silent, vacant room. Stripped of wares and customers, the empty shell was exactly as it had been before we opened shop — before shelves were heavy with goods, before throngs of shoppers and many volunteers breathed life into the idea and lifted it off the launchpad of conception into an orbit of financial success. Since opening, over fifty volunteers had worked here and more than $24,500 had been raised. We'd passed out 400 brochures and acquired two board members who had first volunteered for the store.

I smiled at my custom-built 20-foot-long black iron clothes rack. Naked of clothes, it lay like a dinosaur skeleton on the floor. I recalled the lonely Saturday I had spent in the store putting it all together. It became the sturdy backbone of the new enterprise, displaying thousands of clothes over the two and a half years we'd been open. I chuckled as I remembered Sharon's shocked face about the disorganized way I tossed the clothes on the rack, my surprise at her offer to help, and how she'd become an invaluable member of the team.

There was no parking in front of the store, so everything had to be carried along the sidewalk and up to the parking lot behind. It took four trailer loads to deliver the shelving, the clothing rack, and all the well-labelled boxes that the team had packed. As Friendship House was vacant, we unpacked and set things to open a week after we'd closed the other store. Sandy, Sharon, and the other volunteers were keen to be back in business.

On the day of the big office move, one trip from a five-ton truck resettled all the office furniture in its new location. Things were chaotic for a while: "Where's the fax machine?" "Where's the printer paper kept?" "Is there a washroom upstairs?" "Anyone seen the bathroom tissue?" Like a pack of cards, we'd been reshuffled and dealt new rooms, but things gradually fell into place. Without the continuous roar of traffic, days slipped by serenely in our new, residential neighbourhood, and a relaxed peace spread over our team like a comforting blanket.

I looked out of my new office window at the picnic table on the front lawn, trees, and houses beyond. Stepping outside without the sound of monolithic trucks pounding past the building brought inner joy. Usually, I brought lunch from home and ate sitting in front of my computer while I worked, but for the first week at our new location, I treated myself by walking to a different restaurant each day: Greek, Chinese, Japanese, Malaysian, and, on Friday, fish and chips at Jim's Cafe. Although I came from a fish and chip culture, Malaysian food was my favourite.

We had switched banks after the house-purchase debacle, and I sometimes walked to Vancity to make our daily thrift store deposits. I let the Vancity manager know of our move, and she suggested I put a notice up at the bank announcing the location of our new store. On the bottom of the poster, I added, "Volunteers needed, phone Rodney."

Sales in the store dipped slightly after the move, but as we were close to the town centre, more volunteers showed up: Students, clients, and new immigrants who didn't have cars could walk or catch a bus which stopped three blocks away. Residents from our two New Westminster houses could stroll a few blocks to volunteer or take computer lessons or the yoga classes we had just started.

Once the office and store were running smoothly, the last part of our move was to celebrate by having an open house to alert and welcome people to our new location. It felt as though we had been banished to the outskirts of town, but after surviving years in the wilderness, we had crossed the Rubicon and were returning triumphantly to civilisation for the next chapter of our story. We set the open house date for a month after we had moved in. Kevin and Paige got busy painting.

Any event attracts more people if there is food. I knew just the woman. Paulette, one of our competent thrift-store volunteers, had been a pastry chef in Winnipeg before becoming ill and moving to Vancouver. She agreed, after a little persuasion, to cater the event for us. We invited everybody: all our clients and volunteers, our board members, the Vancity bank manager, Fraser Health staff, other CMHA EDs, Barney and his staff, and neighbouring nonprofit staff.

Unlike an AGM or Comedy Courage, there was nothing to go wrong. We were on our home turf, inviting friends of the Simon Fraser Branch to celebrate our new premises. Paulette prepared a fabulous array of food, we had door prizes, and everyone remarked on how much better this location was than the last one.

*Paulette prepared a celebratory feast for our open house*

The Vancity manager surprised my socks off by walking through the door and handing me a cheque for a thousand dollars. "For all the good work your organization does." I was speechless. Every penny scraped together was hard fought for. To have someone hand over an unsolicited donation made me uneasy, for a few seconds. Then I thanked her and gave her a hug.

At the end of the day's open house celebration, I felt pretty good: For the first time since I joined the organization, we were in a decent location and had no immediate financial crisis.

The everyday multiple tasks continued as normal, but nothing loomed ahead, except Christmas, which was no big deal. It was my third time cooking Christmas dinner for a hundred clients, we had a good system figured out, and it all went smoothly.

By January 2008, I had time to take a breath and review operations of both the thrift store and our core work of supporting people with mental illness to be housed and interactive with the community. The slower pace allowed me to spend more time in the store, often dropping in twice a day to say hi to volunteer staff, thank donors, and fix anything that needed repairing. I decided to put some defences in place against bedbugs, always a worry. I built a large tray with six-inch-high plastic laminate sides for sorting all the clothes. Any bedbugs on the clothing would fall into the tray and be trapped as they can't climb up plastic surfaces. Most of the clothes also went into the washer and dryer to kill any possible bugs. I had equipped store staff with the bedbug spray and posted a blown-up picture of a bedbug in the clothes sorting area so staff knew what to look for. Bedbugs were a serious concern, but either by luck or by vigilance, we never had an infestation.

To recognize and value all the time our volunteers contributed to our organization, I had initiated a system of tracking their hours, which were posted monthly in the store. By the time we moved to the new location, Dave had logged in over 1800 hours. Above this monthly tracking sheet, I pinned a large sign:

**This store is successful thanks to our valued volunteers.**

This display of volunteer hours was a small way of letting our volunteers know their efforts were recorded and appreciated. On a more practical side, it bothered me that many of our volunteers, especially our clients, were not able to afford the donations they were putting on the shelves for others to buy. After discussing this with Sharon and Sandy, we decided to award a dollar an hour credit to all volunteers. That way if a beautiful painting or piece of jewellery came into the store that a volunteer really wanted, the credit accrued gave them an ability to purchase a small luxury. We were making up our own rules, but it felt right to offer a tangible reciprocal gesture for the volunteers' hard work. But the credits would start from the time we moved to the new location, not retroactively; otherwise,

Dave could have bought half of the store.

It was a tricky walk: Every donated item that came into the store had to go on the shelves. Nobody got favours. To respect the donors, I wanted an honest in-and-out flow of goods. Nobody was special or could stick things away in a corner to buy later for themselves or friends.

We were changing not only the way the store operated but also the way it was promoted. In the newsletter, I was rebranding it using a relatively new term. Our thrift store was now a social enterprise — a new term I had been reading about. The description seemed to describe our store.

> Social enterprises seek to make a profit while maximizing benefits to society and the environment. Their profits are principally used to fund social programs.

It sounded more upscale and differentiated us from other for-profit thrift stores, like Value Village, which internet sources say donate between 8-17% of their profits to charities.

The store benefitted our community in multiple ways: Donating to our store was a greener solution than taking things to the dump. Once a week, Suzy and two volunteers from Bluebird House bagged up all the unsellable clothes and took them to Big Brothers which bought them by the pound. We threw little away. Sandy had also negotiated with two consignment stores in town to give us their unsold goods that the owners no longer wanted. One was a women's clothing store, the other a furniture shop. Quality donations from the public and businesses were a trickle-down way of wealth redistribution.

Our client volunteers gained confidence by engaging with the public and working on a team to help CMHA. Some found paid work in similar stores. Paulette, who had prepared our opening celebration feast, ran into my office one day, gave me a hug, and said, "Rodney, I got a real job working at Value Village because of my experience working here."

The major benefit was that the funds generated were used to cover overhead deficits and offer free programs like yoga and computer training to our clients and volunteers.

While the store was important to our finances, I wanted to measure the competency of the services we provided to our clients. As we had around 90 people living in their own apartments, 23 in the transition houses, and about 100 homeless clients per year, this was a large undertaking.

Every nonprofit has good intentions and likes to believe they are providing valuable services. In the business world, if customers are not treated well, they stop coming. No such potent feedback loop existed for us. Not asking questions about the quality of our service minimised client importance and maximised our own by assuming we were doing everything right. I was also concerned that Fraser Health, which funded all our housing contracts, might insist we become a member of the Commission on Accreditation of Rehabilitation Facilities (CARF). However, with an annual budget of well over $2,000,000 but only three of us in management, adopting CARF would have mired us in a morass of extra paperwork — a situation I dearly wanted to avoid.

By formulating our own annual client satisfaction questionnaire, I hoped to avoid the need for CARF. The questionnaire asked clients to evaluate twenty aspects of the services we provided, 1 being the lowest mark and 5 being the highest. Even though I'd bought donuts, the staff were unenthused. Some read it; others gave the form a cursory glance and started chatting.

"My clients won't want to fill this in," Stephanie said.

"This is a waste of time," Lisa chimed in, waving her copy of the survey in the air. "I can't think of one client who would want to do this."

"It depends how you ask," I said. "You could tell them that by filling in this survey, they'd be helping you. Or blame me and say 'Rodney's got a bee in his bonnet about everyone filling in the survey. Could you help me out by filling it in?' Most people want to be helpful if given the opportunity."

I handed out enough surveys for all the clients and got a grumpy acquiescence from the staff.

When the clients mailed in the surveys to me about a month later, they were excellent — between four and five on each question except for one: "Your support worker asks your opinion on how your goals could be achieved?"

This had the low average of less than three. The poor result on this question was discussed at the weekly staff meeting. The consensus was that they felt embarrassed asking their clients how best to help them because it might erode client confidence in their abilities.

I shared something learned from being a counsellor called feedback-informed treatment: At the end of each session, the counsellor asks clients what had or hadn't worked for them. This allows the counsellor to fine-tune the sessions by learning from the client what was needed.

After much discussion, most staff agreed to try asking the client's opinion of how they could best help them. Over 50% of the surveys were returned, and the results were published in our newsletter and forwarded to Fraser Health. I also initiated an annual 20-question, 360-degree review of my own performance. The staff, board members, volunteers, and sister nonprofits like Fraserside or the Senior Services Society were asked to complete the evaluation so I could get some idea of my own efficacy. My results averaged the same as the staff's.

When opportunity arose, I tried to get to know our clients on a one-to-one basis to keep in touch with the reality of our everyday work. As I walked into the office one morning, I got a call from SIL worker Lisa. "Rodney, we've got a problem. I'm sick, and there's no one to fill my shift, but we need to help John today." She explained it was John's food shopping day. "He has paranoia and OCD, is almost blind, and gets upset if we are late for his appointment."

Yes, I would fill in for Lisa! Working in the field with a client I hadn't met before sounded much better than being stuck in my office all day.

"Okay, I'll go, Lisa." It was too urgent to leave till staff were available in a few days.

"Thanks, Rodney. You'll need to drive. Be there at ten o'clock sharp and take him to Safeway. Good luck."

One hour later, I approached the pink and green low-rise building and rang the buzzer. "It's Rodney. I'm replacing Lisa today. She's sick." Silence. "Are you there, John?"

"Are you new?" I could barely hear him.

"Yeah, we haven't met. But Lisa said you needed to go shopping today, so I'm here to help."

"Okay. Come in."

The ground-floor apartment was neat and tidy. I stuck my hand out, but John either didn't see it or ignored me. He was medium height, with a touch of grey hair, and wore jeans.

"Do you have a car, Rodney?" he asked in a low, gravelly voice.

"Yes."

"Good. Let's write a shopping list. Do you have a paper and pencil?"

"No."

"Lisa brings her own. Look on top of the dresser in the living room."

As John said, I found mauve notepaper and a red pen on the dresser and returned to write the list. John took a deep breath, pursed his lips, and listed off about 20 items — five types of canned soup, canned vegetables, fresh vegetables, fruit, milk, instant coffee, bread, cheese, and crackers. He spoke in a monotone as though he were seeing each item in his head.

"Did you get all that?"

"Yes, I think so."

"Okay. Read it back to me to make sure it's all there."

After giving his approval, he instructed me on the next step.

"I will hold your arm to the car. When we get there, open the door and put my hand on the back of the seat."

John carefully locked his apartment door. As he lowered himself into the front seat and reached for the seat belt, he asked me if I had a dog.

"I'm looking after my son's dog. How could you tell?"

"Your car smells like dog."

We set off the few blocks to Safeway.

"Park near the entrance."

I helped John out of the car and guided him toward the buggies.

"Put my right hand on the left side of the buggy and walk slowly."

"Sure." Once in the store, I walked around a bit but couldn't find anything on the list. Grocery shopping is not one of my strengths.

"If you can't find something, ask one of the employees," John directed. "They know where everything is."

"Good idea."

After gathering a few items, I put the list down to check each tomato selected was perfect. John wouldn't be able to see any rot. Shortly after, we came to a halt.

"What's the matter?" John asked.

"I'm trying to remember what's next."

"Where's the list?"

"I can't seem to find it."

"You've lost the list?" John said in disbelief. "You *are* new at this, aren't you?"

"Yes, it's my first time."

"When is Lisa coming back?"

"Next week."

John suggested we backtrack to find the list, and we did a slow 360 to retrace our steps. I was relieved to find it sitting on the tomatoes and resolved to double my efforts to be a better shopper. It was a new skill, shopping with someone attached to the cart. I misjudged the space a couple of times. John bumped into a fellow shopper and a rack of bananas. John pursed his lips and gave a heavy sigh at my poor steering. I was relieved to finish grocery shopping without further mistakes and drove carefully back to John's place. He took my arm to his apartment, and I unloaded the groceries on his kitchen counter.

"Well, that's it, John. Lisa will be back next week."

"I need you to put everything away, Rodney," he said in a loud voice. "The soup cans lined up in the cupboard in alphabetical order left to right."

"Alphabetical order?" Lisa told me that John had OCD, but this seemed over the top.

As I seemed confused, he spelled it out, "Chicken noodle soup is first, then clam chowder, corn, oxtail, and pea."

"Oh, I get it. So you know what you're choosing."

"Yes, most people like to know what they are eating." John waited till I'd placed the cans in order, then gave me instructions how to load up the fridge.

"Okay, that's it for this week. Next week is shopping and I get help doing my laundry. I hope Lisa is back."

"I'm sure she will be," I said, thankful to have escaped laundry.

"You did your best, Rodney," he said in a resigned voice. "Thanks."

I drove slowly back to the office, wondering what on earth it would be like to live alone, be almost blind, and have a mental illness. I spent a while looking at my screensaver of Mount Baker and sipping coffee before I could get back into the rhythm of work. On the drive home that evening, getting stuck in traffic on the freeway felt like a trivial inconvenience.

For the first time since I had joined the organization, everything was running smoothly. We had a great location, a full board of directors, and no looming financial crunch. The thrift store was operating better than ever, supplying us with financial security, a tangible connection with our community, and volunteer opportunities for our clients.

We had expanded the number of houses we operated from three to five, managed to buy one of them, and provided transition house living for a total of 11 more clients. The outreach program was helping many homeless people achieve more stable lives than couch surfing or living on the street. I had even found a volunteer to help with the quarterly newsletter so that it actually got out on time.

With no emergencies to cope with, I should have felt happy. But within six months of moving to our new location and completing the fine-tuning of our programs and operations, I began to feel flat, like a listless surfer looking for the next big wave.

However, wallowing in calm waters was not to last. The next challenge wasn't work related but blindsided me with a phone call from my sister.

# Leaving

Alison was my only sibling left in England and lived over three hours' drive from our mother. Our brother, Al, lived in Scotland and was often away on Greenpeace missions. Ali's twin sister, Lindsay, lived in Montana. By default, Alison became Mum's carer. Although not well herself, she arranged home care, helped with Mum's frequent calls asking how to turn on the TV, and cancelled around-the-world luxury cruises ordered from some "nice young man" on the telephone.

My mother's needs were ever increasing, and Ali reported that the house needed plumbing and electrical work. Neither Al nor Lindsay were in a position to help, and the repairs were too complicated to manage from a distance.

"You should come over, Rod, have a visit with Mum and fix whatever needs doing in the house. Revitalize your relationship with her while she still remembers you. Might be your last chance."

Her words were a sombre reality check and foreshadowed the beginning of the end of my mother as I knew her. Mum had always been self-sufficient, lived a full life, and been very independent until her diagnosis of Alzheimer's eight years previously at age seventy-five. She had a resilient nature, formed in part by growing up in a large family of strong characters and further tempered by being a teenager in London during the Second World War.

Now 83, she still lived in the bungalow my father had built for our family 50 years before. Still feisty, she often lost the thread of her conversation but would say, "It's because I have a mental illness — something beginning with A. I think it's called autism."

Yes, I would go back and help — take a three-month leave of absence. There were no more fires to put out at work, so everything should be fine.

A stray thought slipped into my mind and wouldn't go away — like a song you hear and you keep humming even if you don't want to: What if I took a whole year off? Deprogram myself from CMHA and get a different job when I got back. One where I wasn't in charge of everything. A year off became a magical idea, a release from being a worker drone. I would escape the hive — fly out of bounds, become someone different, for a while.

Since becoming the ED of CMHA's Simon Fraser Branch four years earlier, it had been an uphill grind. It felt rewarding to have steered the branch into calm financial waters and a great new location, but I had lost some of myself along the way: I went to bed earlier and did less bike riding, hiking, badminton, and socializing. Anna said I'd become "less fun." I told her it was due to aging.

After repairing the family home and spending time with my mother, maybe Anna and I could spend some time in Italy. Anna could revisit her homeland that she missed so much. I could relax and improve my Italian, volunteer for a nonprofit. Italy's Malpensa Airport was just over an hour's flight to Gatwick Airport, close to Mum's house in case I was needed.

The day after my conversation with Ali, I started off by pitching the three-month-off idea to Anna as we were having a drink before dinner.

"Baker, that sounds like the best idea you've had in years. Let's do it."

So far so good. Then I blurted out, "What if we went to Italy after England. Took a whole year off. Give ourselves a real break?"

She flipped her head toward me to see if I was serious and didn't speak for a while, then started laughing. "Why not? Our kids are grown, and we both love travel. I could still work a bit as a travel agent while we're away. When we return, you could get a more relaxing job."

I had expected an argument. Instead I got affirmation.

"Okay. Let's do it," I said. It was decided. We would have an adventure and leave for a year.

The most critical element in moving forward with the plan was renting out our house to pay for the sojourn abroad. The logistics were tricky: Should I give my notice at work first or rent the house? If my notice was tendered and we couldn't rent the house, I would be out of a job but stuck in Canada. We decided that renting the house first, then telling the board of directors was the best option. Writing the ad for the house felt like a covert action which, if successful, would airlift us out of our lives for a year. I put an ad in the *Vancouver Sun* and listed it with a rental agency.

Five-bedroom house in North Vancouver for rent. Great view. July 1st 2008 - July 1st 2009.

If the board saw the ad, would they fire me for planning to leave without telling them? While pondering this dilemma, I got a phone call from Jill Bloom that created another.

"Got some interesting news, Rodney, given your affinity for houses."

"Why, what's happening?"

"Fraserside's decided to sell the house you're renting from us for your office and thrift store."

"What about our lease?"

"It will go on the market a couple of months before your lease is up."

"Find out how much they want, Jill. We may be interested in buying it."

"Ha, I knew it," she said. "I think they're asking about $550,000."

I hung up the phone and poured myself a coffee. My heart raced. I wanted a cigarette, but my emergency pack was finished. Should I delay going to England and try to buy the house? Instead of paying monthly rent, we would be buying our very own office and store premises. If we could get a down payment by re-mortgaging Bluebird House, the thrift store earnings should more than cover the monthly mortgage. I almost skipped into Trevor's office and laid out my idea in a torrent of words. "Do the math for me, Trev, see if you think it would work."

"It will take a while."

"C'mon, Trev. I need to know right now!"

He smiled and got out his calculator. I decided to walk around the block, maybe pick up some lunch. Arriving at the Greek restaurant, I stood outside scanning the menu. Consumed with the idea of buying the house, I no longer felt hungry and killed some time walking to Queens Park and back. Twenty minutes later, I returned to Trevor's office. "Well?"

"If we can get $30,000 from the bank, the mortgage payments on this building should roughly equal the rent we are paying now." He explained that with the money earned from Comedy Courage, we now had $180,000 of equity in Bluebird House. That would probably allow us to refinance an additional $30,000 from the bank on that property, which could be used as a down payment on the house we were currently occupying. Always erring on the side of caution, he reminded me that he was not a mortgage expert or banker.

I phoned my new Vancity manager, the one that had made an unsolicited $1000 donation to CMHA during our open house, and made an appointment to see her regarding financing. Maybe I could delay my departure to England and get the deal done to buy this house. I decided to phone my sister the following morning and test the waters for postponing the trip. My ideas of how to tell her were hazy. How would she react to my coming over being put on hold?

That evening, Anna claimed she could tell by my eyes something had changed.

"What's going on, Baker?"

"What do you mean?"

"You've got a different look to you, but I can't tell if you are happy or worried."

Glad she'd opened the door, I dived in. "Well, it's both. It seems like we might be able to buy the house we moved into at work, but it would take a while and we'd have to delay our trip."

She looked at me with big eyes. After some moments of silence, she smiled. "Well, it would be great if you could buy it. What would your sister say?"

"I'll phone her tomorrow and test the waters."

Saying it was easier than doing it. When I phoned Ali and casually asked how things were, the news wasn't good: Her own MS had new complications, and her husband was having major problems with his hip. New challenges were coming up with Mother's behaviour each week, and more things needed fixing on the house.

"You're still coming soon, aren't you, Rod?"

I said nothing.

"Is something wrong?"

"Something's come up at work."

"Please don't tell me you're going to be delayed. I'm relying on you, Rod."

"No, it's gonna be fine. I'm coming. No worries, Ali."

Family commitment won over work. I'd done little to support my mother. Maybe I could figure out the financing to buy the house, and the replacement ED could push it through. I didn't have to do everything.

After six weeks of advertising our house, we found a confirmed renter for the year we would be away commencing July 1, 2008, just over seven weeks to go.

That was a positive development. I was unnerved about the next step — telling the board of directors.

I sat alone in the boardroom at the head of the long table, waiting for the directors to arrive, and remembered my first board meeting almost four years earlier. In our new location, our meeting room had windows and normal lights. Two large pizzas with a free litre of cola were delivered to each meeting. Ada the president had resigned. I'd found new board members, moved to a better location, fixed all the funding deficits, and brought the organization to a sound emotional, financial, and client-focused footing. Every venture I presented to the board had a positive underpinning, which made my upcoming announcement feel like a reversal, a betrayal.

The board filtered in and sat chatting around the table. I took a breath. My voice wavered. "I have to return to England to solve some family problems and am leaving in just under two months on June 28th. After that, I'm taking some time off to recharge my batteries and plan to be gone for a year."

The seven board members sat in stunned silence — open-mouthed, swallowing, wide-eyed, looking at one another.

The room remained uncomfortably empty of words. I tried to fill up the vacuous space.

"I can help by posting an ad for hiring my replacement. I also told

Kevin, a reliable staff member, about my plans, and he has agreed to take over my work if an ED isn't found before I leave."

"This is most unexpected news for us, Rodney," stammered our president, Richard.

"Yes, I realize it's kind of sudden, and I apologize for that. But I feel an obligation to help with my mother's problems, plus I'm feeling kind of worn down after fixing all the challenges here." Most of the board nodded in agreement.

"Maybe we should meet in two weeks instead of a month," Joan suggested, still our treasurer after four years. "We need to decide right away on an interview team for the new ED."

"Good idea," I said, relieved the board seemed to be moving forward. "I'll put an ad for a new ED on Craigslist and the *Vancouver Sun* newspaper and will email you the details of any viable candidates."

"Run the wording by me before you put the ad in," Richard said.

I nodded.

Mary broke a long, uncomfortable silence. "I wonder if you'd be interested in coming back to resume your position as ED after your year away?" Mary was a new board member in her 40s, who had volunteered to be vice president.

"Yes, we're going to miss you, Rodney," Joan said, smiling. "You started the thrift store, new programs, two houses, moved us here, and got us back on a sound financial footing." The rest of the board nodded.

"What if we treated it as a sabbatical?" Mary suggested. "Would you consider coming back?"

I'd wondered about this possibility but thought it too big a favour to ask. Way back at my first board meeting, when our president had told me I needed to fundraise to pay my wages, I recalled thinking *if* I could pull the place out of the dumpster, maybe I would get some recognition. Perhaps this was it — recognition — the offer of a one-year sabbatical. After a year away, surely I'd be well rested and keen to take up the reins again.

"Is this what everybody agrees, for me to come back in one year?"

Each of the seven board members either nodded or said yes. A warmth flushed through my body. My first inclination was to get their offer in writing, but I put my business instinct aside. It seemed like a callous response. We all trusted one another. The rest of the meeting flowed by in a gratifying haze.

Arriving home that evening, I announced to Anna that the board of directors had offered me a year's sabbatical.

"Baker, they should give you two years off for all you've done for them. Of course they want you back!"

I informed my sister I would be coming on the first of July just seven weeks away. Ali was pleased and relieved. I phoned my mother to let her know.

"Why are you coming, darling? Is it a holiday?"

"Yeah. Thought I would bring Anna over for a visit and repair the plumbing and wiring problems for you while we are there. Be nice to see you."

"What wiring and plumbing problems?"

"I'll explain when I'm there. Looking forward to seeing you soon, Mum."

I built a small shed in the atrium to store all the personal items we weren't leaving for the renter — photo albums, books, Anna's heirloom silverware, and our kitchenware. We stored everything in

Rubbermaid tubs piled high in the shed. It was cheaper than renting storage and more convenient.

At work, there was little response to my ED employment ad, so I expanded the distribution to newspapers in adjacent municipalities and reworded the job description to sound more appealing.

The board was sluggish in addressing the task of finding a new ED. When meeting two weeks later, they were unable to decide on an interview team and what questions to ask prospective candidates. As we discussed hiring procedures, Richard announced in a grumpy tone, "You have created quite a dilemma, Rodney, leaving with such short notice."

*Nothing compared to the dilemma the board dealt me when I started here, Richard.*

He was still peeved about not being involved in writing the lease for our current location. Seven weeks' notice was short but not impossible. Hiring an ED was one of the board's main responsibilities. At least they wouldn't have to tell a new ED there was no money to pay their wages.

"What kind of questions should we ask?" Mary asked. "Is there some kind of standard list?"

"If you want, I could email you some questions after the meeting," I offered, glad they seemed to be getting down to brass tacks.

After the pizzas were eaten and everyone left, I returned to my desk and wrote an email to the board titled, "Suggested ED interview questions."

1) Why do you want this position?
2) What relevant experience have you had?
3) How would you cope with the following: a

depressed staff member, a volunteer stealing from the thrift store, a client suicide, a staff member abusing a client, staff bullying staff, a union grievance, firing a staff member, firing a volunteer?

4) How do you look after yourself emotionally in times of stress?

It was easy to come up with the list. I'd coped with most of these situations. By staying after the meeting and firing off an immediate email to the board, I hoped it would indicate that hiring an ED was urgent. I also suggested they have a staff member and a client on the interview team. Having both those perspectives would be valuable in determining if prospective EDs were a good fit.

I worried about the board's ability to hire an ED. This was a new experience for them. Before I joined the organization, the position had remained unfilled for six months. Nonprofits without an ED at the helm tend to be like rudderless vessels at the mercy of random winds and currents. Another major factor in securing an ED quickly was so we could buy the property we were using for our office and store. Owning our own building would be a major step in securing a solid future for the Simon Fraser Branch.

Even with the expanded job circulation ad, the few applicants that replied were not qualified. I put another ad in the *Vancouver Sun* and listed the job with Charity Village, an excellent resource for nonprofits. Not finding anyone was a nail-biter and added to the stress of all the other preparations I was making to leave for a year.

Two weeks before leaving, I began to see my office in a different light. Instead of being a comfortable shoe that I wore daily, it would soon be a new ED's workplace. I cleaned the junk out of my drawers, dusted my desk, vacuumed the floor, and wiped dead flies off the windowsill. *Why do flies die on windowsills? Failed attempts to escape?* I cleared the recent searches from my computer — no point having a stranger know what I didn't know. All emails were deleted. Comments between Barney and me were far too honest for general consumption. I checked that the 78 subfolders under my CMHA Day-to-Day Business folder would be understood by a newcomer and finished by deleting unnecessary files from the desktop. For a final touch, I borrowed Trevor's screen cleaner and sprayed a couple of bursts onto the monitor and keyboard. Now that my whole office space was spruced up, it looked wonderful and inviting. It hadn't taken that long. Why hadn't I kept it like this all the time?

One week before my departure, just as I was closing up at 5 p.m., I got a phone call regarding the ED's position.

"I saw your ad and would like to take a look at the premises," said an assertive female voice.

"I'm just about to head home. Would tomorrow work?"

"Well, my van is outside your office. Maybe I could take a look now?"

I was primed to leave, but it was hard to say no as we were getting desperate to hire someone. Looking out of the window, I saw a grey-haired, rotund lady on crutches, lowering a wheelchair from the motorized platform at the rear of her vehicle. She let herself carefully down into the chair and headed for the wooden disability ramp that Fraserside had installed one year earlier. I went out to meet her and introduced myself. She didn't offer to shake hands.

"I'm Veronica," she said, powering her chair toward the ramp. As she navigated the first corner, her chair became stuck. I tugged the front of her vehicle around the first ramp corner and again on the second one. "The bends on this ramp weren't built to code," she said. Manoeuvring through the back door and kitchen, she came to a halt in the boardroom and swivelled her chair around to face me. "So tell me what this job is about," she said, fixing me with a stare.

She had a sallow face and hawkish green eyes, which locked onto mine.

"The largest part of the work is helping people with mental illness to find housing in apartments around the city or acquire skills for independent living in five transition houses we run. We do our best to help them live more autonomous lives. You know...make their own life choices. There is a smoking cessation program, funded by the Federal Government, and an outreach program for homeless people. I've learned a lot from our clients. They..." I had more to say, but she waved her hand to one side.

"Okay, I get the general picture. I can see this work means a lot to you."

That caught me off guard. I stared out of the window for a moment, digesting her comment. She coughed. I turned back, resumed my role as host, and handed her our brochure listing all our services.

"This pretty much sums up what we do."

She gave it a brief glance, then tucked it into a side pocket of her chair. "I thought I'd drop by and look the place over — check out the access. Perhaps you could just assist me to navigate past those bad corners going back down the ramp?"

"Sure." I handed her a card. "If you are interested in the job, I can forward your email to Richard, our president."

"Yes. I'd like that!"

If she got the job, how would she cope? She couldn't get upstairs to my office.

I left 45 minutes late. By that time, the traffic had plugged up the freeway. I spent almost an hour getting home. As the car trundled along in bumper-to-bumper traffic, Veronica's comment, that she could see the job meant a lot to me, kept bubbling through my head. I had never stopped to think about what the job meant to me. I had been too busy. The line of traffic came to a complete halt in the Cassiar Tunnel, and the radio went dead.

What *did* the job mean to me?

I liked the people I worked with: Trevor, the accountant, was so polite and competent. Donald's youthful energy and his earnest intent to do a good job as housing manager were admirable. I appreciated Kevin's solid housing work in the trenches and that he always stepped forward to volunteer. Most of our staff were competent, caring people. I admired the excellent work they did with our clients day in and day out. I was okay with the occasional black humour that sometimes slipped back and forth between them. It was a tough job and a way to let off steam. Their mutual support helped them to keep encouraging our clients to lead more autonomous lives despite their disabilities.

Then there were the volunteers; without their friendly, competent help underpinning our finances, we would be out of business. It was heartwarming to see so many people selflessly giving their time.

Most of all, I was inspired by our clients and admired their courage and resilience as we worked with them to help navigate pathways through loneliness, poverty, and psychiatric symptoms.

Like the rest of our staff, if I made good decisions and worked hard, it could make a positive difference in our clients' lives. Veronica was right. The reward of being on a team effectively helping people meant a lot to me.

Sitting in the dark tunnel of stalled traffic, the realization swept over me that my work, and all the people I knew, would soon be 5,000 miles away on the other side of the planet. Was I doing the right thing? After struggling for so long to get the organization straightened out, I was leaving. Handing it all to someone unknown. Would the new ED follow through and buy the house from Fraserside? I decided to leave a financial plan for buying our building on my desk. No point worrying about it now, I'd done what I could. The die was cast. After fixing Mum's house, maybe I could find some worthwhile cause to volunteer for in Italy, a mental health nonprofit — learn some helping perspectives from another culture.

Two weeks after showing Veronica the office, no ED had been hired, and my last day had arrived. I spent the time wrapping up last-minute details and saying goodbye to my colleagues and volunteers. Although excited about leaving, my stomach started to churn at the thought of walking away from my job. Not having a party or any hoopla allowed me to slip away with no fuss. After all, I was coming back. My throat felt hoarse echoing goodbye after goodbye. When my last day arrived, I could hardly believe I was leaving. At four o'clock, I handed the office keys to Kevin who would serve as the interim ED and walked down the front steps on shaky legs along the street to my car.

It was the last time I would ever set foot in that office.

Although full of traffic, the drive home felt empty.

On Canada Day, July 1, 2008, with our suitcases packed for a year, Anna and I caught a cab to Vancouver Airport and boarded a plane for London — a world away.

# England

When our turn in the Heathrow Hertz Rent-A-Car queue came, I couldn't recall our home address in Canada. Anna reminded me. Hurtling through the air in suspended animation for nine hours and touching down on a different continent had made me lightheaded. It was 5 a.m., Vancouver time.

The paperwork over, we wandered on stiff legs around the giant parking lot and spent 20 minutes searching for the right licence plate. Relieved to finally find the car, I jumped in. There was no wheel! Confusion turned to laughter. I would repeat this mistake a few times due to driving on the left. If car rental agencies had any idea what it was like to get off a long transatlantic flight, hop into a car, and drive 110 miles through busy traffic on the wrong side of the road with no sleep, I'm sure it wouldn't be allowed.

It was the roundabouts that threw me. Going in circles made me confused about which side of the road to exit on. The first one I went around twice to figure it out.

"Why are you going around twice," Anna yelled.

Busy concentrating, I ignored her because it should have been obvious. I got it wrong on the third roundabout. Oncoming cars honked when they saw me approaching them head-on.

Anna screamed, "You're on the wrong side of the road."

I made a quick correction.

England is full of roundabouts, sometimes three in a row. I laughed and said to Anna that maybe there was a secret Ministry of Roundabouts that produced them on commission. She told me to quit joking and concentrate on driving. Anna was an anxious passenger and yelled at any hint of danger.

The trim green hedges, red brick buildings, and ancient stone churches of my birth country flashed by — familiar sights welcoming me back. After miles of quaint scenery, roundabout confusion, and the occasional shriek, we arrived at my mother's house, a brick bungalow overlooking the small port of Newhaven on the Sussex coast.

Ali texted me she'd let Mother know we were on the way, but she seemed surprised to see us.

"Hello, darling. What on earth are you doing here? Don't you live in America?"

"Canada. We've come to visit you for a while. I phoned you last week about it. Ali mentioned you need a few things fixed around the house, so we've come to help."

She gave us a big smile and hugs. "How lovely, darling. I've been having trouble with the TV lately. Your father used to go in the loft and turn the aerial round a bit."

Mother's TV had been on cable for at least 20 years, and Dad had been deceased for over 40.

"I'll see what I can do. Is it okay for Anna to make dinner tonight? We stopped at Sainsbury's and picked up a few things."

"Lovely. How thoughtful. Maybe you could look at the TV while she's cooking." Her short-term memory wasn't completely gone. The TV worked fine, but she had five remotes, two of them without batteries and one for another TV. She couldn't recall in which order to press the buttons, a situation that didn't improve despite numerous explanations during our stay.

The words mother, home, and family retained a strong resonance within me, mixed with tinges of guilt for leaving the country. As an impetuous 16-year-old, I had decided to go to sea. Travelling the world was also a way of broadening my horizons. University wasn't on the radar for people of the lower class in that era.

After a dinner of *risotto rosmarino* and a bean salad, jet lag drew us to bed early. Lying within the four walls of my youth, long-forgotten ghosts invaded my mind: As my parents' first child, I had unwittingly trained them to be parents, smoothing the way for my twin sisters and brother. I lay in my sisters' former bedroom, with Anna sleeping soundly beside me, as disturbing memories hijacked my ability to sleep. The smell of familiar rooms, and my mother's voice, triggered childhood traumas: Mum's tales of my misdeeds to Dad that provoked his anger. In the dark of night, I returned to feeling small and ineffectual.

*Get a grip. They were doing their best. You made lots of mistakes parenting your own kids.*

Mother was no longer in her late 20s acting as the behaviour police but an elderly woman with dementia deserving of my help and understanding. I needed to show love, be patient, and listen to her stories.

At daybreak, the first rays of consciousness flickered into my brain and delighted in the dawn chorus of long-forgotten birdsongs trilling in the morning sunshine. The familiar smell of Mum's rosebushes wafted through the window. I resolved to be the perfect son/caregiver.

I was mostly successful, drawing disapproving looks from Anna if I slipped up and approving nods when I shut up. I learned to let my mother keep her own truths.

Using Dad's tools still hanging in the garage we'd built together when I was fourteen, I fixed the plumbing leaks, replaced the defunct electrical receptacles, and oversaw contractors putting in a new hot water and heating system. The weather was the usual British forecast, scattered showers with sunny periods. I worked inside during the showers and mowed the lawn, straightened out the garden, and fixed a leak in the conservatory roof during the sunny periods. It was satisfying to know I was making things better for my mother, even though she was past noticing the improvements.

Mum was a Scrabble aficionado and insisted we play every day. Remarkably, she'd maintained her word prowess. When being tested for memory, Mum explained, a nurse had asked her how many words she could remember starting with the letter P. "I got up to 23, and she said, 'Stop, Mrs. Baker, stop. That's enough.' I wanted to say 'persimmon,' but she wouldn't let me."

The games were pretty equal. Anna is multilingual and likes competitive word games. English is my native tongue, and I had no dementia. Mother, Scrabble expert for 40 years, played to win and was not above covertly discarding Qs. I learned it was best not to protest after receiving under-the-table corrective kicks from Anna.

I often awoke at night to a plethora of questions coursing through my mind about CMHA: How was Kevin coping as acting ED? Had they hired someone to replace me? How were all the programs running? Was the volume of business at the thrift store still increasing? How was Sandy managing without me? And the big one, did they buy the house at their current location?

The unanswered questions never stopped — like a dull background buzz of uncertainty. I couldn't phone Canada from the house phone because Ali had asked the phone company to restrict Mum's calls. She had been running up huge long-distance bills phoning an unknown person in Argentina. Maybe I shouldn't worry about work. That was the point of leaving.

With no internet in the house, I decided to walk down to McDonald's half a mile away in the hope I could get online. The familiar aromas of coffee and French fries tickled my palate as I stood at the counter. I sat down with my apple pie and tea, punched in the password, and waited for Gmail to boot up. After a month away, nothing from my former colleagues arrived in my email. Maybe there was nothing to report. Why would they report? I was out of the country, no longer their ED. Nonetheless, it felt strange, even eerie, not to hear from any of the folks I had worked with daily over the past four years. I sought comfort in another apple pie and sent cheery emails to Kevin, Donald, and Trevor. "Hey, how's things at CMHA? Miss you all. Say hi to the team. Regards, Rodney." I sent emails to President Richard and Vice President Mary enquiring if they'd had any success in hiring an ED. Having satiated my need to reach out to my former colleagues, I emailed a few friends, slipped my computer into my backpack, and walked through scattered showers back to the house.

A big change for us at my mother's house was the lack of internet. We'd become used to online communication with friends and family, and instant information on Wikipedia. As an independent travel consultant, Anna had decided to do less work while we were away, but having no internet meant zero work.

Without the phone calls, multiple meetings, or deadlines filling my day, life became very quiet except for Mum's constant chatter. If you were in the same room as her, she was talking. We sometimes escaped to the bedroom or went out walking.

After seven weeks visiting Mum and the repair list completed, we decided my duty was done and that it would be fun to spend a week with my sister in Suffolk before leaving for Italy. Lisa, the brilliant caregiver that Ali had found to look after Mum, would resume her daily visits. It felt strange hugging Mum goodbye and knowing in a few days she would barely remember our visit.

It was good to see my sister. We talked about Mum and the possibility of her going into a care home one day. We were unsure how to handle this as our mother decried any loss of liberty. She still complained bitterly to anyone who would listen that Ali was responsible for taking her car away two years before. It was a pleasant break to stroll down to the local pub with Ali and her husband, have a pint of bitter, and watch the world roll by at a slow village pace. Cows mooed in the distance. Wind ruffled fields of barley. People left fruit, eggs, and flowers for sale outside their houses and a can to put the money in. After a pleasant, relaxing week, Anna and I packed our cases again, and at 5 a.m. on an unusually chilly September morning, we drove the rental car to Stansted Airport.

# Italy

Arriving in another country often brings challenges you hadn't considered. As we stepped off the plane into the warmth of Italy, my green corduroy trousers, flannel shirt, and jacket were immediately too hot. Beads of perspiration rolled off my forehead. Trundling my case through Milan's busy Malpensa Airport, I found a lonely washroom, 150 metres away from anything, and squeezed into a tiny toilet cubicle. Opening my suitcase and rummaging through a year's assortment of clothing, I located a pair of khaki shorts and a T-shirt. Contorting my body like a yoga master, I managed to change into cooler clothing. Emerging from the cubicle, I headed for a sink and ran cold water over my head.

I found Anna in a bookstore buying her favourite Italian crossword magazine.

"Your hair looks funny," she said. "Where's your comb?"

"Somewhere in my case."

One does not "look funny" in Italy, especially Milan, the fashion capital of Europe. Anna did her best to smooth my hair out with her hands.

I was cooler, and Anna had her crossword. We were set for the train ride to Anna's hometown of Arona and pulled our cases toward the station. Two months earlier, she had negotiated the purchase of a Fiat Panda hatchback, which was promised to be ready for us on our arrival that day.

An hour and a half later, we arrived at the dealership to hear a smiling salesman explain that our car "wasn't quite ready." The car dealership was air-conditioned, and after 20 minutes of waiting in my new cooler clothes, I grew chilly, wandered outside, and sat on a low stone wall.

Unlike air travel in Canada where you can fly for five hours and land in the same country, a 90-minute flight in Europe parachuted us into a change of weather, language, culture, currency, and the side of the street you drive on. I'd be able to exit roundabouts on the correct side if I remembered to switch back to driving on the right.

The cheeky sparrows fluttering down to pick up crumbs from the restaurant tables next door were just like their English cousins, but other differences were notable: The people were more eloquently dressed; unlike the squat English bungalows, the houses were tall and stately; and the driving was more frenetic.

The speed of the car dealership's service did not compare with the hustle of local traffic. Despite the repeated smiles and assurance of the salesman that the car was almost ready, we waited almost two hours for our car to be prepped — longer than our flight to Italy had taken.

"This guy's an idiot. He's been telling us for two hours it's almost ready."

"Relax, Rod. He is a nice guy and trying his best."

*Incredible. She is standing up for him.* "I'd hate to see him doing his worst!"

Surrounded by the beautiful buildings, lyrical language, and long-missed culture of her beloved Italy, Anna was not going to let a small delay or grumpy partner spoil her mood.

The smiling salesman approached, avoided eye contact with me, and with a wave of his arm announced the car was ready.

*"Finalmente, signori!"* I said in my best loud Italian voice. Taking a deep breath, I swallowed further comment and loaded our suitcases into the long-awaited red Fiat, and we departed for the Cicin Hotel.

The hotel was located on a busy street close to the small town of Omegnia and known for its hard beds, mediocre rooms, but amazing food. We dumped our suitcases on the bed and, feeling very hungry, walked down to the restaurant — the shortest and best journey we'd made all day.

Mario, an older waiter with tight curly hair, smiled broadly as we entered the dining room.

"Good evening, sir and madam. I show you to your table." His English was excellent. He had worked at the Dorchester Hotel in London but returned to Italy three years earlier to look after his sick mother. He pulled Anna's chair back for her to sit down. "I hope you are both well this evening?"

"Yes, thank you, Mario, and you?" Anna said.

*"Si bene, bene, senora.* Welcome to the Cicin. And now, I tell you about tonight's menu." His eyes lit up as he explained the dishes on offer, each described like a precious jewel. Opening his arms, he said, "For antipasto, we have *prosciutto melone, e pesci di lago in carpione...*" I lost track of the Italian after the first two dishes. As Mario drifted on with the list, I looked around the restaurant. About 15 families were seated around the tables, grandparents, mothers, fathers, and children all chatting, laughing, eating dinner together — happy, animated people enjoying one another's company. The festive mood had been largely created by the sumptuous dishes placed in front of them — excellent food prepared with pride and skill. The warm scenes of family pulled unexpected chords in my heart. Maybe we should learn from the Italians: Surely, this is how the world should be — families sitting down together at the day's end, enjoying each other's company and amazing food.

Mario returned with a bottle of Barolo. We sipped wine, chatted, and snacked on appetizers and antipasti, the wonderful flavours wiping away the travails of the day.

A beaming Mario reappeared and, with a flourish, presented us with two small portions of pasta *vongole* — clam pasta with a garnish of parsley — one of my favourite dishes. The *prima piatti*, or first dish, is usually pasta.

"Anna, this is fabulous!" We locked eyes. "Instead of finding our own place, let's live here."

She giggled. After wiping our plates clean with bread, the tagliata dish arrived — thin, lightly brazed strips of beef tenderloin laid on a bed of arugula, garnished with flakes of parmesan, and sprinkled with reduced balsamic vinegar. Heaven! We smiled at one another. At the end of a long day's journey, we had slipped into the soul of Italy, where food is art and enjoying it with loved ones is an essential part of life.

Before leaving Vancouver, our discussions about where to live in Italy conjured up an air of freedom and adventure: Should we live in Rome or Calabria in the south, by the ocean or in the mountains?

Lying in the Cicin hotel bed, the morning after our wonderful meal, the decision about where to live demanded our immediate attention. The novelty of not going to work every day had made us more relaxed and less organized. We had neglected the important question of where we were going to live.

"Why don't we start off living at Hélène's cottage in Liguria. See how it works out?" I suggested.

"We should have phoned before. Maybe she's away or has guests staying there," Anna replied.

When Anna's friend Hélène heard we were coming to live in Italy, she offered us a small cottage at a marginal rent. We had prevaricated because while it was a wonderful location, we worried that Hélène, while an interesting friend, might prove to be a challenging neighbour.

"Well," Anna said, "let's phone her and see if it's available."

Anna called on speakerphone, and I could hear Hélène's French-accented voice saying "Yes, yes, you can 'ave it."

"How about the day after tomorrow?" Anna asked.

"Yes, I can make it ready."

It was a relief to know that our lapse in finding accommodation had been resolved. I admonished myself for being lazy and resolved to be more organized in the future. I decided it was time to check my email and see if there was news from CMHA. I opened my laptop and tried to connect to the internet. I waited and watched a little blue circle go around and around with no result. "Anna, can you phone the front desk? See if I have the right password?"

I had the right password, but the internet was "not working" today. Contacting the outside world would have to wait.

We spent the following morning browsing through shops and bought adapters for our cell phones. Anna bought a hair dryer. I bought some tea bags but couldn't find peanut butter. It was a beautiful sunny day, and after shopping, we parked and strolled along the shore of the jewel-like Lago d'Orta. We stopped at a newsstand. I bought a *Guardian* newspaper and Anna a *Republica*. We found a small lakeside restaurant and ordered a pizza Napolitana and two beers.

"Pizza Napolitana is the real pizza," Anna exclaimed. "It's what the poor fishermen in Naples used to eat. Simple ingredients — mozzarella, tomato, anchovies, and oregano. North Americans have vulgarized pizza with pineapple and chicken toppings."

Maybe she had a point. Our pizza was delicious. I sipped my Peroni beer, unexpectedly good for a country of wine drinkers. Pure relaxation — sitting by a lake in the sun with a beer and a good pizza.

As I glanced at my newspaper, the headlines grabbed my attention. "Banking Collapse. Lehman Brothers fail — more than £90 billion wiped off the value of Britain's companies in the city's worst day of trading."

"Anna, what are the headlines in the *Republica*?"

"President Berlusconi is accused of having sex with a 17-year-old girl from Morocco."

"Anything about a banking collapse?"

She flipped to the front page. "Oh my god, what's happening? Is the world economy collapsing?"

"Yeah. Looks like it. Scary! Hey, I'm just thinking, the guy we rented the house to was in the financial field. If he loses his job, we won't get any rent."

It seemed smart salesmen had sold houses to people who couldn't afford them, wrapped the mortgages in hard-to-decode bonds, and sold them around the world to people eager to make a quick buck. When the homeowners couldn't pay their mortgages, the whole scam collapsed, taking the world economy with it. Hundreds of thousands of people lost their houses, their life savings, and their jobs. The avaricious, quick-buck financial snake had choked on its own tail.

As though a harbinger of doom, the sun became obscured by a cloud and a wind ruffled the flat waters of the lake. The breeze fluttered our newspapers and brought a chill to the table. I finished my beer in four straight swallows.

The long, cold fingers of the subprime mortgage crisis had expanded around the globe and reached our little lakeside table in Italy.

"Well," I mused, "there's nothing we can do about it now. We'll just carry on and hope for the best." We drove back to the hotel. I continued reading the *Guardian* while Anna watched *I Love Lucy* in Italian. We had another wonderful meal from the Cicin kitchen, which lifted our spirits, and we went to bed in a better mood.

In Italy, there is a distinct driving style. For Italian men, it appears that speed is equated with personal virility. Even when driving above the limit in the fast lane, a car will arrive out of nowhere and fill your rear-view mirror. The new arrival appears attached to your bumper and flashes his headlights continuously until you move over. Failure to move aside results in faster headlight flashing and rapid horn honking. We usually drove in the slow lane.

We set out for Hélène's house and breezed along past the industrial area around Milan toward Parma, the home of Parmesan cheese and prosciutto. We turned off the freeway and meandered our way south up to the 1,260-metre-high Passo del Cerreto. The slow drive past quaint farmhouses and grazing sheep relaxed us. Coasting down the other side of the pass, we entered Tuscany and drove through rolling hills of olive groves toward Lerici in the province of Liguria — a thin strip of land along the west coast of Italy.

Hélène seemed pleased to see us and ushered us into a little four-room cottage a few metres from her house. This would be our new home, high on the mountain with stupendous ocean views. Hélène was in her mid-70s, a little forgetful, and unable to share her internet with us because she couldn't recall her password.

*Anna at our rental cottage in Italy*

We unpacked, and Anna busied herself sorting out the kitchen. Stretching my legs after the five-hour drive, I strolled around the property, discovered an infinity swimming pool and fig trees, and picked a few kumquats, tiny oranges you eat whole.

"Look what I've found, Anna. Taste one. So citrusy!"

"Yes. Really good!" She poured us both a glass of wine, and I pulled two chairs outside. From our high perch on the mountain, we sat in the warm afternoon sun and gazed over the stunning gulf of La Spezia cradled in the Apennine Mountains.

Everything had worked out: We had somewhere to live, a car, and the rent from our house in Vancouver provided enough money to live on, as long as it kept coming.

Anna was delighted to be in Italy: She chatted with relatives, caught up with old friends by phone, watched Italian TV, and planned meals with Héléne.

It was different for me: Not going to work, unable to watch TV in English, and having no access to the internet left me little to do. I had gone from having too much work to too much leisure. So much for the work-life balance I had often reminded the staff about. I had preached this but wasn't practicing it.

For the first two days in our new location, I practiced speaking Italian with Anna and Hélène, finished the book I was reading about an English soldier trapped in Italy during WW2, and helped with the grocery shopping.

On the third day, I awoke early feeling restless and scribbled a note to Anna that I was going exploring. Walking past the pool, I came to a five-foot-high grey stone wall on the perimeter of the property. I peeked over the wall and saw a grass track running down the mountain. The iron gate was locked, but I managed to clamber over the wall and start walking. After many days of inactivity, I could feel the blood pulse through my calf muscles. It felt good. The steep trail would be tough on the return journey, especially as the sun rose in the sky. I decided to keep careful note of left and right turns to avoid getting lost. I wasn't sure my Italian was good enough to ask for, or follow, directions back to the house.

To my left were small plots of land where people were growing vegetables. I spotted a cluster of green grapes overhanging the wall and picked a few. Though small, they were sweet and delicious with an unusual aromatic flavour. Further down, I spotted a tree laden with deep purple figs and plucked several from an overhanging branch. The juice, fruity sweet and warm, dripped off my chin. The grass trail turned right, and I sat down on a large rock beside a huge green and yellow agave to finish off the succulent figs. The panoramic view and exotic fruit enchanted me. The land fell away below my feet, swooping down through a smattering of houses and woodland to the small town of Lerici.

I sucked my fingers then wiped them along the broad agave fronds to get the juice off, stood up, and continued down. As I turned past a copse of tall Cypress trees, a small collection of red roofs slid into view. Like a limpet, a tiny village clung to the steep mountainside that fell into the sea. Close to the buildings, the pathway changed from two tracks into a narrow brick road. I was soon walking among grey stone houses of a small village, so close, so intimate, I felt like an intruder.

Loud sounds of Italian daily life spilled into the street through open windows. A baby crying, someone singing, cooking pots clanging. Close by, a loud voice made me jump. *"Davide. Vieni qui. Mangi qualcosa."* — a woman calling her son to eat.

My solitary walk came alive with the clatter of family life.

A loud peal of church bells rang out, bounced off the stone houses, and startled me. It was Tuesday morning. Perhaps someone was getting married. I passed through the village and came to a busy road. Should I cross or go back?

Adventure! I crossed the road and walked down a steep cement driveway then veered right onto a footpath. Ten minutes later, I spotted a faint trail leading to a set of cement stairs zigzagging down through a grove of holm oaks.

I started to descend, feeling like Alice disappearing down the rabbit hole. Crispy brown oak leaves lay uncrushed on the stairs — no human feet had passed this way for months. I counted as I descended, the sound of my voice reassuring under the dark canopy. One hundred and sixty-four steps. The stairs ended abruptly at a roadway, thrusting me out of the trees and into the sunlight.

I sat on the last step to let my eyes adjust to the light. I saw a stone wall across the street and the sparkling blue sea beyond. The country roads were twisty and the drivers so fast I usually avoided walking along them, but having descended so far, I pushed on. It would be great to find access to the sea. After 20 minutes of walking, flattening myself against the wall as cars passed, a faded blue-and-white sign, *Spiagga Publica*, came into sight.

Great, a spiagga, even better, a public beach where I could avoid paying the 40 Euros demanded to lie on a private beach. The wide cobblestone path descended 50 metres to a horseshoe-shaped beach of sand with low, scattered rocks to the right, all surrounded by a semicircular high stone wall.

Finding a secluded spot among the rocks, I slipped off my clothes and sank into a cool pool of seawater, tingling my skin and refreshing my body from the long trek. I clambered out, dried myself with my T-shirt, pulled on my shorts, and stretched the T-shirt over a hot rock. I lay on my back, with my runners for a pillow, and watched white mare's tails float across a brilliant blue sky. The rhythmic ebb and flow of waves sloshing up and down the rocks slowed my heartbeat. Cool zephyrs brushed my skin like a soothing balm. My eyes fluttered shut for a while until thoughts of the long uphill journey home pulled me back to reality. I slipped on my shirt and shoes, picked my way back through the rocks, and started the steep trek back to my new home.

That walk helped set a pattern for much of my time in Italy. I set myself the job of exploring my new environment by hiking the trails that spiderwebbed across the surrounding countryside. I would keep fit and feel a sense of adventure exploring unknown territory. I needed something to do in Italy that was mine.

With two competent Italian women preparing dinner, there was no opportunity to help in the kitchen. As mealtime approached, I laid the table. Hélène monitored my efforts.

"Don't put the forks on the table like that. It's too agresseeve." She turned one over with the tines facing down — illogical, but it was her table.

The menu was antipasti, *risotto rosmarino*, followed by a fresh shrimp salad washed down with glasses of Hélène's favourite Chilean wine. We watched the large golden orb of the sun slide to the distant blue sea as we ate and chatted leisurely about Hélène's former life in Algeria and our day's activities.

I mentioned I had found a beach. Hélène told me it was called Fiascherino and that D. H. Lawrence, "your countryman," had rented a house there on the low cliff overlooking the sea. "'Ee was writing *Women in Love* while 'ee lived there."

After dinner, my efforts to help attracted more guidance.

"Don't wash the glasses. They must sit overnight in water before we wash them." Our hostess had odd ideas about culinary procedures.

A couple of weeks later, Anna and I drove along the narrow road to Tellaro, a tiny village with its feet washed by the ocean waves, its back glued to the steep mountains, and closely packed, bright-coloured houses wedged in between. I had heard there was a café with the internet there, and we'd hoped to get in touch with the outside world. While the café did indeed have internet, it required paying the café owner five euros and showing our passports; we drove back to get them. Since leaving CMHA three months previously, I hadn't received a word from anyone there. Gmail was very slow in loading. I sipped my latte and crunched on a biscotti. When it finally loaded, the first message was from Steve, my 36-year-old son:

> Dad, I found work building tower cranes for

construction sites and am really getting into it. Could you send pix of Italian tower cranes so I could see what they have over there.

A warm glow spread over my body. He had been unemployed for some time and hadn't seemed concerned about finding work. This was a big improvement, and it sounded as though he liked the job. Yes, I would certainly take pictures of tower cranes.

My happy mood evaporated when I found zero replies from Donald, Kevin, or Trevor — nothing from anybody at CMHA. Puzzlement gave way to sadness ending in a pit of worry and self-doubt. Why was there zero response? We'd been friends and colleagues working together for years. A cold sweat came over me. Had I somehow been blacklisted as an embezzler, or a pervert, or some other type of pariah? I couldn't accept getting no response and fired off brief emails to people I trusted outside the office —Sandy, the thrift-store manager; Heather, the outreach worker in Maple Ridge; and Jackie, the Comedy Courage volunteer. For the office employees, I tried Kevin again. They all got the same message:

Hey, guys, I emailed a bunch of people to see what was going on at CMHA, but NO ONE replied. I'm wondering why? Has a new ED been hired? Did you buy the house from Fraserside? Is the thrift store running okay?

I hoped that would do the trick. It was unnerving not hearing from anyone.

Although enjoying the break from the daily problems of work, I began to worry about not knowing what the problems were.

The weather remained warm enough to swim into November. I got used to the steps and hiked down to the beach three or four days a week. The strenuous hike up and down felt like I was achieving something — fitness and time spent doing my own thing. It would have been nice to meet someone at the beach, but it never happened. I often swam out, looked back at the house D. H. Lawrence had rented, and imagined him writing as he looked across the bay. With time on my hands, I thought it would be fun to try my hand at writing, like my "countryman." I decided to write a biography so my children and their children would know about an age when the milk came to the front door by horse and cart and my grandfather trained me how to march when I was seven so I'd be ready for the next war.

I relished this new mental focus. This area, the Gulf of La Spezia, was also known as *Il Golfo dei Poeti*, The Gulf of Poets, due to its popularity with writers: Percy Bysshe Shelley, Henry James, Lord Byron, Charles Dickens, Virginia Woolf, and a host of others had spent time here. The climate and visual beauty of Liguria were enchanting and, apparently, inspiring.

To keep in touch with the world, Anna and I drove to the café in Tellaro once a week to check our emails. In the second week of October, we paid our five euros, ordered coffee, and chatted as we waited for Gmail to load. I got the shock of my life as I read the first message from a CMHA address.

# Bad News    Christmas with Mother    Missing my Tribe

A chill ran through my body at the stark words on my laptop screen.

> I've been hearing rumours circulating among staff that you are coming back to CMHA. You resigned, and your former position has been permanently filled.
>
>    Veronica Blumfeldt, executive director, CMHA Simon Fraser Branch

A slow rage welled up inside me. I should have insisted on getting the board's offer of a year's sabbatical in writing as my gut had told me. I had been worried that due to the financial crash, our renter might lose his job, but now I had lost mine. So much for the recognition of a job well done!

"Anna, I've lost my job. Look at this email."

She put her glasses on and tilted the laptop toward her. "Incredible that the board of directors would go back on their word after all you've done. Who is this Veronica Blumfeldt anyway?"

"I think she was the woman in a wheelchair that I helped up the ramp a week before I left. This whole thing is weird. She can't fire me. Only the board can hire and fire an ED."

The next email was from Sandy, the thrift-store manager:

> Rodney, I have resigned from the thrift store. I can't work with the woman the board hired. She is unappreciative of my efforts. I'm very sad, but it's over.

Heather also replied:

> Rodney, re your query about what's going on — I don't go to the office much. The new ED has told the staff not to contact you. They didn't buy the house.

How could she tell the staff not to communicate with me? Not emailing me during work hours was fair enough, but after work was their time!

I had been desperate for information from CMHA, but not *this* information. I was angry at the board's broken promise of a year's sabbatical and worried that I had no job to go back to.

Using an international call card, I tried phoning CMHA three times. The receptionist was new. Each time I said who was calling, she responded, "The ED is busy right now," and hung up.

Although my job loss seemed like a fait accompli, I emailed the president and vice president of the board to ask for an explanation.

A week later, Mary replied that Richard had resigned and she was the new president. In the next email, I asked her why they hadn't honoured our agreement for a one-year sabbatical. She explained, "We can only go by what was written, not just by what was said." She was wrong: A verbal agreement is just as binding as a written agreement, but proving its existence could be problematic. When I challenged the truth of her explanation, she repeated the same explanation as though programmed.

I had wanted to help my mother, get some breathing space, and de-stress from work by having a different life experience. The disturbing news that I had lost my job dried up my creative writing ability. The poor state of the world economy cast a shadow over my prospects of finding work on my return to Vancouver.

Further bad news was that Anna's relationship with our host was deteriorating. I tended to ignore Hélène's odd opinions and unusual ideas. She had once said to Anna, "Well, of course, people of your class know nothing about life." That was rude and hard to ignore.

We ate dinner with Hélène once or twice a week, and she sometimes dropped in during the day. After her many put-downs of Anna's ideas, I remarked to Anna, "She keeps poo-pooing whatever you say." Anna was amused by the term, and Hélène became known as Madame Poo-poo. If I spotted her walking across the few metres from her house to ours, usually to impose her strident opinions on Anna, I'd yell out, "Poo-poo's coming," so Anna could escape into the bedroom. I'd greet Hélène by saying, "Hi, Anna's not available right now. I'll tell her you dropped by."

We decided to have a break from our close proximity to Hélène and take a trip away. Christmas was first on the list: Anna wanted to spend the holiday season at a stone cottage her family owned in the mountain village of Rima. Friends from her youth would be there. Her son Johnny, who was studying in Germany, would also join her.

At my sister's request, I agreed to spend ten days with my mother. Ali had spent every Christmas with Mum since she'd been diagnosed with Alzheimer's. I emailed my brother, and he agreed to join me. He worked for Greenpeace and didn't have another action until February. Spending Christmas with my family members felt like a good plan — a rare occurrence since emigrating. I perceived my brother as having rather anarchistic tendencies. He probably thought of me as boring. I hoped for the best.

On December 20, Anna drove me to Pisa Airport. It would be our first Christmas apart in our ten-year relationship. After a short flight to Manchester Airport, I was picked up by my brother, Al, and his new girlfriend, Rachel, on their drive down from his house in the Scottish Highlands. This would be our first-ever Christmas together. I was 17 when Al was born and had left home to join the merchant navy. I came back from my first trip at sea to find him occupying my bedroom.

Al was driving a blue VW Jetta recently given to him by an aging neighbour. He drove the new machine like a test pilot checking out its limits. Rachel had a big smile and long raven hair. She seemed unconcerned about driving at 100 miles an hour down the motorway, so I followed her example and chit-chatted about Christmas arrangements.

We pulled up outside the three-bedroom brick bungalow.

Mum's face lit up when she opened the door. "Can it be true? My two big boys home for Christmas!" Her eyes filled with tears. We had a group hug. "And who's this young lady with you?"

"It's Rach, Mum. She's my girlfriend. I mentioned I was bringing her."

"Did you, dear? I don't remember. My memory doesn't work well these days. They say I have a mental illness —something beginning with A. I think it's called…autism."

Each day, we did our best to entertain Mother by playing interminable games of Scrabble, going for walks, or taking drives in the countryside. Rachel was 20 years younger than me, and I appreciated her upbeat, youthful energy in helping with cooking, playing Scrabble, and walking together. Mum's constant chatter pervaded all activities, but we just swallowed and made the best of things.

On Christmas Day, we walked around the neighbourhood in the morning. The frosty garden hedges sparkled in the sunshine. Other walkers greeted us with "Merry Christmas." Mum's hip was aching, so Al and I each held her arm. We put the turkey on at noon, played Scrabble, and watched a Christmas play on the BBC. Delicious aromas filled the small kitchen, and we left the TV room and seated ourselves around the table. I carved the turkey while Rach served the veggies. We pulled crackers and put on funny hats.

"Such a good price and very tasty too," Mum remarked, biting into a drumstick. We all agreed and toasted one another's good health.

Thoughts of my father flooded into my mind as we sat at the

dinner table. I looked at the yellow and white cupboards on the kitchen walls and remembered him building them. We sat under the fluorescent light Dad had installed. I wondered what he would say seeing us all sitting there — his youngest son, Al, all grown up; poor Mum's dementia; me 61 years old, 17 years older than Dad when he died. It felt unworldly being in the house I grew up in, with my mother so changed, and chatting with the brother I never knew. I couldn't seem to fit it all together. I had another large glass of wine.

"Not eating, Rod?" Mum asked. "You won't grow up to be a big boy."

Al and I laughed; it was a sentence we'd both heard often. I was 6'2". Al was 6'4".

"Yeah, just thinking how nice it is to be with you all," I said, giving her a big smile and squeezing her arm.

I admired Al's ability not to get rattled by Mother's non-stop talking. We exchanged catch-up tales about our youth— covert antics — both getting in and out of the bedroom window at night. We'd had similar adventures 17 years apart. It was good to get to know Al — better late than never, and we were bonding over Christmas with Mother.

Two days after Christmas, Al and Rach dropped me off at McDonald's as they left to go home. I ordered a coffee and apple pie, opened my laptop, and struggled with the unfamiliar Wi-Fi. I finally got into my Gmail but immediately wished I hadn't. My heart raced as I read the message.

> We are moving. Leaving Friendship House. The new ED has rented four rooms below the Fraser Health offices for our new office. The thrift store is being relocated to a new building on Carnarvon Street. Paige will manage it full-time. We are not supposed to be in contact with you so please don't quote me. Don't want

to lose my job. Kevin.

I slammed my computer shut and marched out of the door. It had taken me almost five years to get the Simon Fraser Branch back on track, but in a few months, things seemed to be unravelling: The relaxed atmosphere that came from having the office and thrift store in a residential house was over. How could you keep an eye on the thrift store 12 blocks away? How could it make money with a full-time manager? Sandy had been getting $10 an hour as a part-time contract manager. Paige would get $25 an hour full-time plus benefits. Renting another location for the thrift store would be expensive, at least double what "we" paid now. But of course, it was no longer "we."

On the way back to my mother's house, my heart was heavy with the latest news from my former work — heavier because there was no one to share my grief with. My mother wouldn't understand, and it wasn't fair to phone Anna just to tell her bad news. I was listless, couldn't focus, and lost two games of Scrabble.

"I think I'm doing well today," Mum said with a smile. "Maybe my memory is improving. Did I tell you about the time the doctor was testing my memory?" She continued on without my having the chance to say, "Yes, at least ten times." I smiled weakly as Mum continued the story.

"You did very well, Mum. Why don't we see what's on the telly? There might be a nice Christmas show." I fished out some leftovers. We ate lunch on trays and watched TV while my mother talked.

I rode out the next four days, cooking, watching TV, and listening to Mother's multiple stories punctuated by escape trips to McDonald's. On the other hand, I felt good about doing my Christmas duty and giving my sister a break.

The flight back became very bumpy as we crossed the Alps. I arrived at night, got the train from Pisa to Sarzana, and hailed a cab. The driver wasn't sure how to find the rural address. Scanning for landmarks from the back seat in the dark, I gave him directions in poor Italian for the 12-kilometre ride back to Hélène's house on the upper slopes of Monte Rocchetta. I only got two wrong turns.

Relieved to have found my way, I approached the front door and reached into my pocket. "Damn!" There was no key. Anna wouldn't be back for two days. I knocked on Hélène's door, but there was no answer. She always turned off her phone at night. I cussed my stupidity for not hiding a key outside for my return. A chill wind blew up the mountain as I walked around the house checking possible entry points. The kitchen window was closed but not locked. Prying it open, I balanced on a rickety wooden chair, managed to hoist myself in, and crawled over the kitchen sink back into our home. The heat was off.

After the non-stop chatter in England, the stark silence of the house bit into me. I poured myself a wineglass of scotch, put the heat on, found some cheese and crackers, wrapped myself in two quilts, and lay on the couch. The strong wind rustling the grapevines against the windows reminded me of the rough flight.

Memories of my trip crowded into my mind: Meeting Rachel, speeding down the motorway, Christmas dinner around the kitchen table, Mum's constant chatter, and countless games of Scrabble. Disconnected memories flitted across my mind. I poured myself a second glass of scotch and wondered how my children's Christmas had been. They'd always come for dinner during the holiday season, but this year, Alexis was visiting friends in Europe and I was far away from Steve and Mike in Vancouver. I missed their laughter and the sound of their voices — part of my Christmas since becoming a father 38 years before. I hoped Steve's job was going well and that he was keeping himself safe. As safe as you can when you're working hundreds of feet aboveground building cranes. As he had asked, I'd taken lots of pictures of tower cranes in Italy, mostly while I was driving — much to Anna's loud protests. It was one way of keeping in contact with him.

Whisky and quilts were warming my body, the buffeting wind my sole companion. I had flashbacks of the previous year — cooking and serving Christmas dinner for a 100 clients. I missed the camaraderie of daily contact with my people, my tribe.

Anna returned in good spirits with tales of a wonderful Christmas. "Everyone was there. The snow was two metres high. We put all the champagne outside the window to keep cold in the snow, sang traditional songs, and went to bed at 3 a.m." I was glad to hear she'd had a great time. She loved visiting Rima and seeing all the friends from her teenage years.

"How was your Christmas? What did you do?" she asked.

I explained our Christmas dinner, many walks, and multiple Scrabble games — that Al's girlfriend was fun and had helped entertain Mum. "After they left, I got a little overwhelmed with Mum's non-stop chatter but stuck it out."

Anna laughed. "Well, you've done your duty."

Our time in Italy wasn't working out as we'd envisioned: I hadn't found a volunteer position, and I'd lost my job. While Anna loved being back in Italy, she found our landlady challenging.

We decided to take advantage of being in Europe and make secondary escapes from our current escape: We drove to Slovenia and stayed in Ljubljana with a friend I had met some years before when touring Europe. We drove to France and meandered around Nice and Arles.

For a completely different pace, we flew to Tunisia, rented a car, and completed a two-week tour by driving as far south as the Sahara desert and visiting multiple Roman ruins. During our travels, I kept an eye out for homeless people but saw none. Even in Tunisia, a poor country made worse by the lack of tourists due to the worldwide recession, I saw no beggars or people sleeping on the streets as I'd seen in Vancouver. I wondered why it was so different in North America.

The day after we arrived back from Tunisia, Anna left early to go shopping, I pulled on my walking shoes and stepped into the sunshine for another hike, but my hand stayed on the doorknob. I gazed at the olive trees and the blue Mediterranean Sea sparkling in the distance. Everything was the same — except it wasn't. I stepped back into the house and stared at the white marble counter. Perhaps a cup of tea. Boiling the kettle and pressing the bag against the side of the cup with the spoon was reassuring, familiar.

I brought my tea to the table and opened my laptop to resume my writing. No words came. The screen faded to black.

The tea got cold. The hard kitchen chair made my buttocks ache.

*What am I doing here?*

Only the rustle of leaves responded.

I had escaped days rushing by so fast I could barely grab hold of them but had overreached, gone too far, and ended up in a tiny cottage in Italy disconnected from everything I knew.

At first, meandering along lonely trails in the sunshine, plucking figs, enjoying ocean and mountain views seemed sublime. But since losing my job, each day drifted by like an empty cloud. I was no longer sojourning from work. I was out of work.

At age 50 when my marriage ended, I started a new career

working with people who had mental illness. The work had lifted me up and become my life's purpose. Staring out the window and listening to the wind, I understood that I needed to be helping people for my life to have meaning.

Energized by that realization, I slipped my laptop into my backpack and set out on the four-kilometre walk to the internet café in Tellaro. As I drew close, I could smell the coffee mixed with the faint scent of oleander. I flashed my passport at the owner, paid the five-euro Wi-Fi fee, and bought a latte. I'd be glad to get back to Canada where internet cafes were numerous, Wi-Fi was free, and I could find paid work.

Time in Italy had improved my Italian, but not using any mental health terms for eight months, I struggled to find the right words to respond to job ads. Consuming another latte helped brighten my mind. I updated my resume and applied for four jobs. After three weeks of applying for multiple positions, I got one positive response from a Vancouver-based nonprofit. Following a 25-minute discussion on the phone with the vice president, she asked me to come for an interview. Excited and hopeful, I explained it would take me a couple of weeks before I would be back in Vancouver.

We packed our bags, said goodbye to Hélène, and drove North. Anna rented a small apartment overlooking Lago d'Orta and planned to join me in Vancouver when our house became available. We hugged goodbye at Malpensa Airport, and I boarded the plane in a hopeful mood.

# Return to Disaster

My lifestyle of Italian indolence ended abruptly when I stepped off the plane in Vancouver. Being jobless, carless, missing Anna, and without a house to live in, I had problems to solve.

Ada, the former president of the Simon Fraser Branch, was away in Europe for three weeks and lent me her apartment. My new job was to water the 43 plants she shared her apartment with, which resembled a greenhouse.

A friend took me to the car auction in Richmond where I tendered the winning bid on a well-used red Kia for $350. I bought a dark suit and went to the job interview I had travelled 9000 kilometres to attend.

The president of the nonprofit interviewed me alone and asked a lot of questions about how to solve the problems the organization was experiencing. She took notes then informed me she didn't think I was suitable. The Kia quit on the way home from the interview and cost $120 for the tow and $75 for a new spark-plug harness.

I was keen to find work and applied for positions as a therapist, nonprofit ED, and mental health worker without success. Ada returned from Europe, and I moved into my friend Daphne's house. She was on vacation in Greece and needed someone to look after her house, feed the dogs, and ensure her late-rising son got to summer school on time.

In order to be a nice guy as well as the adult rule enforcer, I agreed to play a few games of tennis with him on the court behind their house. On the first game, not wanting to lose to a 16-year-old kid, I overreached to make a winning shot. Something snapped in my lumbar region. A violent pain ripped through my back as though I'd been stabbed by a hot knife. I yelled out loud and clutched my back. I bore the pain for a while, hoping it would subside. It didn't.

Acupuncture and trigger point therapy didn't help; neither did visits to a chiropractor or massage therapist. I had played my last game of tennis and added another injury to my long-suffering back. Not wanting to look like a 60-plus bent-over applicant, I took muscle relaxants before each job interview. They dulled the pain but made me drowsy — not helpful when trying to appear as a sharp candidate.

In early August 2009, I stopped by to visit Louise, my former wife. We sometimes met to discuss our three children. As we sat in the sun on her front porch drinking tea, my cell phone rang. It sounded like Steve's girlfriend, Christine, but the reception was bad. She was barely coherent, sobbing more than speaking. She said they'd been in a car accident.

"Christine, calm down. The reception is bad, and I can hardly hear you."

"Steve's been killed in a car accident."

The colour drained from my face. Louise asked me what was wrong.

I looked at Louise, the lawn, the trees in the yard. A robin sang. Everything looked normal except that time had stopped and I could hear my own heart thumping.

Christine must be mistaken. What she was saying could not be true. At six feet seven inches tall, Steve was an upbeat, indestructible giant: He had survived motocross crashes, a head-on car crash on the Sea to Sky Highway, a gunshot wound, and lately working hundreds of feet in the air building construction tower cranes. I was going to visit him at his new place in Vernon in two days. He was my son. He couldn't be dead. "Christine, slow down. I can hardly hear you. Tell me again what happened to Steve."

"What is it, Rod, what's happening," Louise asked, looking worried.

"It's Steve's girlfriend, Christine. They've been in a car accident." I needed details. "So, Christine, tell me what happened?"

"We were all in the car this morning, going to get coffee. It went off the road, and Steve was killed. The other three of us are fine."

*She must be on drugs.* "Is anyone with you now?"

"Yeah, Jason. He was driving."

"Can I speak to him?"

Jason could hardly speak. "I didn't mean it. I didn't mean it. I wasn't my fault." He stuttered as he explained that Steve had let him drive his new Mustang convertible. He had overtaken a camper on the inside lane. The camper pulled into the inside lane and flipped their car down an embankment. Steve was thrown from the car and died immediately from massive head injuries.

Louise took the phone from me. She had to hear it with her own ears.

It was hard to believe, to understand. We didn't want to believe. Steve had sometimes been involved with a few unsavoury characters. We thought maybe someone was mad at Steve and trying to hurt us by getting people to phone us with false news. After talking to the RCMP in Vernon where the accident happened, they suggested we talk to the coroner. The coroner confirmed our worst fears. Steve had been killed in a car accident that morning.

We contacted our daughter, Alexis, who flew home from England to join us. Louise, Mike, Alexis, and I drove to Vernon and stayed in the house Steve and Christine had just rented.

The neighbours heard why we were there. They quietly brought gifts of food, paid their respects, and left. No one felt like cooking.

Mostly we sat on the deck, smoked cigarette after cigarette, and shared our disbelief, our grief, in the soft Okanagan rain.

The carpenters working next door made a white wooden cross. We wrote our thoughts of love for Steve on the cross, bought flowers, and went to the site of the accident. We dug into the gravelly earth, planted the cross, and placed the flowers beside.

We walked down the embankment to where the car had landed. We wanted to be at the exact place where his life had ended. He must have been terrified as the car plunged off the road and down the slope. The grass was scarred with deep brown furrows where the car had flipped over. Mike found a half-smoked cigar on the ground — the brand Steve smoked. He put it in his pocket. No one knew what to say.

"He didn't suffer."

"No. Must have been instant."

"Yeah."

Everything takes time — even the official process of death. We had to wait until we could identify the body. After an uncomfortable two days, we drove to the local funeral parlour with Christine.

Seeing him stretched out cold on a gurney in the funeral home made me gasp for breath. His long body with tattoos up to his neck was unmistakable. Part of his head was covered with a cloth to shield us from seeing the impact that had killed him. We stood close to his body in horror, stunned into silent disbelief — minutes ticked by. I looked at all the haunted faces around me and took a deep breath. To break the stunned silence, I grasped Steve's cold hand, flinched, and asked everyone to join hands.

"Steve, we are here with you holding hands, your loved ones and family. We care for you so much and are standing by your side today. We are devastated you are gone from our lives, but you will live on in our hearts forever, son. God bless you, Steve." I felt like crumpling to the floor, but as his father, I needed to be stoic, join us together, and say something for Steve, for all of us. Lots of "father duties" had tested me in the past but nothing like this.

When I heard myself saying the words, they felt like a lie. Steve had always been bursting with energy, full of ideas, plans, pranks, and humour. I wanted to deny the cold touch of his body, half expected he would suddenly sit up and say, "Ha, fooled ya, Dad!" But he didn't. He couldn't. He was dead.

Two days after his cremation, we left with his ashes for the drive back to Vancouver. My life felt cold and alien. Time hung in the air. Each day, I awoke to the worst realization possible — that I would never ever see my son again. He hadn't been easy to parent, and I regretted the times I'd been angry with him. Now it was too late to say sorry. We'd also had fun times and shared lots of adventures. I had coached his soccer team for four years, and we'd gone dirt-bike racing together.

A third of my father persona was gone forever. Steve, my firstborn, had been my son for over half my life. We were imbedded in each other's DNA, understood each other's thoughts.

The next three weeks were a blur as the family tried to cope with Steve's passing while putting together a memorial service, writing an obituary for the *Vancouver Sun*, and contacting friends and relatives. I pride myself on being a logical person but when alone kept repeating, "I don't want Steve to be dead. I don't want Steve to be dead." It stopped after the finality of the memorial service when about 120 people showed up to grieve and pay their respects.

Steve's death was the most devastating experience of my life. Future fears and challenges could be diminished by reminding myself, "I have survived Steve's death, this is nothing compared to that." Not working had its benefits: I allowed myself to cry a river of tears — draining, hopeless, healing, accepting tears, unlike when I was 18 and my father had died. People around me had said, "Don't cry, be a man, you have to stay strong for the family." My mother was 40 and my twin sisters eight. They cried all the time, but I had held my grief in, being "strong," not allowing myself to properly grieve his death. This time, I knew better, did better.

I thought losing my job, not finding another, being out of my house, being broke, and having a crappy car were low points in my life. Compared to losing my son, they were short-term inconveniences.

As I weathered the storm clouds of loss, positive events started to occur. Anna returned from Italy, and we moved back into our house. After multiple interviews, I was offered a position as lead counsellor at a well-respected nonprofit in the municipality of Delta. I looked forward to working for a new organization, meeting new people, using my counselling skills, and not having to raise money or be in charge of everything. They knew of my recent loss and suggested I start in three weeks.

Meanwhile, the trajectory of CMHA's Simon Fraser Branch continued on a downward path. I had been in contact with the staff. Most had come to Steve's celebration of life service. They were unanimous in condemning the current executive director and had recently aired their grievances to the board via the annual ED evaluation — the one I designed.

Veronica was furious at the totality of negative evaluations. During the staff meetings, she demanded to know who had written what. Officially, staff were not to contact the board, but in this case, three or four complained to board members that they were being harassed about the evaluation. The board instructed the ED to cease and desist from any further questioning.

Veronica became incensed when she heard the staff complained to the board about her. She told the board the staff were usurping her authority and demanded to know who had spoken to them. Instead of desisting, she doubled down on questioning the staff. When the board became aware of this, they decided not to renew her contract. Shortly after this, the board resigned en masse except for the president. CMHA's Simon Fraser Branch was without a board of directors or an executive director.

## Back to CMHA

I heard from Ada that she had rejoined the Simon Fraser Branch board and had volunteered to be president again. She was looking for new members, and I let a couple of people in my network, Graham and Rahim, know there were positions vacant, as well as Barney, who no longer worked for Fraser Health. Two clients joined the board to make up the required six board members. I was happy my former organization seemed to be rising from the ashes. However, this regeneration created a dilemma: Two weeks after the new CMHA-SF board had been formed, I received a call from Ada.

"Rodney, on behalf of the directors, I have been asked to offer you your previous position as executive director of this branch."

"Ada, are you serious?" I explained that I'd found a good job and was starting the following week. The news literally gave me a headache. After three months of searching, I was relieved to find a job and really liked the ED of the new organization. I spent the following day deliberating. In the end, the temptation to get my former job back was too strong. I phoned Ada to accept. My logic was that New Westminster was a lot shorter daily commute than Delta. But who was I kidding? A big part of the decision was to right the wrong of the board reneging on my sabbatical, plus the branch was in deep trouble. Hard not to reach out and help.

Feeling guilty, I phoned the Delta organization, informed them I'd been offered my original job back, and apologised.

The weekend before starting back at CMHA, Anna and I drove around to look at the new location of the office and thrift store. The thrift store was in a brand-new building on low-pedestrian Carnarvon Street. Half the store's floor space was elevated nine inches higher than the rest — a big step running the width of the store. My iconic black iron clothing rack was missing. The store was empty except for the weekend staff person.

"Didn't you say the temp ED was in a wheelchair?" Anna said.

"Yeah, that's right."

"Strange she would open a store that was only half wheelchair accessible."

I nodded. Anna had a point. We drove up Sixth Street and looked at the new office building.

"It's those four rooms there," I said, indicating the bottom floor of a three-storey brick building.

"What an awful place. It looks like an abortion clinic."

I laughed. "Why do you say that?"

"All the windows are over six feet above the ground. You can't see in."


Accelerating onto the familiar freeway route to work brought a smile to my face — once a mundane, everyday journey, now it was the road back to my mental health tribe, using my skills, and earning a living.

I arrived at the new location, pushed through the door, and walked down the hall looking for my office. A few staff saw me, smiled briefly, then averted their gaze. Their faces looked strained. It wasn't the happy team I had left.

Trusty Trevor, our accountant, pointed me toward my new office, one of four rooms connected by a single hallway. After a warm handshake, he clenched his jaw and frowned as he sat down and briefed me on the current state of affairs: Donald, our competent, friendly housing manager, was on sick leave, and Robbie had replaced him. The lease on St. John's House in Maple Ridge had not been renewed, so we no longer ran that house and lost the administration revenue of $8,000 a year. The volunteers for the computer training program had quit as had most of the thrift-store helpers, including Sharon and Sandy. Instead of the thrift store making $3,000 a month profit, it was losing almost $3,000 a month at the new location on Carnarvon Street. Veronica had signed a multi-year lease and hired Paige full-time to manage the store. Trevor explained we were headed for a $30,000 deficit for 2009.

"One piece of good news, Rodney. We have a new program called Bounce Back that comes with a small amount of admin money."

"Yeah, Kevin emailed me about that. Sounds like a really good program. I guess this whole organization needs to bounce back! Is that everything, Trevor?"

"Yes. Nice to have you back, Rodney," he said with a grimace as he drew in a deep breath.

"Thanks. I've come back to a bloody mess, haven't I?"

I made myself a cup of coffee and sat down at the desk, stunned by all the bad news, and flicked my computer on. Someone had anonymously emailed me their evaluation of Veronica. I read through it, open-mouthed. Each of the ten questions were answered in extremely negative terms. I felt sorry for Veronica. If that was typical of how the staff felt about her, each day at work would have been spent in unfriendly territory.

I called the staff together for our first team meeting but decided not to reveal our dire financial circumstances — I didn't want them to quit and look for more secure employment. They were already stressed enough. We squeezed into the small meeting room at the end of the hall. I brought donuts as I had at our very first team meeting six years previously.

Before I could speak, Stephanie yelled out, "Rodney's back! He's come to save the organization like he did before."

Her vote of confidence put a smile on my face — made me feel like I could do it. She and I often differed on many occasions, but perhaps things had changed for the better. Good, we all needed to pull together to get out of the dire situation we were in.

"Thanks, Stephanie. It's good to be back and great to see all of you again. Perhaps we can do a round-table check-in, just to see where everybody's at."

Instead of discussing their clients' challenges as they had done in the past, each staff member vented about the wrongs they experienced from the previous ED. I wanted them to be able to vent and have their voices heard but didn't want it to consume the whole meeting. We needed to make plans for the future, not dwell on the past.

"Guys, we are going to have to limit this to five minutes a person." This brought a rash of sour looks and covert grumbles. I didn't want to turn the staff against me at my first meeting back and decided to ignore the time limit and let the whole meeting be a venting session. I hoped it was a one-time thing. Their barrage of questions were unanswerable.

"Why did she limit our time on the computers?"

"Why did she move us here?"

"How could she fire someone on maternity leave?"

"Why hadn't the board done something?"

I was saddened my colleagues' spirits were at such a low ebb. Their caring work was the lifeblood of the organization. The good name we had earned and the reason we got our contracts from Fraser Health was solely due to the staff's stellar work with our clients. Bitter feelings of injustice negatively affected the staff's well-being. As well as addressing our failing finances, I needed to validate the emotional suffering of the staff but somehow raise fresh hope and move toward a brighter future.

To end the meeting, I stood up, took a deep breath, and looked around the room to gain eye contact. "Listen, I understand you've obviously been through a rough patch, but now it's over. Remember why you are in this line of work, why you bust your butts every day. It's for the satisfaction you get from making a positive difference in the lives of our clients. Let's try to move forward together and hold that goal in mind." I felt good about my meeting wrap-up. A few wan smiles and nods were exchanged around the room.

Stephanie stood up across from me. "Sisters and brothers, as your union rep, I want you all to remember that I was here for you during the past year, and I'll be here for you now and in the future whenever you might need me." Everyone applauded.

*What the hell? I was here for them too!*

Stephanie had stood up for the staff against Veronica and filed multiple union grievances. While I was out of the country, she had gained their respect and admiration. When I first came to CMHA, the staff members were a challenge because they'd become semiautonomous through lack of a leader. Now it seemed they had become radicalized against management due to too controlling a leader. Despite my heartfelt words, I was still management.

For the following three months, instead of the normal business of discussing our clients' challenges, the staff meetings ran hot with tales of unfairness at the hands of Veronica. Not only were they informing me of recent history, but they were also processing their own feelings of anger and loss. The atmosphere was often so dark it crossed my mind that I should have taken the counselling job in Delta.

After the first staff meeting, I returned to my office deflated and sat staring up through the high windows at white clouds floating across a blue sky, back down to my swimming fish screensaver, then back up at the sky. The clouds and fish moved slowly. I felt like a slow fish too, sluggish, bogged down by bad energy: The staff were traumatized and angry. I missed Donald, my trusty housing manager. We were heading for a huge deficit. The thrift store was losing money. Overarching all this gloom was Steve's passing — still raw and cutting. Only three weeks had passed since his death.

Jumping up from my seat, I walked out of the office, escaped onto the sidewalk, and gasped in lungsful of fresh air. I strode past the Greek restaurant and into Royal City Centre Mall. It was a relief to be anonymous, an impersonal window-shopper, cruising along with my hands in my pockets looking at things I didn't need — women's shoes, party balloons, fish tank equipment — bleary visions through damp eyes. Trancelike, I passed by the dollar store and continued on to Safeway to pick up something for lunch. I stopped in my tracks as I spotted Lisa. She was shopping with John, our partially sighted client, as I had done over a year ago. He was holding onto the shopping cart as she pushed it. She was selecting tomatoes. They were laughing about something. She walked slowly, steering the cart carefully around the other customers toward the checkout.

Legally blind John, with a mental illness, who lived alone, was laughing. I pictured him at home feeling along the shelves for the right cans of soup.

To run this organization effectively, I needed to put my personal grief aside and start solving the problems at hand. I bought a couscous salad in a plastic container and headed back toward the office. Just past the locksmith, there was a For Rent sign on a storefront. I looked through the grimy window at a big retail space. My mind started whirring — high pedestrian traffic but kind of grungy, so the rent shouldn't be too high. I stepped back onto the street to get a better view. There were rooms above. Maybe the upper floor could be used as office space. My heart started to thump. I walked back to the office with a spring in my step and bumped into Carmela, the former manager of Bluebird House. "Hey, how's the new job going?"

"Great, I'm really liking it," she replied with a bright smile. At least we had one happy staff member and a positive new program.

During my absence, Bev Gutray, CMHA's CEO, had found funding for a great new program called Bounce Back Regain Your Health. A Scottish psychiatrist pioneered the program to help people overcome negative thought patterns. With a doctor's referral, people suffering from depression or anxiety used a workbook and coaching sessions by telephone from trained staff to support them in reaching self-directed goals. Doctors dealing with depressed or anxious patients typically could only prescribe meds. Patients getting empathy and guidance in cognitive behavioural skills from the comfort of their own home was a big improvement on medication alone. Carmela had stepped up, taken the training, and ran the Bounce Back program at our branch.

Enlivened by John's spirit, Carmela's smile, and thoughts of the empty retail space, I sat down to make a list. Writing down what needed to be done helped me organize my thoughts and put me in charge of the problems rather than vice versa. I was going to eliminate them one by one.

    1) Check out the retail space

    2) Set up interviews for the housing manager's job

    3) Visit the houses we run. Check for repairs

    4) Address unresolved union grievances

    5) Set up the union-required safety committee

    6) Visit Heather in Maple Ridge to check on the

outreach program

7) Check the lease length of our current office space

8) Phone Moira about setting up a cleaning business for clients

9) Restart the computer-training program

My list-making was interrupted by a call from a member of the CMHA survey team who wanted to set up an appointment. This was a new idea of Bev Gutray's: Each CMHA branch in the province would be evaluated by a three-member team who would carry out onsite inspections to ensure that each branch was heading in a financially sound direction, that staff morale was good, and that we were offering programs in alignment with CMHA values. I had agreed with this idea when it first came up 18 months before, but with the mess we were in, it just added to a feeling of overwhelm. Nevertheless, I booked a date for the team to evaluate us and went back to my list. As usual, I had left the most pressing problem to last.

10) Fix the Carnarvon Street thrift store

How the hell was I going to fix the thrift store? To have a chance of making money, I'd have to fire Paige, renege on our current office and store leases, and find a building that would accommodate running both operations together. I liked and respected Paige, but because she'd quit her mental health position to work in the store, she'd lost her union seniority and I wouldn't be able to hire her back full-time. Terminating the newly signed thrift-store lease would be challenging, maybe impossible in a building owned by a high-profile real estate developer.

When confronted with tricky problems in the past, I'd found it helpful to get out of my office, walk around the thrift store, drink a coffee, chat with the volunteers, and often scrounge a chocolate-chip cookie. It put me in a different mood and made life seem less complicated, more human. With the thrift store 10 blocks away, accessing this trusty over-the-counter "Valium" was no longer practical. I decided on another distraction: As we were now in the same building as Fraser Health, I would check out #9 on my list by going upstairs to hear Moira's plan for starting a cleaning business for clients. For exercise, I ran up two flights of stairs and rapped on Moira's door.

"I'm busy," she yelled.

"Too busy to discuss the cleaning business?"

"I can give you ten minutes."

"You'd better talk fast then," I said, chuckling.

Moira was from Ireland, in her 50s, with dark curly hair and an infectious smile. She was a dynamic combination of hard work and innovation, tinged with occasional dry humour. She worked for Fraser Health as an employment counsellor and had the idea of starting a cleaning business. She found janitorial training for her clients and then located companies that needed office cleaners.

As she worked for the government-run Fraser Health, she couldn't run an entrepreneurial venture but suggested CMHA run the business end of things — do the billing and pay the workers. Great idea. I was happy to help: One thing that often separates many people with mental illness from their fellow citizens is lack of employment. We live in a work-oriented culture. People get their identity and value themselves through their work. When meeting new people, enquiries about what they do is often the first question asked. "I'm a janitor" sounds better than "I'm unemployed."

I admired Moira's proactive energy. Being there for clients was her top priority. We were like-minded about the value of work for our clients, and I was proud to be part of her plan. She was a bright light in a gloomy landscape. We figured out a plan: We would bill the customers she found for office cleaning and pay her clients for the janitorial work they did. Our organization would charge a small fee for the paperwork.

A few weeks later, the CMHA survey team finished their report and informed me that staff morale was awful and that financially we would not last the year. I could have told them that, but it was depressing to hear it officially. They suggested we needed to get rid of the thrift store but had no suggestions how to get out of the multi-year lease.

Three months after my return, Trevor walked into my office looking worried and passed me a notice from the thrift store's landlord. It was a special assessment requiring we pay $784 for an upgrade to something called "common areas."

"That's a brand-new building. What the hell do they need to upgrade in a new building?"

"Beats me. What do you want me to do?"

"I'll get back to you." Paying a big chunk of extra change for a failing enterprise irked me, and it slid to the back of my mind. Two weeks later, the day after the payment deadline passed, I got a panicky call from Paige. "Rodney, the bailiff is here. He says unless you run down with a cheque for $784, he's going to get a truck to pick up the entire contents of the store and put them in storage, and we'll be charged for all the costs."

"Tell him I'll be down within half an hour." Amid everything I was trying to put straight, I'd forgotten about the common area charge. My payment reluctance evaporated with the threat of a shutdown. Having nothing to sell would just increase the losses we were already suffering. I put the phone down and sank back into my chair. My heart started to race, getting ready for a fight: failing nonprofit versus the giant construction company that owned the store. David killed Goliath with a stone to the head. I racked my brain for a stone. Paige said the air conditioning hadn't worked for six weeks in the summer. The store became so hot people could hardly breathe. Customers complained about the heat and left. This would be my projectile — flimsy, but better than nothing.

## A Sliver of Hope

I finally got a call from the landlord of the retail space I had peered into days earlier. We agreed to meet the following day at noon. The owner was in his late 50s, a burly man with a brusque manner.

He gripped my hand hard. "Igor Gretskon. I will open up."

Fluorescent lights blinked to reveal a large, empty space about 18' wide and 30' long. The floor was cement and the walls yellow. A door in the corner opened to three back rooms, which would be great for storage and sorting donations. Igor led me up a pine staircase leading to two large rooms on the next level and three on the top floor, all in a state of disrepair — cracked linoleum floors, paint peeling from the walls, missing doors, and damaged drywall. Two rooms had no ceilings. A musty odour permeated the air.

"Before, was second-hand store, but the guy went bust." Igor was not a real estate salesman. Although in dire need of maintenance, the building was located only two blocks from the Royal City Centre Mall, a high-traffic area, great for retail. The rooms above could serve as offices, and there was parking out back. I hid the flush of excitement rushing through me. I exhaled deeply, shrugged, and waved my arm toward the walls.

"It's in pretty bad shape. How much are you asking? I'm gonna need some rent allowance to fix it up."

"Okay, I talk with my sons. We can meet in my office next week. Maybe we make a deal."

I shrugged again. "Sure. Maybe I could borrow the key so I can get estimates from contractors?" He stared me in the eye. I looked straight back.

"Okay, bring back when you finish."

We shook hands again. His grip was not one to be messed with.

On reaching my office, I phoned Sandy, the previous thrift-store manager, and invited her for a coffee so we could catch up. We hadn't met since my return.

"Good idea, Rodney. Do you want to come to my place?"

"I'm pretty busy, but I could slip out and meet at Tim Hortons opposite the locksmith on Sixth Street."

We met the following day at 10 a.m. It was good to see her. We had been comrades in arms building and running the thrift store at two locations.

She shook her head about the current store. "It will never work there. Not enough foot traffic."

"I agree. It's a disaster. Hey, before we go, I want to show you something."

She looked puzzled, but we dodged traffic as she followed me across the street. The For Rent sign was still in the window. I opened the door and switched on the lights.

She looked around for a while then started laughing. "Rodney, this wasn't about coffee, was it?"

I laughed too.

"I'm not doing it, Rodney."

"Look at the back rooms. There's even a washer and dryer there. We could wash dirty clothes instead of re-donating them. See all the storage? There's three separate rooms back here."

She had followed me in, and her eyes lit up. "The clothes could be sorted on this big bench then stored on all the shelving. What a great space," she said. "And lots of foot traffic."

"Yeah, and there's room for our office upstairs, a staff room, and parking out back."

"How would you get out of the other lease?"

"I dunno, Sandy. But if we don't, we'll go broke and won't be able to pay the rent anyway. I've gotta do something before we go bust, and this is my solution."

She said nothing but walked around inspecting every nook and cranny, holding back a smile. I could see she was planning it all in her head.

"You could do this without me."

"Sandy, you're the best manager the store ever had. You are a natural at retail. But more important, you get what it does for our clients to have a job, a place to go to in the day, where they are valued for the contribution they make. The respect they got from you, their co-workers, and the customers helped them start to respect themselves — maybe for the first time." The truth blurted out of me. We stood in the flickering light, looking at each other. Our eyes were wet. She gave me a hug.

"You con man," she whispered.

For the coming battle, I needed people like Sandy in my corner. Trevor was always there for me, helpful, earnest, and polite. Kevin remained a stalwart supporter — aware of the big picture, ready to pitch in when I needed help. Many of the staff had been traumatised and seemed resistant to change or any extra work outside of caring for clients. I could live with that. Caring for clients was the main focus.

I took a bottle of whisky to Igor's meeting as a goodwill gift. It couldn't hurt. After some hard bargaining about the rent, who would pay the utilities, and how many parking spaces we could have, I stopped at the point where it looked like he was getting fed up. We agreed on our moving into the premises in two months' time. He would give me three months' free rent for all the repairs we were doing. I had bargained my way into a good deal, hopefully.

For everything to work, I needed to get out of the Carnarvon Street store lease, find contractors and money to complete all the repairs in the new premises, relocate the office and store, and get a business licence — all in two months while carrying on business as usual with unhappy staff.

## Restoration

I returned from the meeting with Igor and started composing an email to the thrift store landlord informing him that we would be leaving in two months due to his not living up to obligations regarding air conditioning. I also mentioned that the store was losing $3,000 a month, which would cause our organization to go bankrupt. Not strictly true as we still had two houses as assets.

The six new directors were aware of our dire circumstances and wished me luck in trying to get out of the lease. I reminded them that we carried directors' insurance in case we were sued. I let them know there was a suitable place to relocate available at a reasonable price but that it needed lots of repairs. Graham, a former friend whom I had reunited with at my son's funeral, had an interesting idea.

"My builder is a great guy," he said. "I've given him lots of business, and I think he could be talked into doing some of the work pro bono if we gave him a tax credit and a write-up in our newsletter. Due to the financial meltdown, he's been complaining lately about not having enough work to keep his guys busy. This project could prevent him from laying anybody off."

This sounded amazing, and I asked Graham to set up a meeting with the contractor. Everybody on the board was behind me. It felt great not to be pussyfooting around trying to please divergent factions.

Moving on with my list, I advertised for a housing manager on Craigslist and Charity Village. Before posting it in the staff room, I let Robbie know.

She responded angrily, "Why are you doing this? Aren't I doing a good job?"

"In case of future problems, we don't want anyone saying you were just given the job rather than earning it," I said to reassure her. "When Alice just handed Donald the housing manager position, some staff were still complaining about it two years later when I joined the organization."

She mumbled something under her breath. I valued her caring attitude as a housing worker, and she'd done an amazing job starting the Smoking Cessation course, but she tended to make decisions on her own instead of collaboratively. As housing was our main function, the housing manager played a pivotal role and I wanted to ensure we had the best person for the job.

I set up an interview team of one client, myself, Kevin, a board member, and Jill from Fraserside to make it five in case of a deadlock. We had four questions each and marked the answers out of a possible ten points. It was more challenging for Robbie because we had worked with her and already knew the answers, a fact that she pointed out during her interview.

We had four candidates. Jennifer, a young woman in her early 30s, stood out far above the rest. She showed up for the interview in a stylish black business suit. Her language skills were impressive: She spoke English as her first language plus French, Mandarin, and Cantonese. Jennifer had been the executive director for the Swiss Chinese Chamber of Commerce in Beijing, organized fundraising events, and written many successful grants. Due to a government grant, she came with half her wages paid for six months. On our collective score sheets, Jennifer was way ahead of the next applicant, Robbie.

I delayed telling Robbie. I was pretty sure there would be fireworks. When she asked me about the result the following day, I asked her into my office and explained another candidate had been awarded the position.

Her nostrils flared, and her face turned white. "How could you do that to me? Do all these years I've given to CMHA mean nothing? I want to see the results. I'm not accepting this decision," she yelled.

I felt genuinely sad for her but unhappy she was taking it out on me. "I'm sorry that you're upset, Robbie, but it's not a case of you accepting the decision. The committee of five was unanimous. It's not something you can change."

"How long has this person you've hired worked in mental health? I bet it's not as long as me!"

This was tricky: Jennifer had confided to us that she had "personal experience" of mental health challenges, which we accepted without asking for exact details. It could have referred to either herself or a close family member having a mental health challenge. Unlike most organizations, we had a specific policy of not discriminating against people with mental illness. Along with her well-honed organizational skills and multicultural knowledge, the six months' wages and her fundraising experience were big draws given our depleted financial condition.

"The panel's decision is final, Robbie." I told her we valued her work and that she was welcome to stay with us in her former position. As I didn't answer her question, she smelled a rat and went off to inform other staff members she was sure we'd hired someone with less experience than her. It was the beginning of a rough ride for Jennifer.

About three months after I had returned, Fraser Health cut $6000 from our annual funding. They figured they had been overpaying us for one of the housing contracts. Added to the projected $30,000 deficit, it was like rubbing salt in the wound. When Trevor told me of the cut, I started laughing. With our crappy new office, failing thrift store, depressed staff, and announcement from the audit team that we wouldn't last the year, laughter was the only response left. Trevor threw me a worried look.

Even though we were in dire financial straits and morale was low, the overarching pall of my son's death made work problems seem less overwhelming — created some distance from them. On the other hand, a bonus of working was that being so engaged in solving problems at work took my mind off the cutting pain of losing Steve. I was surviving, gaining more time and space from the shattering loss. At the end of each long day, I walked out of the office tired, sank into my car, and drove along Canada Way toward home. As I turned onto the freeway, a large construction tower crane filled the windshield. It triggered memories of the many times I'd reached for my camera in Italy to take pictures of cranes as Steve had requested. Tears streamed down my face. I took a few deep breaths and exhaled slowly. "It's okay to cry," I told myself.

Allowing myself a private time to grieve in my car happened each day as I passed the crane on the drive home. Each time I saw that tall crane reminded me I would never see Steve again, hear his voice, feel cheered by his big smile, or be a part of his life. Crying acknowledged my pain, kept me balanced — work, grief, home, dinner, sleep. The pain never left, but slowly it became less sharp, less stabbing.

In October 2009, the Simon Fraser Branch was in similar financial circumstances as when I had first come aboard five years before, except this time, I had a proven remedy — the thrift store. I met with Graham's builder, and he agreed to restore all 10 dilapidated doors in the building and change a wall location to make a reception area. I made a list of the work to be done — installing flooring in the thrift store and refurbishing the office spaces — and put an ad on Craigslist for "Carpenters with sharp pencils." Board member Rahim was a contractor and found me a low-cost drywaller to repair all the drywall damage and missing ceilings in the upstairs offices. I took my toolbox to the new site and fixed the smaller items as time allowed.

The new store and office were abuzz with the sound of power tools as it was refurbished into workable premises. I researched, bought, and installed the necessary fire protection equipment and emergency lighting needed for a public shopping space. Trevor applied for a retail licence. Everything was progressing well, but the consequences of bailing from the other lease made me very uneasy. Getting three brothers to agree to let us off the hook, as had happened last time, was a different kettle of fish from getting a giant construction company to forget about a lease.

I got the call I had been dreading from the thrift store landlord. "I'm Giuseppe, your landlord. I wanna meet you tomorrow at the store. Ten o'clock." I had other things planned but decided to bite the bullet and comply with his crisp demand.

Giuseppe was in his early thirties. Dressed in a sharp dark suit, pink shirt, and blue tie, he looked impatient.

I greeted him with a smile. *"Buongiorno, signori. Comme va oggi?"* (Hello, sir, how's it going today?) I assumed from his sharp suit and name he was Italian. It didn't work to lighten the mood.

He shot me a dirty look and said in a loud voice, "You can't leave this store. You signed a lease. We'll sue you."

I pointed out the terms of the lease stated the landlord had to maintain the air-conditioning, which he failed to do, causing us to lose customers. "Another reason we are leaving is that we are losing $3000 a month in this location. By the end of the year, we'll be broke. We want to leave before that happens."

He walked toward me. His lips tightened. "You don't wanna do that."

"I'm telling you the truth." I stared back.

He continued, "We'll close this store down, sell all the stuff, and sue you."

"Surely you have more important things to do than selling used clothing and suing an organization that doesn't have any money." I pointed out that it wouldn't be good press for a large real estate developer to be seen suing a nonprofit that helps people with mental health issues. "I'm sure you need building concessions and permits from the city. How will the mayor and council feel about assisting an organization that's against mental health?" I held his gaze.

Giuseppe stared at me then looked away and yelled, "You'll be hearing from our lawyer."

I heaved a sigh of relief. At least the issue was in the open. I turned to see that Paige had been watching from the sorting room.

"You did well, Rodney. Stood up to him."

I laughed. "Well, we don't have a choice, Paige. How are things with you?"

"Not good. When Veronica was running things, the staff always dropped by and we had a bitch session, but now you're back, no one comes and there's so few customers it's kinda lonely."

"If I get a new location, there won't be enough money to hire you as full-time manager."

Paige nodded and explained with a catch in her voice that Veronica talked her into working as the thrift-store manager. "I wish I hadn't. It means I've lost my union seniority."

"We'll do our best to find you work, but it won't be full time."

I was glad to have broached two difficult topics, dealing with the landlord and letting Paige know she would be let go from the store.

Three days later, Giuseppe asked for another meeting with a lawyer at my office. I prepared myself by bringing a copy of the

CMHA doomsday audit that predicted our financial demise. We met in my office.

The lawyer with greying hair and a serious expression introduced himself. "I'm Derek Smith representing Giuseppe and the company he works for."

I introduced myself and shook his hand. Derek seemed less hard-edged than Giuseppe as he laid out the case against me. I agreed with much of his argument, then passed him the CMHA audit, flipping to the conclusion on the last page that we had less than five months to survive. He read it, nodded, and passed it to Giuseppe who brushed it aside.

I explained that the current thrift store location was pulling the whole organization toward a financial precipice — not his client's fault or mine. "You can sue us, but I will argue you guys breached the contract by not maintaining the store, causing us to lose customers. Another point that rankles is you threatened to seize the goods in the store and shut us down unless we paid a shared-upgrade fee of $784 in the building which was brand-new." I looked the lawyer square in the eye and stated that if we went broke in five months and couldn't pay the lease, it would make little difference to his client's bottom line than if we left immediately. "If you let us off the hook, we would count it as a donation and publish it in our newsletter."

"You guys won't stand a chance in court," Giuseppe said in a loud voice, unimpressed by my offer.

"We'll see," I said, looking him in the eye. "If I show the judge the kind of services we've been providing since 1958 for the people with mental health challenges, he may think us continuing in business is more valuable than adding a micro percent to your company's bottom line." I gave a nonchalant shrug. I wanted to give the appearance that going to court didn't scare me. The lawyer thanked me for my time, shook my hand, and suggested to Giuseppe that they leave.

A week later, I got an email from the lawyer saying if I sent them three months' rent, while not admitting any fault, they would allow us to cancel the lease. I figured Giuseppe had needed a token payment so as not to have lost face to an old guy running a failing nonprofit. I sent the lawyer a letter with a cheque for two months' rent, with the proviso that cashing it meant we were free of any further rent obligations. I never heard back. The outcome had been better than I could have hoped for: Instead of years paying killer rent, we had got off with only paying two more months.

More good news was that I discovered the landlord for our office wanted to upgrade the building and was happy for us to move out any time. I gave two months' notice. The new location might not be completely finished, but it would probably be good enough to move into. Setting a moving date kept me focused on getting it done. I pushed on, supervising the contractors and doing small jobs myself.

Later that day, I was up a ladder replacing a burned-out fluorescent tube in our future store when my cell phone rang. I slipped the tube in, gripped the ladder, and flipped the phone open. It was Suzy, the new manager of Bluebird House.

"Hi, Rodney, the sewer has backed up. We can't use the toilets. The shower downstairs became full of sewage and overflowed. The smell is god-awful."

Damn! As soon as one problem was solved, another popped up. "I'm on my way back to the office, Suzy. I will try to get you a Porta-Potty by the end of the day. Can you cope till then?"

"Yeah. I'm sending the residents down to the gas station when they need to use the washroom. We scooped a couple of buckets of sewage from the shower and dumped them into a hole we dug in the backyard. I've got all the windows open. The house smells a bit better now."

"Holy shit, Suzy!" We both laughed. I admired Suzy's can-do attitude. In her late 50s with grown kids, she always put the clients ahead of the job description, rare in the more radical union atmosphere I had returned to. The housing managers were only responsible for the well-being of the residents. Approving construction upgrades, repairs, and new furniture was my domain.

I got a portable toilet delivered to the backyard and flipped through the yellow pages trying to locate a reasonably priced plumber who could be available immediately. It would need a camera pushed down the four-inch sewer outflow pipe to find the blockage — a $300 fee before anything could progress. I found a plumber and gave the go-ahead. They found tree roots had invaded the sewage pipe in the backyard. It would take three days to fix.

Two days later, Suzy phoned again. "Rodney, we've got bedbugs."

This was really serious: No one wants to wake each morning with fresh red welts on their body, especially people with anxiety, psychosis, or depression. The remedy was a costly and disruptive fumigating procedure that didn't always work.

Later that day, I phoned to check on Bluebird House. "Suzy, just wondered how are you coping with the bedbugs and sewer problems?"

"Fine! We're sitting around the Porta-Potty in the backyard burning the couches and singing 'Kumbaya.'" I erupted into laughter. I loved Suzy's spirit — coping and making fun of the awful circumstances.

"Sounds great! Keeping warm, burning bugs, and having a sing-along. I might drop by later with my guitar."

I hired a pest control company to eliminate the bedbugs at Bluebird House. Bedbugs were a widespread problem. Some clients in apartments were hoarders — increasing the risk. Even smart hotels in downtown Vancouver were reporting bedbug problems. My other major concern was that the thrift store might become infested. I wanted to make a pre-emptive strike and found a safe chemical that, watered down ten to one, peeled the shells off bedbugs and killed them. I ordered five gallons of this state-of-the-art liquid from Ontario. At the next staff meeting, I distributed the spray bottles and printed instructions to staff and encouraged them to get clients involved in bedbug elimination and prevention. I also distributed special sticky pads to place under the bedposts, which the bugs would stick to on their way up or down the beds. Prevention was far cheaper than fumigating and gave the residents a sense of control over their environment. I shared my find with Jill Bloom and Dave Brown to use for their clients' housing. The new product was a hot find in a world where bedbugs seemed to be taking over.

Similar to the first store, I installed a change closet with a curtain for privacy. With new paint, working lights, and a new laminate floor, the store looked great — ready for action.

A few days later, I met a city official to inspect our refurbished store premises and certify it for retail use. He was in his thirties and gripped a clipboard. We shook hands, and I invited him into the store. He noted the two extinguishers and emergency exit light in case of a power failure had been recently added to comply with retail space regulations. After writing a few notes on his clipboard, he peered into the back room.

"Aha, what have we here?" he said, stroking his exquisitely clipped moustache.

"That area is not open to the public. It's not part of the inspection."

"Everything attached to the store is part of the inspection," he said in a sharp tone. "If something catches fire in another part of the building, it will affect the retail space."

After multiple jottings, shaking his head, and muttering, he left the storage space and started up the pine stairs to the reception room and offices.

"It's not finished up there yet," I yelled after him. "People are still working up there."

"Yeah, I can hear that. I'll take a look anyway."

I was mortified. I had put all my eggs into this basket. Without it, we would have no store and no office. The building was over 100 years old. He was bound to find all kinds of issues that were not up to code. Thirty minutes later, the inspector walked out with a lengthy list of issues that needed attention.

"You've got a lot of work to do before you can open a retail space here. For a start, you'll need to rewire the whole place."

The location had been operating as a store for years prior to us renting it. Why was it suddenly up to me to fix everything? After successfully wiggling out of the lease with Giuseppe, my bright hopes for a fast, cost-effective store relocation were getting dashed. I walked around in circles on the new laminate floor, my shoes squeaking loudly, muttering to myself. I cussed Veronica, the city building inspector, the landlord, and everyone else I could think of.

When my self-pity ran out, I came to a standstill, sucked in air, and blew it out in a long hiss. Hot blood started coursing through my veins. I wasn't going to allow my hopes to be trashed by a clipboard-wielding city nitpicker. Slamming the door shut, I walked briskly along the street to my office, grabbed the phone, and dialled city hall.

"Good afternoon, how can I help you today?" said the genteel voice of the receptionist.

"I need to speak to the mayor on an urgent matter concerning a local nonprofit mental health service," I said in a loud voice. "And I'd like the meeting as soon as possible." She booked me for a meeting in a week's time. I was surprised it was so easy to get an audience. Maybe it was my determined tone.

I scrawled the meeting date onto my calendar and made a list of arguments on my computer while my surge of righteous feelings ran high.

Hoping the meeting with the mayor would be successful, I continued with repairs at the new location.

Due to the economy still reeling from the subprime mortgage meltdown of 2008, work was scarce, and my ad for contractors with a "sharp pencil" had yielded some excellent bids. Repairs to the whole place had come to about $14,000, of which Graham's building contractor had contributed about $5,000 for free. However, Trevor warned me that due to the past year of thrift store losses, lack of volunteers, moving expenses, and refurbishing our new location, we were running out of money. Even if the store went into operation in two months' time, he calculated we would need to borrow almost $40,000 to survive the year.

He suggested we could get the money by re-mortgaging Bluebird House; it was worth about $350,000, and we owed $155,000. It irked me to take out money after all the hard work Comedy Courage had done to help pay down the mortgage. At the next board meeting, I got the directors' approval and made an appointment to see our friendly Vancity manager.

She gave me a welcoming smile. After telling my story and sharing the figures, I was relieved to see she was still smiling. She took a pen from the top pocket of her red blazer and scribbled a quick note. "Rodney, take this to Lillian in the far office and tell her you've got my okay to write you up a home equity loan." She stood up, flashed me another brilliant smile, and shook hands. I felt like hugging her.

What a relief — secure funding till the end of the year. As long as we could get the thrift store up and running, things should be fine. Another hurdle overcome. Now for the mayor.

I felt tense walking into the council chambers — not my usual space. There was a faint aroma of lemon oil, and the hall was so large our voices echoed. Mayor Wright was a friendly-looking guy in his 60s dressed in a navy blazer, light blue shirt, and dark tie. We shook hands, and he introduced me to three other people. Being nervous and focusing on my important message, I immediately forgot their names; one was a bylaw guy, another an engineer, and the third never made it into my memory.

I explained that CMHA had been helping people with mental illness in New Westminster since 1958, that the work we did was unseen but valuable to the community. As examples of people we helped, I told them about legally blind John living alone and Big John the thrift-store volunteer. I slipped in the fact that the Maple Ridge mayor had given us a house to use.

"However, due to recent unfortunate circumstances, we are on the brink of financial collapse and need the thrift store to pull us back into fiscal viability." The mayor scribbled something on his notepad. "Even though the premises had been a retail store for many years, your inspector came up with 27 issues that need repairing, the cost of which would be prohibitive."

The mayor and engineer paid attention, but the other two seemed to have zoned out when I started talking about mental illness.

"Thank you, Rodney, for letting us know of your dilemma. We'll be in touch. And thank you for the good work that you do," exclaimed the mayor with a friendly smile. The others nodded.

I thanked everyone and left. The mayor had listened attentively to everything I said and appeared moved by our plight. I hoped hearing how helpful the Maple Ridge mayor had been might encourage this mayor to be equally supportive. A week later, I received a revised scope of work in the mail: We needed to replace the old breaker box, install 5/8th-inch drywall on the back room's ceiling as a fire barrier, and cover any bare wiring. For the upstairs, we needed to install ventilation panels in the soffits under the roof. I was relieved and happy that the to-do list had shrunk to four items. The need to install vents in the roof soffits of a hundred-year-old house baffled me, but it was a small price to pay for such a reduced sentence.

Within two weeks of getting the new specs, I had enlisted a friendly electrician to complete the wiring, Rahim's drywaller installed the thicker ceiling, and the rest of the list had been completed without exceeding our budget.

A different inspector came the day after we finished the work and approved the repairs. With a big smile on my face, I went down to collect the business licence, framed it, hung it on the wall of the store, and breathed a huge sigh of relief.

The office space was ready, and the next job was to pack up and move. As the new location was only a hundred yards up the street from our current office, I talked some of the staff into helping. We wheeled a lot of office items along to the new building on a dolly. I loaded heavier items onto my utility trailer. After a couple of days carrying on our normal work, interspersed with sporadic bouts of moving, we were almost done.

An old fridge in the new staff room needed manoeuvring down the back stairs to the parking lot so it could be taken to the dump. My injured back was sore from lifting furniture. As I was wondering how to manage, Kevin walked in. "Hey, Kev, could you give me a hand getting this fridge down the stairs to the parking lot?"

"That's not in your job description, Kevin. You don't have to do that," said Stephanie, the union rep, as she was sorting through a filing cabinet.

I pursed my lips and glared at her. I was seething but just clenched my teeth and shut up. Angry words could be reported as "bullying."

Kevin didn't shut up. "When we signed on to the union six years ago, they said it wouldn't mess with the day-to-day operation of this place, but that's exactly what you are doing," he said in a loud voice. "We are just two guys moving a fridge. Get over it!"

The union rep stood up without looking at either of us, lifted her chin, and marched out of the room. She had probably been upset by my asking the staff to help move to our new office and was trying to claw back some "job description" power. I realized her point. If we'd had the money, I would have been happy to hire movers. I shrugged and gave Kevin a wry grin, and we manoeuvred the fridge onto the porch and down the back stairs.

Now that we were all moved in, staff could concentrate on their work with clients and I could focus on my three main concerns: looking after our clients, the staff, and our finances.

# Gaining Traction

To get the thrift store up and running, Sandy phoned all the volunteers who had quit and asked them to consider helping at the store again. Most agreed to return, and we invited them to a welcome-back lunch. We sat around on donated chairs eating Tim Hortons wraps while admiring the new space and discussing old times.

"This is gonna be great. The best location ever," Dave said.

I thought back to when he first volunteered in 2005 and committed to coming in "maybe once a month." Sadly, Sharon, our erstwhile scheduler, was not there. She was not well enough to attend but still wanted to help by arranging volunteer shifts and playing a role in the store. We planned to be open six days a week from ten to four, which meant twenty-four volunteers a week — a lot to schedule. We were tight on volunteers; sometimes if they were sick, people volunteered to work double shifts until we found more volunteers.

Three trips with my trailer transferred all the goods and racks into the store. As this space was bigger, we needed more clothing racks. Sharp-eyed Sandy noticed a women's-wear store advertising a going-out-of-business sale in the Royal City Centre Mall. As no one answered their phone, we walked up to take a look. Yes, they had four large chrome clothing racks for sale, only ten dollars each. A great bargain.

"Sandy, how are we going to get them back?"

"Well, they're on wheels. Why don't we just grab them and head for the store."

First, it was embarrassing, then funny. Laughing, we grabbed two each, pushing one ahead, dragging one behind, and set out toward the exit. They were a challenge to get through the revolving doors, but after that, it was just a three-block trundle to home turf. We passed the Greek restaurant where three of our staff sat outside eating lunch.

"Rodney, how come you're pushing clothing racks down the street?" Lisa asked, always a quick wit. "Is this some new kind of fundraiser?"

I laughed at her comment. "No, it's a fund saver," I replied and carried on behind Sandy with our 16 wheels clattering on the paving stones as we trundled along. Lisa's comment gave me an idea: A fundraising event that went past the thrift store would really kick-start the new location.

Sandy and the volunteers set everything up, and we slid into business with a minimal crew. The toughest hurdle was finding competent people to cash out at the end of the day and making sure the cash in the till matched the sales receipts. Sandy took on the job until she had trained six people. Ads on Craigslist, word of mouth, and a sign in the store window produced more volunteers. We had roughly a 50/50 mix between clients and people from the surrounding community. We got more volunteers from our two New Westminster houses in the city, now that the store was within walking distance again. The first month in business we netted $2,340 — pretty good for a brand-new location and a lot better than the $3,000 a month loss at the last location.

The challenge of getting out of the lease, bargaining for low rent, firing Paige, interviewing contractors, and battling city hall had paid off! Surely, the worst was behind us.

The new housing manager, Jennifer, arrived for her first day of work. I welcomed her aboard and mentioned that it would be much appreciated if she found ways to streamline operations so she would have some time to use her fundraising skills. She wore stylish bell-bottoms and a red high-collared blouse. I hoped her strong resume, polished look, and can-do attitude would translate into improvements in how we delivered our housing service. She learned about her new position from a disgruntled Robbie; it must have been demeaning to teach Jennifer the job she had wanted so much. Things were a little tense with them both in the office. I felt uneasy about the situation — like something was brewing.

About two months later, Robbie applied for a job in another nonprofit and asked me for a reference. I recommended her highly, stressing the excellent work she'd done, writing, funding, and running the smoking cessation program as well as her housing work. I was happy that she got the position and happy for myself that there would be one less person to challenge new initiatives. I didn't feel resentful; that's just who she was — questioning every management decision, trying to ensure we were heading in what she thought was the right direction. The value of her challenges was that I spent longer thinking through new initiatives before presenting them to staff.

Jennifer seemed busy, often staying late, but after three weeks, I didn't see much streamlining and asked why there appeared to be no change.

"The paperwork is in utter disarray. I'm striving to catch up before BC Housing and Fraser Health find out how bad it is. There are reports tied to our funding that are six months behind."

"Really? I wasn't aware of that. Do you need help?"

"No thanks. You don't really understand the housing manager's job."

That was true. Donald just did his job, and I never bothered to ask him all the details of what his work involved. I felt a little sheepish at having this pointed out to me.

When Jennifer finally brought the paperwork up to date, changes began to appear in the workings of our office: She trained the staff to use Google Docs, an information-sharing technology that made inter-office communication more efficient. When someone couldn't make a shift at one of the transition houses, she made that staff person responsible for finding a replacement, which saved her time. The union challenged this and said scheduling staff was a management function, but somehow it slipped into practice and became accepted procedure. We had a list of 10 casual staff who had to be phoned in order of seniority to fill in a shift.

As the housing manager was also responsible for disciplining staff, the job shouldn't have been union in the first place. I tried to de-unionize her position, a three-month procedure which failed. Stephanie complained that fundraising wasn't in the housing manager's job description. I got around this by upgrading the housing manager's job to include fundraising. Having to parry and thrust with the union was frustrating. The union wasn't interested in making the connection between fiscal health and the ability to pay wages. Their sole focus was the well-being of union members and maintaining union protocols, which I understood. However, my broader goals sometimes put us at odds.

Jennifer wrote grants for summer students. Fresh faces appeared in the office, bringing new skills: we were soon on Facebook, Twitter, Pinterest, and YouTube. While not completely convinced this made a difference, not having a presence on these sites would indicate that we were behind the times. Our main website was revamped. I was enthused by the new energy and faces joining our daily work life. However, change, even for the better, was not universally welcomed. In staff meetings, frowns and whispered comments behind hands were exchanged as I announced exciting new milestone events. I thought the lack of enthusiasm would pass as the benefits began to show — a miscalculation.

New people in the office overloaded our limited parking space. Stephanie complained that paid staff should have parking priority, but I felt that as volunteers were donating their time and staff only dropped by to fill out reports, it would be first come, first served.

The thrift store gained ground every month, and a stream of new volunteers appeared: A herbal doctor from China sorted donations all day Friday, an international lawyer from Luxemburg handled cashing out on Saturdays and Sundays, and an accountant from Romania ran the till on Tuesday mornings.

I still maintained control over who became a volunteer, hoping to weed out any unsuitable candidates. After each successful interview, I handed them a written list of expectations for the store and introduced them to Sandy. I was surprised to learn from her that Mike, a new volunteer, was working out really well.

"I haven't interviewed anyone called Mike."

"The young guy with a beard that comes in every Friday at ten and sorts all the books."

"Sorts all the books?"

"Come and look."

The bookshelves were 15 feet long and 6 feet high. Incredibly, all the titles were in alphabetical order.

"He does all this by himself. Sorts all the titles, adds new donations, throws damaged books in the bin. Doesn't speak to a soul."

The following Friday at 10:15 a.m., I walked down to the store. Sandy nodded toward the book section. A young guy in sandals, jeans, and a t-shirt was deftly arranging the books with librarian-like skill.

I walked closer and watched from behind. "Looks like you've got your work cut out here."

He paused, frowned, and glanced my way. "Yeah. Would do better if I had some signs for different genres."

"Genres?"

"Historical fiction, memoir, biography, romance, thriller — that kind of thing."

"Have you been working here long?"

"About a month. Dave Brown from Lookout said the store might need help. Saw a sign in the window, 'volunteers wanted.' Saw why. The books were a complete mess. I come in once a week."

"That's really helpful. I'll print up some signs for you."

"You work here?"

"Yeah, upstairs. I have a list of store protocols for volunteers. Usually I interview people before they work here."

"I just come to sort books. Books have powerful messages."

"Yeah, I agree. You're doing a great job. Nice chatting with you."

I walked past Sandy. She was giggling. "How did the interview go?"

I laughed. "Different. He told me what he needed, instead of me telling him."

"Yeah, he doesn't speak, just sorts books and leaves."

"Maybe he has anxiety challenges. What if you offered him one book a week for his services?"

Sandy nodded. "Good idea. You going to interview him?"

I shook my head. "Maybe not. He doesn't seem to like talking much, and he's been working here for a while with no problem."

Sandy nodded in agreement.

I often went online looking at other thrift stores for new ideas and spotted one in Arizona called Twice Nice. Surely our store deserved a better name — something more distinctive than the "CMHA Thrift Store." Twice Nice kept rolling off my tongue. I had to test it on someone and walked into Jennifer's office next door. "What do you think of Twice Nice as a name for the thrift store?"

She looked up slowly from her computer. "Thrift stores aren't really my thing, so I'm not the best person to ask."

She was right; as the people most involved, the volunteer staff should be part of the decision. I always emphasized it was their store and posted a notice in the sorting room:

Thrift Store Naming Competition — $10 Prize for the winner

Write your best name below. Votes counted and announced June 4th

I was pleased to see the following list form under my choice, hoping that being first past the post would help.

Twice Nice

Neverland

The Treasure Chest

The Thrifty Shopper

Best Drest

An empty pineapple juice can was placed below the sign for the votes.

At 4 p.m., on the fourth of June 2010, eight of us stood watching as Sandy counted the 28 ballots.

She took a deep breath. "Our store has a new name suggested by

David." She paused. "From this day forth, it will be known as the Treasure Chest." We all clapped — me less enthusiastically, disappointed my favourite name wasn't chosen. But I was happy handing the money to David, our longest-serving volunteer.

A few days later, I continued mulling things over. Maybe Treasure Chest *was* more apt: It really had become a treasure chest of surprising gifts — a vibrant feel-good connection with shoppers and donors in the community, a sense of purpose for volunteers, a feeling of renewal as fresh volunteers brought new ideas and skills, a recycling alternative, and the all-important source of revenue that kept us afloat.

After six months in the new location, we were averaging $4,300 a month profit, the most ever and still increasing. More volume meant more pressure on Sandy. I gave what help I could by finding and vetting new volunteers, picking up donations from two consignment stores, and meeting weekly with her. She seemed a little worn down. I was becoming concerned about her and suggested she take a break. She smiled and readily agreed. Jennifer found a competent paid student from UBC to run the store for a month.

Because the store was so busy, we upped the staff to three people per shift: one in the back rooms sorting donations, one tidying the store and helping customers, and one at the till. Jennifer found another student to handle scheduling. Sharon had become too sick with multiple health problems to continue. Sandy went to visit her once a week and often helped tidy up her tiny suite.

Another improvement was that the store now accepted VISA and Mastercard. I had never learned how to process credit cards. Occasionally, I filled in for the cashier if they were a little late for opening time; most antipsychotic meds have the side effect of making people sedated and drowsy, which can make for slow starts in the morning. Customers marched through the door promptly at 10 a.m., and I would stand at the till hoping they wouldn't buy anything, in case they wanted to use the credit card. Ridiculous, but I never learned.

The Treasure Chest ran so well I mused about opening a second store in Maple Ridge. Maybe Heather could have her homeless clients working there alongside volunteers from our two houses and the general public. I retained feel-good memories of the help we received from the Maple Ridge community and mayor in starting two houses and the outreach program. The idea tantalized me, like an unpursued romance. In reality, at 30 kilometres away, it was too far away to look after properly and never reached the point where my fingers drummed out a list on the keyboard. List-making was the signal that my enthusiasm was boiling over into action.

As a way of measuring volunteers' satisfaction with working in the store, I started asking them to fill out exit surveys. People left for a variety of reasons: finding paid work, end of summer vacation, moving out of the area, etc. I noticed one promising teenage girl quitting after only three weeks. I always felt a pang of remorse when a volunteer left the store. I reviewed her reason for quitting, "Didn't work out as planned," and asked her what hadn't worked out.

She looked flustered and asked me to come into the sorting room for privacy. "My mother has schizophrenia. I thought if I volunteered here, she would come and work with me. Something we could do together in a friendly environment, but she wouldn't come — too scared to be in the limelight." She bit her lip and wiped back a tear.

I was impressed by her caring spirit. At an age when many kids were pulling away from their parents, Mary was looking for ways to include her mother. Her explanation showed me that the Treasure Chest had limited appeal. Maybe a citywide family-inclusive activity might provide an alternate option — something more elevating than sorting and selling used goods — a supportive activity for the whole family. Mary's disappointed face stayed with me for the rest of the day.

## Miles for Mental Health    Team Discord

At the next team meeting, I shared Mary's story and asked staff for ideas about activities we could sponsor that would have a broader appeal to families. Silence prevailed; perhaps they didn't want to embark upon yet another of my extracurricular projects.

Not a fan of silence, Lisa quipped, "How about holding an egg-and-spoon race around city hall?"

"Thanks, Lisa. Maybe you and your son could do a few laps, show us how it's done?"

A few titters echoed around the table.

"Nah, can't do that, Rodney, I'm limping. Stubbed my toe playing soccer with him last night."

"Maybe an annual run could work," Carmela suggested.

"I don't think a once-a-year activity was what Mary had in mind," I said.

"I can see you've never been in a run, Rodney," Lisa said. "You have to train for it."

"Good point," I conceded. Running was not my thing.

I liked the idea of training together, definitely a beneficial shared activity, but running was less suitable for people with schizophrenia, who formed the majority of our clients. Psychosis is correlated with excess dopamine activity in the brain. Antipsychotic medication reduces dopamine, which is also used for muscle activity; this results in lessened limb control, making it difficult to run. In the movie, *A Beautiful Mind*, John Nash's shuffling gait was typical of someone on antipsychotic meds.

"Maybe we should have a walk and run combined for people who aren't runners," I suggested.

"Yes, we could encourage our clients to participate," Kevin said. "Exercise is healthy. Instead of taking clients for coffee, I could take them for training walks — better for me too."

A few "Yeahs" echoed around the room, suggesting the idea was gaining traction.

"We'd need a catchy name," Jennifer said. "Something that rolls off the tongue and pulls people in."

"Rodney's Money Run," Stephanie suggested, bugging me about my perennial fundraising focus.

Other suggestions flew across the table: "Limping with Lisa." "Kevin's Kilometres." "Kilometres for Health."

"Miles for Mental Health," Carmela said in her usual calm voice.

"That's a great name," Jennifer said. "Catchy and descriptive."

"But we'd have to make it the Miles for Mental Health Run/Walk to attract both kinds of participants," I said.

"Putting on a run event is a huge amount of work," Jennifer said, nodding and looking around the table.

"So, you've put one on before?" Stephanie asked, looking around the table at her colleagues.

"Yes, I have, Stephanie."

"So, you gonna tell us about it?"

Jennifer took a slow sip of coffee before answering. "I was in charge of organizing the first Terry Fox Run in Beijing."

No one spoke.

In 1980, having lost one leg to cancer, Terry Fox started his Marathon of Hope run across Canada to raise funding for cancer research. At age 22, he succumbed to cancer, but his courage had inspired worldwide fundraising runs for cancer research.

We all stared at Jennifer. I didn't recall her mentioning that in the job interview. Her statement took me a moment to digest. She had organized the Terry Fox Run in Beijing, a city of twenty million people.

"Sounds good," I said. "We have a great name and an experienced run organizer. Where should we go from here?"

More silence.

While it was great to have such qualified help for our new event, I sensed the relationship between sharp-dressing, multilingual, uber-organized Jennifer and our competent female housing staff had just widened from a gap to a chasm.

"We need lots of people for this project," Jennifer said, "and a run support committee that meets regularly." She noted there was still time for her to write summer-employment grants for UBC students to help get us started.

We followed Jennifer's suggestion, formed a committee, and started holding biweekly walk/run meetings. Kevin, myself, Jennifer, and board member Graham volunteered to work on the Miles for Mental Health project. Carmela offered to chair our embryonic committee meetings of the "Run" as it became known. Yet another meeting for me to attend, but at least for reasons I believed in: encouraging the social inclusion of people with mental illness, bringing mental health into the public eye, and raising money. We decided on a catchy slogan: "Help fight the stigma of mental illness and join the Miles for Mental Health Walk/Run."

Fighting stigma and participating in the Run were only connected because we said they were. We were making our own truth and inviting the community to join in and make it their truth. If we could get people walking and running to eliminate stigma, it would encourage them to think and talk about the effects of stigma. After diagnosis, stigma was the second huge slap in the face for people with mental illness. If the world around us believes we are deficient, it easily becomes part of our self-view.

I had stumbled through the first days of running the store, gradually learning to correct any mistakes over time, but as Jennifer explained, the Run was a time-sensitive special event that had to tick along like a Swiss clock: "In three hours, participants need to arrive, park, resister, pay, receive bibs, have their shoes fitted with shoe timers, listen to a couple of welcome speeches, line up for the start, navigate around the course, attend the prize ceremony, buy a burger, hang out with their family, and maybe dance to the free band."

"We're having a band?" I asked.

"The more pizazz we create, the more people will come," she explained. "I've got people looking for a band. That's the easy part, we need to find financial sponsors, dignitaries, donors, barbecues for burgers, and about 40 volunteers."

"Why do we need burgers?"

"Another way of increasing revenue. You get a couple of hundred people turn out for the event. You sell a hundred burgers for five bucks a burger."

"It seems like a lot of setup for a three-hour event. When are you thinking we'll have it?"

She looked me in the eye and tilted her head. "In May."

I was shocked. May was eight months away. "That's 16 meetings."

"Yes, lots to do. I'm going to look for funding for a couple of part-time people to help us."

Where Jennifer got the funding from, I had no clue. She appeared to be a fund-finding machine.

"Great, good idea. Let me know if you need any help." She didn't reply. We both understood I was out of my depth. The Run was like a huge hot-air balloon lifting off in public view with the CMHA name emblazoned on the fabric. If things went right, our organization would look successful. If they went wrong, the executive director would get the blame.

With no experience working in mental health, Jennifer's acceptance by the staff as housing manager had been lukewarm. Introducing changes to streamline housing operations gave her more time to fundraise but caused resentment. Most of our client-focused housing staff didn't appreciate her fundraising activities. Being the brains behind the Run widened the rift. At staff meetings, she delivered housing manager reports followed by her fundraising news and Run updates. I had hoped her relationship with staff would improve when they saw how much she was helping our branch, but it had the opposite effect. Jennifer became persona non grata: She was not included in the casual banter around the office, and female staff stopped talking when she entered the room. At the Christmas fundraiser attended by all the staff, the situation became blatant. She sat at a table eating pizza by herself. This upset me, and I sat with her for a while. The evening was supposed to be about the team pulling together to raise money, not an opportunity to demonstrate division. The breach in team spirit concerned me, but I was unsure how to help. You can't order people to speak to someone. After the fundraiser cold shoulder, Jennifer always sat next to me at staff meetings. I hoped the split would heal over with time. It didn't.

## Everyday Challenges

While our Run preparations hummed along in the background, the day-to-day work of supporting our clients to live lives of social inclusion remained our main focus. Having 97 people with mental illness under our care, and the outreach program helping about 100 people a year, the operation was like a large multi-purpose garden in need of nourishing, watering, weeding, and occasional pruning.

As there were no overnight staff, I initiated a practice of adding my cell number below the emergency instructions posted in each of our four transition houses.

Phone Rodney if unsure how to handle a problem when no staff member is present.

The residents all knew to follow emergency procedures posted in prominent locations on each floor of the house, with instructions to phone 911 in case of fire, medical, or other emergency. When a member of the public goes missing, police usually wait 24 hours before taking action. However, for people with mental health challenges, I sometimes called the local RCMP and got them involved earlier. My phone number was supposed to be used by residents for emergencies when staff were not available after 5 p.m.

Shortly after my number was posted, I got a call from Mandy, the weekend staff person at Sheppard House.

"Rodney, there's a problem at the house. Barry is not home for dinner yet. He's half an hour late."

I was out of breath, hiking by Cypress Falls Park in West Vancouver, and the reception was poor. "I'm sorry, who is this?"

"It's Mandy from Sheppard House."

"Being a little late for dinner isn't an emergency, Mandy," I said, stopping to gather my breath.

"I'm worried. He's not usually late."

"You're only supposed to phone me in an emergency. Please ask one of the other residents to phone me if he's not back by 8.30. Okay?" Mandy was on duty till 5 p.m.

"Okay, sorry."

Mandy suffered from anxiety, which made life challenging for her and those in close proximity. During the H1N1 flu virus outbreak, she showed up for work in white coveralls with a hood and a heavy black charcoal-filter mask, which unnerved the residents: One thought she was a thief, two got scared and left, another who suffered from delusions went to Starbucks, phoned 911, and reported that his house was being invaded by aliens. Part of the problem was that the weekend staff in Maple Ridge didn't attend our Monday morning team meetings in New Westminster and were somewhat disconnected from our mainstream operations. As the union minimum block of work was four hours, plus the mileage, it was too expensive to bring the weekend employees from Maple Ridge to our New Westminster office for a one-hour team meeting.

After Mandy had been working weekends at Sheppard House for about three months, she started leaving Post-it notes everywhere outlining procedures for the clients to follow during the week. After many complaints from the residents and weekday staff person, I went to Sheppard House on Sunday morning to see for myself.

"Hi, Rodney. Didn't know you were coming by. Want some coffee?"

"No thanks. I just stopped by to talk about all these notes you're writing." I explained once again that the reason we ran the houses was to try and replicate normal everyday living.

"That's why I write the notes, to remind residents of everything they need to do."

"Mandy, the notes have to stop. Having every room in the house covered with Post-it notes doesn't represent normal living." I explained the staff person who worked there five days a week was upset about the notes, as were the residents. I knew she meant well, but her anxiety was putting her behaviour over the top. She looked crestfallen at the news. Her eyes filled with tears, her lips quivered, and her yellow pigtails bobbed on her shoulders as she shook her head.

"Hey, I know you were trying to help, Mandy, but it's not working. Please help me out by not writing any more notes." Asking for help usually had better results than top-down instructions.

She nodded. "Okay." She went to hug me, but I shook her hand instead — wary of her tendency to misinterpret situations.

The following week, there were yet more problems at Sheppard House. Occurrences like these made me realize that starting another thrift store in Maple Ridge wasn't a smart idea. Each time I went there to problem solve, it was a 60-kilometre round trip. The next issue was a complaint from Mandy that Jeff, one of the residents, had threatened her with physical violence.

I knew Jeff quite well. Sometimes, when I was at the house, we'd sit outside and chat. He was in his 50s, had owned a house painting business, and was the breadwinner for his family before being diagnosed with schizophrenia. Jeff observed all the house rules, cooked a meal once a week as requested, attended Monday morning house meetings, and generally was a helpful guy but liked his privacy. The only house rule he contravened was to hang out of his bedroom window and smoke. You could tell by the mound of butts beneath the window. His logic when confronted was that he wasn't smoking *in* the house.

Mandy walked her dog by Sheppard House most weekdays. One day, she saw Jeff smoking from his bedroom window and yelled at him to stop. They got into a shouting match, and he threatened to "stuff her into a garbage can" if she didn't shut up. She reported the threat to me Tuesday evening on my cell phone.

"I don't feel safe working there next weekend, Rodney."

This presented a dilemma on many fronts — one of Mandy's specialities: First, she was only supposed to phone me at home for emergencies. Second, she wasn't supposed to be monitoring Jeff's activities when she wasn't working there. Third, it was my duty to provide a safe environment for my employees. The threat of being "stuffed into a garbage can" could certainly be construed as unsafe.

I reported this incident to Cuthbert Kaufman, my new Fraser Health contact in Maple Ridge to let him know what had occurred. Cuthbert was in his late 40s, had a pointed Van Dyke beard dyed jet black, and held very firm ideas about how those working under him should behave. Unfortunately, those ideas were often shared after infractions had occurred rather than before. I found working with Cuthbert to be a constant challenge after my relaxed relationship with Barney.

Behind his back, our workers in the Maple Ridge houses called him KFC, Kontrol Freak Cuthbert. Despite my best efforts, which mostly consisted of trying to figure out how I and my staff could avoid running afoul of his many "pop-up" demands, we often failed. As he represented the funder, I tried to avoid mishaps. Despite this, he always seemed to be upset with our two staff members and/or me. The week before the incident with Jeff, I received an angry phone call from him.

"Rodney, I wasn't informed that a new staff person would be at Riverside House. I need to be informed of every aspect of what goes on in those houses you are supposed to be running."

"Sorry. I did send you an email saying Marylou would be off for a day to attend a funeral."

"I'm too busy to read emails. Make sure I'm informed in person next time."

Before phoning Cuthbert, I engaged in calming self-talk and repeated, "Don't get triggered. Don't engage," for about a minute, then turned on my placid swimming fish screensaver, and took a deep breath. "Cuthbert, how are things in Maple Ridge?"

"I don't have time to chit-chat. I'm just heading out the door."

"I need to talk about Jeff. He threatened to stuff Mandy into a garbage can. I'm thinking we should encourage him to apologize and make it a condition of his staying there. Thought I'd check in with you as he is on your caseload."

"I don't think so, Rodney. I don't see the point. He should be allowed to express himself. He obviously didn't mean that. It would just make him feel inferior. Your worker is the problem, not Jeff."

I heard the phone bang down. For some reason, Cuthbert liked Jeff. I wasn't sure why he was okay with Jeff issuing threats, but it caused a problem for me. Mandy had filed three union grievances when I was away but dropped them all when I returned. Something I was grateful for. Grievances took lengthy meetings with the union to resolve — a drain on my time. I didn't want Mandy filing a grievance about my failing to provide a safe work environment. This could mean she would be off with pay until the matter was resolved. If Jeff apologized in a written note to Mandy, saying he was sorry and didn't mean her any harm, I figured it would be proof that the situation had been resolved. I needed to act before the weekend so that Mandy wouldn't have an excuse not to show up for work, but had to fly under the radar so that Cuthbert wouldn't get wind of Jeff apologising. On Wednesday, I made the call to Sheppard House I hoped would provide a solution.

"Jeff, I'm heading out to Maple Ridge later today. Thought I might drop by. You gonna be in around three?" Jeff confirmed he'd be home. I bought a pack of Rothmans on the way to Maple Ridge, parked by the garage, and knocked on the door to Jeff's basement suite.

We shook hands. "Wanna sit outside and have a smoke?"

He smiled. "Sure, what's on your mind?" He pulled on a black hoodie and followed me outside.

"Maybe you could help me solve a problem?"

He nodded with a wisp of a smile on his face. I explained that it was my duty to provide a safe environment for the workers and the threat of one of them being "stuffed into a garbage can" wasn't meeting that requirement.

He tossed his head back and laughed. "I guess not, Rodney, but that bitch drives me crazy." The words flew out of him in a torrent. "There's no way she should be walking by the house telling me what to do. She's outa control. She used to leave notes in my bedroom telling me how to make the bed and set the fuckin' alarm clock. She bought me a used dressing gown I never asked for, then bitched because I never wore it." He laughed out loud. "The damn thing was mauve, for Christ's sake." He puffed deeper on the cigarette and shook his head, blowing the smoke from side to side.

"You're right, Jeff. She sometimes gets too involved with clients. Any ideas how we can figure out how to solve the problem between you and her?"

"Yeah, I've been thinking about that. We could put up an eight-foot-long fence panel six feet high in front of my bedroom window so she couldn't see me when she's walking by."

"Great idea, Jeff. I could just get one of those panels delivered here."

Jeff looked surprised, then smiled and reached for another

Rothmans.

"Keep the pack, Jeff." He nodded and slipped them into his pocket. "Did you really mean you were going to stuff her into a garbage can?"

"Hell no, just said the first thing that came into my head because there were garbage cans out front of the house. I was pissed off with that interfering cow yelling at me."

"It's caused me a big problem with worker safety. It would really help me out a lot if you could write a note apologising and saying you didn't mean what you said. Would that work for you?"

"Sure." He nodded, went to his desk, and started writing.

"This do the trick?" He handed me the note.

Sorry, Mandy. I was just in a bad mood. Didn't mean what I said. You are safe here. Jeff.

"Wow, great, Jeff. Just what I needed." I shook his hand. Problem solved. I took a picture with my camera for the record and put the note in an envelope to drop through Mandy's door.

"Just one question," Jeff asked. "Where can we smoke when it's raining? I'm not quitting smoking. It's one of the few pleasures I have, that and walking along the river dike."

"Good point, Jeff. I'll check into funding for building a gazebo on the back lawn. Riverside House has the same problem."

The provincial government had recently enacted tough anti-smoking bylaws prohibiting smoking within six metres of any exterior doorway or window, making it difficult for our house residents to find a place to smoke legally.

I left Sheppard House, popped the apology note through Mandy's front door, and drove home pleased with the result but questioning my ethics. Had I bribed Jeff with a pack of smokes to write an apology to Mandy?

Four months after applying for gazebo funding for Riverside and Sheppard Houses, I received the money, ordered the gazebos, and found an out-of-work carpenter to assemble them for $150 each. I informed Cuthbert ahead of time. I mentioned it was Jeff's idea, and he approved.

Every Maple Ridge conflict made me nostalgic for working with Barney's easy style. He was a straight shooter who spoke his mind. I recalled a remark he made when I asked him why Fraser Health had changed their policy on funding more satellite houses.

"Well, Rodney, here's how it works at Fraser Health. We're all ants, see, and we follow our leader. Every six or seven years, we get a new leader, then we turn around 180 degrees and march back in the opposite direction. People around here think change is leadership."

I laughed out loud at the image of marching ants. Maybe his forthright manner was why he no longer worked for Fraser Health.

Barney still had contacts high up inside Fraser Health, and one day he phoned to give me an urgent warning. "I heard that Cuthbert is upset with cleanliness issues in Sheppard House. It's possible he could use that as an excuse to close it down."

I thanked him and phoned Marylou, our house manager at Sheppard House, and warned her. This could mean Marylou would take on some of the cleaning even though she wasn't supposed to. The whole idea of transition houses was to help residents get in the habit of becoming self-sufficient — a challenge for people coming from an institution where the focus was on medication and safety, not encouraging self-care and living more independent lives. Like any new learning, skill acquisition moves forward in fits and starts. If one resident failed to clean their bedroom and Marylou did it for them, the wrong lesson was learned. I could also see it from Fraser Health's perspective, that they wanted the houses they funded kept clean.

I also sent an email to both Cuthbert and our local New Westminster branch of Fraser Health noting our wish to adhere to all aspects of our contracts and requesting them to inform us if they were unhappy with any aspect of our work. The email created an official record of our good intentions and put the emphasis on Fraser Health to be upfront with any dissatisfaction. Without their contracts, we'd be doomed.

Just as one dilemma in Maple Ridge died down, another one arose. We had always worked as partners with Fraser Health in selecting suitable clients for placement in our transition houses. In the past, Barney, myself, and our housing manager interviewed potential new residents for suitability before they were offered a placement in Riverside or Sheppard House. It seemed as though we had been demoted to being a silent partner when I got a call from Cuthbert. "Rodney, I'm sending you a young man for Sheppard House. His name is Roger. He's 20 and has problems with depression."

I asked why the normal meeting between our organization, Cuthbert, and the client was not being followed.

"I'm too busy for that. He should be fine. Besides, he's in Burnaby General Hospital right now so we can't meet at the house."

"What if I went to Burnaby General and interviewed him there?"

I heard an impatient exhale. "I suppose you could, if you have that kind of time."

I didn't want our participation to be brushed aside and set out immediately for Burnaby General, a half an hour's drive from our office.

While navigating traffic, my reactive mood gave way to logic: How would I find Roger? Would he be available to talk? Where could we talk in private? He didn't know me; what if he refused to talk? How could he decide if he liked Sheppard House without the usual tour of the house? My response had been too impulsive, but I didn't feel like turning back.

Roger was a tall, shy, soft-spoken youth who didn't make eye contact. We met at reception and walked to the cafeteria.

"I'm here to talk to you about you moving to Sheppard House when you leave the hospital."

He tilted his head and shrugged, a listless gesture suggesting he did whatever people in authority requested. I explained to him about the transition houses we ran, why we ran them, that he'd have his own bedroom, that he'd be expected to help with chores, and that there was a cat called Ginger.

"Do you think you'd like it there, Roger?"

He gave the briefest of smiles, shrugged, and whispered, "Maybe."

I asked why he was in hospital.

He heaved a deep sigh and gazed at the floor. "I tried to commit suicide three weeks ago." He looked up to get my reaction. His soft grey eyes reflected deep pools of sorrow.

I put my hand on his shoulder. "Sorry to hear that, Roger. Life can be tough sometimes."

He nodded. We sat in silence for a while. He wiped his eyes with his sleeve.

"My mother overdosed and died a month ago. They found her on a sidewalk on Hastings Street. I was hoping she'd clean up and we'd have a normal relationship. Then it hit me. That was never going to happen now." He started sobbing. I held him. Cafeteria customers glanced at us then looked away. "I don't like it here. They just give you medication and tell you how to think. It's...I dunno...cold."

"You've had a rough time, Roger. My father died when I was 18. It takes a while for things to get better. Medication can often help. You can also help yourself to feel better by choosing to do things you like. I call it personal medicine. Can you think of anything?"

He looked at me with sad eyes, as if he wanted to believe. I squeezed his arm. We sat for a while.

"I like fishing," he said.

"That's cool. The house is not too far from the river, maybe we can set something up for you."

"Yeah, that'd be good." His eyes showed a spark of interest.

"Anyway, if you decide to come to the house, I'll drop by and say hi. The lady running the house is Marylou, she's really nice. Hang in there, buddy. Things get better, it just takes a while," I said, nodding. Hope is sometimes all people have left. His father had been absent and his mother an addict. Through no fault of his own, he had got off to a very rough start in life.

I was worried about Roger's state of mind and listless demeanour. Previous suicide attempts are a major predictor of future attempts. He didn't seem to have much to live for. I had taught suicidology courses to counsellors and had presented on the topic to high school kids so was all too familiar with the signs. In an email to Cuthbert, I suggested that Roger needed weekly loss and grief counselling with a competent therapist and that I knew someone in Maple Ridge who could help. Cuthbert responded like a wounded tiger stating in his email that I was unqualified to interfere with suggestions for his clients' treatment and to keep my insubordinate opinions to myself.

Perhaps Cuthbert was right. I apologised by email. I had become too involved with Roger and overstepped a boundary. The recent trauma of my own son's death may have thrown my judgement off.

Squeezed in between the challenges of our everyday work, our next big event was gathering momentum. The Miles for Mental Health Run/Walk had been sparked into life by imaginative minds blowing on hot coals at a team meeting. Early Run meetings were like a heavy train pulling out of the station; forward motion was barely perceptible. But fed with the high-octane fuel of enthusiasm and hard work, six months later, the train was blasting down the tracks at full speed. The where and when of the event had been meticulously planned. I had hoped to have it pass right by the Treasure Chest but found having an event on public streets involved large policing costs so we decided on the free venue of Queens Park. While the event planning had to be flawless, marketing was the key to success. If no one knew about it, there would be zero participants no matter how well it was planned.

Jennifer's promotional efforts lit up the Run in flashing neon lights: She talked nearby Douglas College into being the prime event sponsor. Once big names were on board, more followed. The Foot Locker agreed to manage the running race and supply bibs, shoe timers, and start and finish banners. Two high-profile local politicians, Dawn Black and Fin Donnelly, promised to spread the word, speak at the event, and participate in the Run.

Jennifer enlisted volunteer Jessica, a fashionably dressed girl from Beijing, who drove a Mini Cooper and had just completed an MA in economics in Ottawa. Jennifer put her in charge of finding sponsors, getting and tracking donations, collecting registration fees, monitoring expenditures, and selling raffle tickets. We found Jessica a spare computer and a small table and wedged them into my office by the window. I worried it might be intimidating sitting in the same office as the boss, working in her second language in a city she didn't know making cold calls for donations.

My fears were groundless: She conjured up a Vancouver Canucks jersey to raffle, initiated an alliance with Vancouver Fashion Week, and got multiple donations from local businesses. We needed donated prizes for all the Run categories: first to fourth place in both run and walk, another for the oldest and youngest participant, and six prizes for best kids' superhero costumes. We thought having a kids' costume event would pull in families.

Jessica talked her friend Cici, winner of three beauty pageants, into presenting the prizes on race day — bound to haul in a few more runners. Board member Graham convinced Darlene, a former business associate, to join the board of directors. She worked her magic and somehow got us free ads in the newspapers and offered many useful marketing suggestions.

Jennifer found temporary funding to hire Adnam, fresh out of university. "He reminds me of me when I was his age," she said. "He's very ambitious." She put him in charge of finding 20 volunteers and training them as race marshals. On event day, he would oversee the erection of routing signs, welcome participants, shepherd them to the registration kiosk, outfit them with bibs and shoe timers, and guide them around the course. He was deferential, politically astute, a good public speaker, and quickly grew into the job. In his early twenties, well-groomed, and with a slight English accent, he earned my appreciation with his keen efforts to find and train all the volunteers.

A month before the Run was set to take place, Jennifer walked into my office and closed the door. "I know you're not going to be happy about this, Rodney, but I'm giving you three weeks' notice. I'm quitting."

"Jennifer, you can't leave now, before the big event. It's all your doing, your planning, your child!"

She pursed her lips and looked at me with watery eyes. "Everything's in place. You'll be fine."

"You agreed to stay for two years. It's only been a year."

"Look, I can't take it any more from your staff," she said with a catch in her throat. "Most of them don't speak to me. They minimize my ideas. I go home every day almost in tears. I walked into the staff room just now, said hi to a couple of them, and they turned away and ignored me." Her lips trembled, her eyes welled up, and tears ran down her cheeks. She turned away and sat down heavily.

I laid a hand on her shoulder. She put her hand on top of mine and sat looking out of the window. She stood up and blew her nose. "Sorry, that wasn't very professional."

"I know you've been having a tough time, Jennifer, but you're telling me I'm gonna lose my Run director, fundraiser, and housing manager." She didn't bite on my guilt trip.

"That young guy, Adnam, that I hired is smart, ambitious, well-liked by the staff, and doing a great job helping organise the event. Maybe you could offer him the housing manager position?" Jennifer was right, but he was young and had no mental health experience. She could see I was considering her idea. "The housing staff like him. That seems to be the main criteria around here," she said in an edgy tone. "I'll be in my office if you need me."

She had done a great job despite not being accepted by her colleagues. I felt incompetent for not knowing how to stop the tension in the office. Sometimes, during team meetings when Jennifer spoke, people would turn and chat to one another. "Okay, everybody, let's just have one voice speaking. You'll all get your turn," I said in my best schoolteacher tone. This had been my feeble response to the problem and made me question my leadership ability.

I'd encouraged Jennifer to use her creative abilities, but her successes had alienated the other team members. I truly believed that young, talented, multilingual, multicultural people like Jennifer were the answer to the world's future problems — finding innovative, collaborative solutions for a small planet. It was disheartening to have her leave.

# Run Day

Sunday, May 8th, 2011. At 7 a.m., I startled awake to the sound of rushing water. Stumbling out of bed and rubbing my eyes, I lurched toward the window. Pulling up the blind revealed buckets of rainwater cascading off the roof, overflowing the downpipe, and flooding across the driveway. The lead-coloured sky barely lit the day, and the deluge falling from the heavens further shrouded the earth. *Please not today, not on our event day!* We'd purposely chosen a date in May hoping for good weather — and now this? I wouldn't want to cross the street on a day like this, let alone run around an outdoor trail.

I pulled my clothes on.

"What are you doing? It's only seven o'clock," Anna said.

"I gotta get up. Going early today for our big event."

"Baker, it's raining cats and dogs. You should cancel. You're going to get soaked."

After downing toast and marmalade, I pulled 250 buns, 100 frozen hot dogs, and 150 frozen hamburger patties from the freezer and tossed them into my trunk. Jessica was bringing the fixings. I tried holding the umbrella while hitching my utility trailer to the car, but it didn't work. Pulling the barbecue from the backyard down 14 steps to the trailer strained my back, and I barely managed to lift the darned thing into the trailer. Completely soaked, I turned my heater on high and set out for Queens Park.

For runners, the course was 5K — twice around the park — and 2.5K for walkers. But on a day like this, a West Coast torrential rain day with water falling from the sky like the biblical 40-day flood, surely no one would show up.

Reaching the lower end of the park, I gingerly lowered the barbecue out of the trailer and started pulling it up the grassy hill toward the shelter. The small plastic wheels didn't work well in sodden grass. My fragile back didn't work well pulling the barbecue. The furious downpour continued. My feet slipped, and I fell backward into the mud, jarring my back and leaving a mud pancake on the seat of my white jeans. I tried stepping sideward so my feet got a better grip, tugging the barbecue with one hand and leaving my other hand free to cushion the impact if I fell again.

When my 15-minute uphill grind was over, I sat under the large shelter soaked, cold, in pain, panting for breath, and thinking about the propane container and food still in the car.

Only an hour to start time and no one in sight. I wondered if our event had been cancelled and no one had told me.

"Hey, Rodney, how ya doing?"

I pivoted slowly around to see Kevin's cheery face. "I'm soaked to the skin, cold, my back hurts, my pants are muddy, and it's raining so hard that if any runners show up, they're gonna slip in the mud and sue us."

"That good, eh?"

We both had a wry chuckle.

"Kev, could you go down to my car and get the propane cylinder and food in the trunk?"

"Sure, no problem."

People began to arrive in the park. I went to the washroom, took off my pants, scraped most of the mud off with the back of a comb, and untucked my shirt to cover the stain. Two more barbecues showed up along with Jessica and her friend Cici. We parked the three barbecues under one of the large park shelters. The burgers and dogs would be offered by donation; selling food required a special licence. We laid out the patties and dogs to thaw on a plastic sheet, although I was convinced we had far too many and no one would show up.

At 9:30, I walked to the registration table. "How's it going, Adnam?"

"Great! We had 120 preregister, another 30 just showed up, and they're still coming."

I tried to answer, but there was a catch in my throat. I turned away. Incredible that all these people would come out on a shit day like this to support Miles for Mental Health. I had imagined people taking one look at the weather and deciding not to come, but no, these were West Coasters. They did stuff in the rain, bless them. Maybe all these participants meant that people's attitudes were really changing to lessen stigma.

Three giggling kids ran by wearing Batman and Superwoman outfits; their mother hot on their heels yelled at them to come back and get their race bibs on.

"Rodney, it's almost ten. They're waiting for you at the podium," Adnam yelled.

Pushing by crowds of people and kids in costume, I hurried to the podium, pulled my shirt further down over my jeans, and grabbed the microphone.

"On behalf of Canadian Mental Health Association's Simon Fraser Branch, welcome to Miles for Mental Health, helping to fight the stigma of mental illness." I named and thanked the sponsors then handed the microphone over to our two politicians, Dawn Black and Fin Donnelly. I appreciated they kept their speeches short so the wet participants could start generating some body heat by propelling themselves around the course. Miraculously, the downpour had abated to a steady drizzle by the time the race started.

I made my way to the burger stand and fired up the three barbecues. Cici, Jessica, and I stood behind our burger stations, started cooking patties and dogs, and placed them on the rack above the flame in case of a sudden demand.

The heat from the barbecue was helping to warm and dry me. Between flipping burgers, I turned my back to dry both sides of my clothing. Chords of the iconic "Chariots of Fire" music were wafting across from the bandstand as the race got underway.

I felt someone pat my butt and whipped around to see Anna.

"Baker, how come these two girls are barbequing with you?" she said, eyeing my comely cooking companions.

"It's a way for us to greet people and thank them for coming. I expect two young female cooks will attract more customers than an old guy in muddy jeans."

A family of five approached. "How much are the burgers?" the father asked.

"If you're broke, they're free. If not, by donation. Thanks for coming here today and supporting Miles for Mental Health."

"You're welcome. We're having fun! Three burgers and two hot dogs, please," he said, throwing a $20 bill and some change into the can. Other people strolled toward the barbecues. The aroma of sizzling meat riding on the air was pulling them in our direction. Sharing food has a way of turning an event into a family outing. Each barbecue station had its own table with a donation can, condiments, and paper napkins. I didn't want any lineups restricting the flow of hungry people. The sudden volume of customers indicated that the running race must be over. I glanced at my fellow cooks. We were all cooking and stuffing hot dogs and patties into buns at full capacity.

As her son was competing, Anna had gone to the finish line and come back with a big smile on her face. "Peter got second place. He's pretty pumped."

"That's great! Maybe you should buy him a burger?"

*The Miles for Mental Health Run/Walk*

The drizzle had almost stopped. People danced beside the bandstand. Kids ran around shrieking in their superhero costumes, chasing one another over the wet grass. Families, participants, and volunteers tucked into burgers and hot dogs while drinking coffee donated by McDonald's. Beauty queen Cici handed over her barbeque duties to Anna and left to present trophies. The three coffee urns ran dry, and the barbecue customers tailed off. I put the eight leftover hamburgers in a bag and gave them to one of Heather's homeless clients who came to watch the event.

Dawn and Fin gave wrap-up speeches and thanked the crowd for coming, for their community spirit, and for helping to support people with mental illness. My downcast mood of the early morning had changed to jubilance: Thanks to everyone's hard work, the generosity of donors, and the Run participants, the day had been a success.

Adnam managed the volunteers superbly and reported 197 entrants in the event. Participants paid an entry fee and attracted donations for each kilometre they completed. Dawn Black won the award for raising the most money individually — an incredible $3,000. My only regret was that Jennifer hadn't been there to see the fruition of her well-crafted plans.

The awards were over, the volunteer band played their final number, and the sky looked brighter as people filtered out of the park.

A couple of volunteers packed my barbecue and gas cylinders into the trailer. After flipping burgers for two hours with an aching back, it was heaven to sit in my car. Even better when I reached home, limped upstairs, and slipped into a hot bath.

"Baker, you did well," Anna announced as she walked upstairs and handed me a gin and tonic. "Who would have thought so many people would show up in the rain to run around the park for mental illness? You've earned a drink."

Topping up the bath with more hot water, I lay luxuriating in the heat, sipping my drink, and reflecting on the day's events: If each of the 200 participants had friends or family members supporting them, there were probably more than 400 people in the park. Given the weather, I was thrilled that so many people had shown up under the banner of fighting stigma.

I mulled over other changes that were happening in the country: Bell Canada had just kicked off a "Let's Talk" campaign for the purpose of informing Canadians about the reality of living with mental health challenges. This effort was spearheaded by Clara Hughes, six-time Olympic medal winner, who openly discussed her mental health problems. On her radio show, CBC's Shelagh Rogers often spoke about her challenges with depression. Politician, lawyer, and radio host, Rafe Mair bravely shared his own diagnosis and dissatisfaction with the treatment of people who had mental illness: "If the physically ill in our province were dealt with as mentally ill people are, the legislature and its lawn would be crammed with irate protesters."

I find it heartwarming when celebrities go public with their own challenges of living with mental illness. Their messages, combined with efforts from mental health service organizations, generate waves of increased understanding and acceptance that begin to wash over the general public. How others see us affects the opinions we have of ourselves: If you don't believe in yourself, it's hard to make and achieve life goals. Reversing that mindset was a large part of our work with clients.

Arriving at work on Monday, I found good news rolling in: There were emails from participants expressing their gratitude at finding a celebratory community event the whole family could take part in — especially if one of them had mental illness. One message explained it was the first time they'd done something as a family since their mother had committed suicide. "Each of us went to counselling, but no one had discussed it until the morning of the run at the breakfast table. Everyone knew why we were participating, and for the first time, we talked about it." The email went on to say how transformational the experience had been and how it helped them move forward to process and accept their loss.

Other emails conveyed a similar message of appreciation for having an event where *everyone* was welcomed and celebrated. It was heartwarming to read accolades from so many families. Miles for Mental Health had touched a nerve in the community — created an event where people with mental health challenges were welcomed and showing up meant you believed in fighting stigma.

The most prized donation that Jessica had received was a Vancouver Canucks jersey. In 2011, the Canucks were doing unusually well and heading for the playoffs. Canucks fever took over our office and the whole province. As an additional incentive to attend, the winning ticket was drawn at the Miles for Mental Health Run/Walk. The sale of jersey raffle tickets efforts by enthusiastic staff and volunteers had raised $2,300. Sales of hot dogs and hamburgers generated $870, and with the balance of pledges and registration fees, the total reached $14,947. I was amazed. Jennifer had predicted we might raise eight or nine thousand. The first Run took endless hours of organization but equipped us with a proven template. Next year, we'd be selling a known entity, the annual Miles for Mental Health Run/Walk, the only mental health run in Canada.

Whereas the thrift store appealed to volunteer staff, donors, and shoppers, this healthy public event in the park with its stigma-fighting slogan reached a far broader range of people. The Run also provided us with the emails of 200 participants, most of whom were unknown to us. I began to understand the idea of finding and stewarding donors and supporters. Any new contacts we made were asked if they would like to receive our newsletter. That way we could keep a growing cadre of supporters informed about our programs by emailing them our brochure and details of future events.

I always stressed to staff that as they did the real work of supporting clients, our Simon Fraser Branch was their organization. To emphasize this, I emailed them the updated 2011 brochure and asked for any suggestions for improvement.

Three days after sending the staff the latest version, I was stunned to get a call from the union informing me we were not allowed to have a volunteer receptionist in our office. A picture of our receptionist had been on the brochure, and someone must have forwarded a copy to the union. So much for my attempt to be inclusive!

During Veronica's year as ED, I understood the union had been the employees' defence against infractions of their rights. But that was no longer the case. I made a point of listening to the staff, addressing their problems, and finding opportunities for them to upgrade their skills.

The union official who phoned me was a lawyer and new on the job. We decided to meet at her office on Canada Way. I pointed out that we'd had a volunteer receptionist since before we were unionized. The volunteer shown in the brochure had been with the organization for ten years. Finally, there was no money for a receptionist in the contracts we had with Fraser Health. I felt like suggesting if the union wanted to pay the receptionist's wages, we wouldn't need a volunteer, but I held back, not wanting to sound antagonistic. I was upset but tried to sound calm. After some back-and-forth discussion, the union said they would let us continue to have volunteer receptionists while they held internal discussions on the matter. I never heard back and never asked.

It bugged me that the union never considered our clients, most of whom weren't employed and lived on the poverty line. If our volunteers were on a disability, they received $100 a month from the BC government for volunteering. Not only was this a valuable financial supplement, but the experience gained was often the first step toward acquiring enough confidence for some of them to find paid work.

At the next staff meeting, I brought up the fact that someone had forwarded the brochure to the union. The receptionist featured in our brochure was very popular, and some of the staff were shocked to think she may have to stop helping us. The polarized atmosphere created by so many disputes over the past year still played a negative role on our team's unity.

## Canadian Mental Health Association
### Simon Fraser Branch

For the past 10 years I have helped with reception and event registration. Volunteering is satisfying because I like to be busy, I like to help and its fun to be here.

It feels like family. *Jerry*

the communities of New Westminster, Maple Ridge, Port Moody, Tri Cities, and Pitt Meadows by offering hope, housing support, outreach & education programs.

We are funded by Fraser Health, United Way, BC Housing, donations from the public, and are also helped enormously by our volunteers corps.

### Our Vision
Mentally Healthy People in a Healthy Society

### Our Mission
The Canadian Mental Health Association, a nation wide, volunteer organization, promotes the mental health of all and supports the resilience and recovery of people experiencing mental illness. CMHA accomplishes this mission through advocacy, education, research, and service.

### Housing Programs

Supported Housing has been the traditional focus of this branch. We currently provide four housing programs which are accessed by referral from local mental health centres.

*Supported housing programs assist consumers in developing skills and obtaining the resources they want and need in their particular living situation.*

*These initiatives represent real hope to people who want to live, learn, work, and socialize in the same way as non-disabled members of the community.*
Psychiatric Rehabilitation, Pratt et al, 2006

#### Supported Housing
We provide two programs for clients who live in apartments in our community. Both the Supported Independent Living (SIL) and the Community Living Support (CLS) programs, provide practical support to clients transitioning to independent living. SIL programs also provide rent subsidies.

#### Transition Houses
Simon Fraser Branch operates six transition houses which support clients acquiring the necessary skills to live independently in their community.

**Barnabas House**    **Riverside House**

#### Youth Semi Independent Living
The mandate of this program is to provide housing and support to youth who are 16-21 years old, who have a diagnosed mental illness & who are unable to live with family.

### Educational & other programs

#### Education
Education is an important deterrent against stigma. We offer "Mental Illness First Aid" courses and other presentations to people interested in learning about, & coping with, mental health challenges.

#### Smoking Cessation Groups
Smoking is the leading preventable cause of death in North America. As individuals with mental illness are twice as likely to smoke as others, CMHA-SF developed the innovative "Breathing Easy" smoking cessation program with funding from Health Canada.

#### Community Kitchen
Our community kitchen programs help people learn to budget, shop, prepare, and cook meals for themselves. This training is made possible by a grant from United Way.

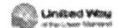

#### Computer Training
We offer consumers one-on-one training to become computer literate.

#### Thrift store
A social enterprise which provides training and work experience for people, recycles unwanted goods, helps the community get to know us, and earns money for our society.

#### Outreach
Helps people who are homeless, or at risk of being homeless, get MEIA benefits and connect to appropriate support services in order to find and maintain housing.

*Copy of the brochure 2$^{nd}$ page*

 I followed Jennifer's suggestion and hired Adnam as a trainee housing manager. He had no mental health experience but agreed to study psychosocial rehabilitation, our guiding theory. He would follow the same course as I had run for the staff a couple of years before by reading each chapter of the course book over the weekend and taking a test each Monday after work.

 I was happy to have him aboard. He was popular with the staff and, as Jennifer had noted, hardworking and ambitious. I hoped after six months, he would be up to speed and I could remove the "trainee" portion of his job description. Adnam was looking forward to the following year's Run and told me he would like to be the Run director as well as the housing manager. They were two big roles, but he appeared to have the energy and confidence to pull it off.

The undertow of putting on the Run had pulled us off course, a worthwhile diversion, but now it was back to business as usual: non-stop phone calls, meetings, and problem solving, but without Jennifer's help. After a year of her supportive ideas, I was back to being the sole person responsible for our financial well-being.

## The Corner of My Desk

I wasn't usually enthusiastic about attending the quarterly meetings of the 20 BC branches of the Canadian Mental Health Association, but it was one of many requirements of membership in the CMHA "family." The meetings took two whole days out of my busy schedule. Both days were chaired by Bev Gutray, the CEO of CMHA in British Columbia. It was her job to lead, pull, push, or drag us toward unified directions and goals — no mean feat to harmonize the direction of 20 different branches with their own boards of directors. Notwithstanding our differing sizes, regions, and programs, discordant notes were usually kept to a low rumble.

In the fall of 2011, I was less apprehensive about attending the upcoming meeting with the other EDs, two men and seventeen women. They were all seasoned managers experienced at running mental health nonprofits. The morning round-table check-in was a good way of learning about the challenges and successes of other branches. My report was usually underwhelming compared to those of the other EDs.

This time was different: I explained our Miles for Mental Health Run/Walk event had netted $15,000 and been attended by 200 participants. The Treasure Chest thrift store was now clearing $6,000 a month on a regular basis. Our commercial office-cleaning program employed six workers and generated funding for our yoga program. Our computer training program had helped 28 people that year, and we just renewed all our housing contracts with Fraser Health. This raised some eyebrows. For once, the Simon Fraser Branch was not the weakest link.

After the check-ins, Bev continued on with a mix of updates and suggested initiatives, one of which was called Living Life to the Full, a program which provided effective tools to maximize people's ability to manage life's challenges.

"It's based on cognitive behavioural therapy (CBT)," she said. "Providers will give presentations to businesses or nonprofits as a paid-for program. Anyone interested?"

*Yes, Bev!* This offered two interesting opportunities, income for our branch and the chance to brush up on the CBT knowledge gained in my master's degree. "Bev, I'm really interested." She wrote my name down as the sole applicant. I was feeling emboldened by my branch's recent successes and decided to become more involved with head office.

On the second day of the meeting, we were joined by each branch's president, making 40 people instead of 20. We moved to a larger venue. I positioned myself at the back of the group, as I had done in school classes, in case my eyes fluttered shut.

I am more of a doing person than a meeting person. When I had my own boat repair company, meetings with staff never lasted longer than 10 minutes. To survive the second day's event, I took advantage of breaks to pick out the best muffins and downed large mugs of snooze-inhibiting coffee.

Bev's energy seemed inexhaustible. One of her latest initiatives was championing a new fundraiser called Ride Don't Hide, an initiative sparked by Michael Schratter: Mike was a Vancouver schoolteacher with bipolar disorder who was riding through 33 countries — a distance of 40,000 kilometres — around the world to raise funds and awareness for mental illness. Bev suggested we send him emails of support which he later reported were very encouraging. I sent him one a week. On his return in 2011, Bev and Michael planned to start a local once-a-year Ride Don't Hide fundraising event. She urged all the branches to become involved, but my branch was already deep into our Miles for Mental Health Run/Walk.

An agenda topic that caught my interest was whether or not

CMHA should accept clients with co-occurring disorders — people who had addiction challenges and a psychiatric diagnosis. From my perspective, it was a no-brainer. It seemed preposterous to be serving clients with mental illness and then jettison them if they developed an addiction. They would need more help, not less.

Our branch was already working with homeless people who had co-occurring disorders. Having mental illness can warp reality and pull someone off the conveyor belt of mainstream life. In the short term, street drugs can help a person feel better, alter their reality, and give them a break from their illness. Crystal meth is cheap, increases energy, and lessens the need for food. Opioids put a person into deep relaxation, a euphoria that helps wipe away feelings of not fitting in. After a while, the drugs become an added problem. To get money for their habit, people often sold drugs or engaged in other forms of crime. I volunteered to join a once-a-month telephone discussion group to resolve this issue and advocate for official inclusion of co-occurring disorders in the CMHA mandate.

I poured myself another coffee. The next discussion topic got my attention: Bev suggested that smaller CMHA branches should amalgamate to save money on office rentals, ED wages, and accounting costs. It made sense, but I didn't want to give up my branch just as we were making a comeback. There was lacklustre agreement from other EDs. It remained unstated what would happen to the displaced EDs when branches amalgamated.

As the afternoon wound on, I slipped lower in my chair. My enthusiasm for further topics was waning. Bev's wasn't. My back ached as I hobbled along to the coffee urn. Empty. I filled my coffee cup with ice water. Maybe the shock of cold water swishing down my throat would revive me. I sat near the front, hoping closer proximity would revitalize my attention.

Bev smiled and clapped as a woman in her mid-40s joined her on the stage. "And now I'd like to introduce you to Helen McDonnell who has flown here from New Brunswick to talk to us."

*She had travelled 5000 kilometres to talk to us?*

Helen walked slowly toward the lectern, switching the microphone between her hands several times before she started speaking. She was a diminutive figure in a stylish red wool coat over black dress pants, her face framed in wavy brown hair. In a soft East Coast burr, she explained she'd travelled from New Brunswick to Vancouver to talk to us about her brother, Duncan. "It was a cold January morning, and I was standing alone in the kitchen when my mother phoned."

I sat up. Her quiet sincerity pulled me in. She took a deep breath and continued, halting and restarting but determined to get the story out. The police and a priest had arrived at her mother's house to inform her that her son Duncan, Helen's oldest brother, had been found dead in his apartment in Vancouver.

"Later, from reading my brother's journals, I was stunned to discover he had committed suicide," she said, biting her lip and pausing. She'd been unaware that Duncan suffered from bipolar disorder most of his adult life. As she read his diaries describing his struggle with depression and suicide attempts, she felt devastated it had all been kept secret. "Maybe I could have helped," she said, running her fingers through her hair. This terrible loss made Helen determined to try to pull back the veil of silence about mental illness and haul it out of the shadows of shame.

She began holding annual awareness-raising events and inviting women to come and share stories of mental illness in their families. On the third year of these Women & Wellness meetings, 300 people attended.

As she wrapped up her story, her voice strengthened and she raised her arms toward us. "I'm inviting all CMHA branches across the country to join me. Let's band together and harness the incredible power created by hundreds of women determined to fight the stigma associated with mental illness." As women were the frontline care providers in most homes, Helen believed they were the right people to initiate conversations about mental illness.

Her fierce determination to make her brother's death count for something shone through. She drew me in. It was the kind of grassroots movement I believed in: real people caring from the heart and trying hard to make a positive difference in the world. The sadness in her voice from the unexpected loss of her brother triggered my own feelings of loss for my son. Unlike the random car accident that took Steve's life, I believed Helen's initiative could help save lives. It would be a worthy cause for our branch to embrace by hosting our own Women & Wellness event in the spring. Five months seemed plenty of time to prepare. Distant events were always easier to embrace.

In contrast to previous meetings, I had been stirred into action by the enthusiastic group bonhomie and signed up for three extra responsibilities: to co-run Living Life to the Full, to participate in discussions about including co-occurring disorders in the CMHA mandate, and to host a Women & Wellness event. While I was enthusiastic about each new endeavour, it would add to my workload. The term EDs use for handling extra events is "running it off the corner of my desk." The corner of my desk was becoming as big as the rest of my desk.

Before my enthusiasm waned, I set things in motion for the Women &Wellness event. From my fellow EDs, I'd learned a new concept. Instead of a fundraiser like the Run, the Women & Wellness event would be a friend-raiser. We were trying to raise community consciousness, not money. At least when I introduced this initiative at a team meeting, Stephanie could not accuse me of always focusing on our finances.

Apart from helping women share their experiences of mental illness within their families, it would introduce new Women & Wellness attendees to our organization and the work we did. If they were concerned about mental health, maybe they would become involved in our organization.

I asked Adnam, my new go-to computer guy, to post an announcement for the new women's event on our website. I also printed a "volunteers wanted" ad to display in the Treasure Chest:

> We will host a Women & Wellness event to promote learning, healing, and discussion about mental illness. Women are often caregivers to those with mental health issues and can benefit by sharing their experiences. Volunteers needed. Contact Rodney.

Just before closing on the following Friday, I posted two event notices in the Treasure Chest and was about to tell Sandy about the program, but she cut me short with a wild-eyed look.

"Rodney, today's money is missing. The till is empty. Teresa's left the building and didn't bring the money up to Trevor. Today's take was $314."

"So, Teresa was cashing out?" I could barely speak.

"Yeah, she's always been so reliable. She's been cashing out for us for over five months. I just don't understand what happened."

Teresa was one of our most competent volunteers. During her interview for the Treasure Chest, I recalled her waif-like body shaking with laughter when I asked her about her work experience.

"You name it, Rodney, I've done it: cook, bookkeeper, restaurant owner, rancher, logging truck driver..."

"Logging truck driver?" I'd never heard of a woman doing that job.

She nodded and laughed again, her straight blonde hair bouncing on her shoulders. "It was difficult at first. They didn't like the idea of a woman driver and used to give me all the loads that weren't balanced. But when I didn't quit or complain, they accepted me. It was fun. I did it for three years but had to quit due to arthritis in my elbows."

I admired Teresa. She was in her 60s and fearless: She could train three new volunteers, handle a store full of shoppers, and accept donations, all while working the till and chit-chatting with customers. I appreciated her skilled help and sometimes had a coffee with her when she took a break in the back room.

Sandy gave me Teresa's home address, and I set off to find her. She lived in a condo by the Fraser River. As I knocked on the front door, it creaked open. "Teresa. Teresa," I yelled. No response. *Why is the door unlocked but no one home?* A sense of foreboding came over me. I worried she'd suffered some kind of seizure or a home invasion. I called her name again and again. Silence. Feeling like an intruder, I took a quick look in each room, a due-diligence scrutiny, and left. The worry and concern kept trickling through my head all weekend.

Sandy couldn't reach her until Monday. Teresa explained she had taken the money home with her by mistake and visited a friend on Bowen Island over the weekend. She brought back the complete amount later that day. Sandy and I sat in my office, shaking our heads. None of it made sense. How could you take the money home by mistake? If she'd gone to Bowen Island, why was her front door unlocked? As no money had been lost and she played such a key role in the store, we made the uneasy decision to let Teresa carry on working at the store.

Shortly after posting a notice for assistance to run the Women & Wellness event, Lorna, a competent Treasure Chest volunteer, walked into my office and said she wanted to help. She was in her mid-40s, had just finished a Douglas College course in social work, and wanted to fill the gap with "something meaningful" until she found full-time work.

"I have some previous event experience, so it would be a good fit." She had a sunny smile and a can-do attitude — a good start. We discussed how she could begin: find a location, make up a poster design, and see if she could attract sponsors. Due to Helen's previous success with Women & Wellness, Shoppers Drug Marts across Canada were contributing 50% of the event costs.

Unlike the Run, AGM, or Christmas dinner, I wouldn't be at this event. When I brought up the idea at a staff meeting and asked for volunteers, the reception was lukewarm. A few folks said they might attend. I smiled at Stephanie and pointed out that Women & Wellness was based on raising consciousness, not money. She commented that as I couldn't be there, women would be doing all the work.

"That's right, Stephanie. My gender excludes me from helping out that night, but not you."

She ignored my comment and focused on embellishing the meeting agenda with artistic swirls of her pen.

Carmela, who ran our phone-in Bounce Back program volunteered to attend the meeting as a wellness coach. I liked the suggestion. It matched the name of the event. It was good to have a safety net in case anyone was triggered by painful memories. We didn't want anyone traumatized by stories of suicide leaving the meeting in a vulnerable state.

I realized it might be challenging for women to come and talk about mental illness in their family in front of strangers. If I could get an outstanding speaker, an expert in the field, it might lessen people's hesitancy to share their stories. I didn't know any big names, except the ever-helpful local politician Dawn Black, but she had just played a big role in the Run.

By the time Women & Wellness came around in March 2012, I would be 65. Retirement age. I didn't feel particularly old but sometimes felt out of touch: I couldn't build a website, write computer code, or make a video. The world was becoming one giant high-tech merry-go-round with everyone clambering aboard the new horses of power: Twitter, Facebook, Pinterest, LinkedIn, and Instagram. There was a list of social media that we needed to be *on* in order to be *in* the game. IT marketing skills seemed to be replacing people skills in importance.

Before leaving, Jennifer persuaded Emily Carr University to make us three animated videos about mental illness, which if they "went viral," Jennifer assured me, "would really put us on the map." The better we were known and "followed," the broader base of people we could appeal to for funding. Securing funding seemed more and more dependent on having excellent social-media skills than providing good programs. The videos never went viral. We remained an anonymous speck on the social-media map.

As the new year started, finding a keynote speaker for Women & Wellness eluded me, nor was it certain we could attract enough participants to make it viable. The response for early registration on our website produced a dismal three people. After dinner one evening, I asked Anna if she would be interested in attending and explained the context of Helen's story.

"Why would I attend? None of my family is suicidal, but it's a terrible thing to happen. My friend Ginny's son, Kelty, committed suicide." She explained how Ginny's husband had been skiing when he got a call from his son saying he was feeling suicidal. Kelty's father raced down the mountain and arrived home to find his son had committed suicide.

"That must have devastated the parents," I said. Unlike many deaths, suicides are often preventable, and I could well imagine the father's grief at rushing home to find he was too late.

"Yeah, it changed their lives. They started a campaign to raise money for mental health in their son's name."

Moved by the story, I googled Kelty Dennehy. The Kelty Patrick Dennehy Foundation showed a plethora of pictures featuring fundraising events his parents had instigated.

Every mile and every smile and every tear and every fear is dedicated to our beautiful boy, Kelty Patrick Dennehy.

I gazed in awe at the multitude of activities the Dennehys had been involved in to improve the help available for people with mental health issues and at risk of suicide. They had dedicated their lives to this cause and raised millions of dollars. I was humbled by their efforts. My own involvement in mental health was just a day job.

Anna was a travel agent. Outside of a shared home life, our worlds never crossed except for this one exception.

"Anna, could you phone Ginny and ask her if she would be the keynote speaker for our Women & Wellness meeting?"

"It's awkward to phone up out of the blue and ask a favour. We were neighbours, and my sons played with Kelty," she explained. "But I haven't spoken to her for a while."

"Please. It's for a good cause!"

After some cajoling, Anna agreed. I kept my fingers crossed, and two days later, she confirmed Ginny had agreed to be the keynote speaker. I was jubilant. Of all people, Ginny embraced the exact ideals Helen had envisioned — going public with family experience of suicide. With such a star speaker, we hoped to attract people out of their comfort zones to attend the meeting. Engaging Ginny gave me courage to ask Dawn Black for help once more; true to form, she offered to be master of ceremonies. I was pumped. Three competent women would be running the evening: wellness coach Carmela, keynote speaker Ginny, and Dawn at the helm.

Lorna used her daughter's media connections to get free advertising from City TV and found a great location, the Westminster Club, at a reduced price. She talked a graphic artist friend into designing an event poster and pasted them up all around the city. During her volunteer shifts at the Treasure Chest, Lorna handed out notices to customers and volunteers, encouraging them to attend the event. I admired her energy and her efforts. She was also helping out a disabled friend with her shopping and supporting her son through a rough patch in his life. Lorna couldn't seem to say no to any good cause. I became concerned she'd taken on too much. As she relied on public transport, I sometimes gave her a lift if we were heading in the same direction. As most of her days were spent helping others, I wondered how she was supporting herself. After Lorna had worked on setting up the Women & Wellness event for two months, I bypassed the usual protocols for hiring and offered her part-time work.

She looked flustered. "I didn't volunteer to get hired. I wanted to help with the event planning."

"I realize that, Lorna, but you're helping us. Can't we help you in return?"

She became silent, then nodded. "Thanks so much, Rodney. I

haven't found any work yet, so a part-time job would be really helpful."

Most of the time, I encouraged people to stretch themselves. With Lorna, it was the opposite. She had such a giving nature I worried she was spreading herself too thin.

When I ran my own business, it would have been inconceivable to ask someone to work for nothing. In my early years of running a nonprofit, asking people to volunteer their time felt embarrassing. I often asked in such a muted voice that people asked me to repeat the question. Many of them were not outgoing and seemed surprised to be asked to help. Was I being too self-serving by asking them to step outside their comfort zones and spend time working in an unfamiliar role for no pay? Did they say "yes" to please me as an authority figure? My concerns lessened as I saw people enjoying their volunteer time — growing, learning, and gaining confidence as they acquired and used new skills.

I treated client and non-client volunteers equally. They were all donating their time and energy. I never enquired if they had a mental health diagnosis, but if they told me, I asked them if they needed accommodating: A person who heard voices might not be suited to answering the phone at the reception desk. Someone who was obsessive about cleanliness wouldn't be asked to sort donated clothes. Although we grew to have over 40 volunteers, they were never taken for granted. Their names and volunteer hours were posted monthly by the reception desk and in the back room of the Treasure Chest. Thanks to Sandy, birthdays were always recognized with a card. She also arranged lunches for the Treasure Chest volunteers and kept track of the credit they had to spend in the store.

Two weeks after the CMHA regional meeting, from the corner of my desk, I started working on the Living Life to the Full workshop. I had studied cognitive behavioural therapy as part of my master's degree in counselling and was impressed by the positive results it produced. I hoped presenting this workshop would upgrade my CBT knowledge, get me away from the ever-ringing office phone, and bring money to the branch and benefits to course attendees.

My co-presenter, Dr. Michelle Haring, was a CBT psychologist who supervised the Bounce Back coaches in all the CMHA branches. She was a statuesque blonde in her mid-30s and was on a first-name basis with the psychiatrist in Scotland who had written the course.

A local nonprofit providing services to seniors asked for their staff to take the series of six two-hour workshops. The course was advertised as "a fun and interactive course that will help you understand your feelings, thoughts, and behaviours, and what to do about them!" I also hoped it would be fun to present.

Pleased that things seemed to be falling into place so quickly, Michelle and I met at my house to plan the first session. I hadn't realized a two-hour presentation would take over an hour to create. We shared tea and gingersnaps as we worked. The idea was to present theoretical concepts followed by group exercises to help anchor them in people's minds.

Michelle claimed she was "geographically challenged," so we agreed to meet 20 minutes early in case she couldn't find the location. Sure enough on presentation day, she was nowhere to be seen at the arranged time and place. I started to worry in case I had to present the course alone. *Is Michelle an unreliable partner?*

Michelle pulled into the parking lot and saw me waving.

"Don't worry, we're still five minutes ahead of schedule," I reassured her. We walked quickly upstairs to the Seniors Support Centre office and were greeted by their ED, Val.

"My staff is really looking forward to your presentation."

We were still on time, and the applause from Val's staff as we entered the room buoyed my spirits. Michelle proved to be an eloquent presenter. She stood up, maintained eye contact, and spoke with conviction.

I sat down and read much of my part from the course manual. I paused to look up at my audience, fifteen people waiting for my words of wisdom. If I stumbled, Michelle took up the slack. My heart rate went up, and my confidence went down. My co-presenter surged through with ease and smiles.

As we walked out to the parking lot, I congratulated her. "Wow, you were great. Do you present often?"

"Yes, I like presenting, but it's usually at conferences to audiences of a hundred or more."

I swallowed. "How do you think it went today?"

"Not bad for a first time. I think it would be better if you didn't read from the manual though. It would seem more professional if you knew the material."

She was right. Michelle was half my age, an accomplished presenter thoroughly versed in her craft. My CBT knowledge was from 12 years previously. My presentation skills dated from when I took a Toastmasters course 15 years before. I had more knowledge of CBT than the other EDs at the regional meeting, but compared to Michelle, I was an amateur. When the rubber hit the road, my tires were flat.

I struggled to get through the remaining five sessions. Michelle was gracious and helpful. After completing the course, Val, the seniors centre ED, sent us both a personal thank you note saying that she and her staff had thoroughly enjoyed the course. The feeling wasn't mutual. I felt less than proficient.

If Michelle hadn't been there, I would have carried it off on my own and reassured myself I had done a good job. At our branch, there was no equal outsider to provide a reflective mirror as Michelle had done. Were some of my other ideas and initiatives less effective than I realized?

Part of my rationale for presenting the course was to reward myself with a break from sitting all day tapping a keyboard and answering the phones; it often felt like my body was wasting away. I noticed that my knee had started to crunch and inflict spasms of pain when I walked up the two flights of stairs from the thrift store to my office. My doctor said it was due to calcium in the meniscus. I started putting more weight on the handrail and less on my knee.

Instead of taking on outside projects as a change of pace, I decided to walk to Queens Park and back every lunchtime to revitalize myself — get fresh air into my lungs and pump oxygen into my brain. I had fond memories of the park: When Steve was two, I built him a red toboggan and pulled him through the snow there. He wore a red woolly hat and matching mitts. I remembered him falling off, laughing, and clambering back on and saying, "More, Daddy. More."

The sleepy road to the park was in one of the earliest developed areas of New Westminster. I loved looking at the stately, well-preserved 100-year-old homes along the way. They were built prior to both world wars and plane travel, before cars and computers had taken over the world. I imagined kids playing in the front yards with skipping ropes and spinning tops. The daily walks were refreshing and less stressful than presenting material I had a sketchy knowledge of to groups of strangers.

I resigned from presenting Living Life to the Full workshops. I needed to think more about living my own life — but making it less full, not more full. Bev wasn't happy at the news, but I recommended she hire a young friend of mine who had studied CBT at the same university I had. It proved to be an excellent fit. Bev hired her to present courses with Michelle and also to work at the CMHA head office.

# People Leaving   Women & Wellness   New Presentations

Most of our staff had been with CMHA-SF since before my arrival. After almost eight years of working together, they were like my day family. Only three full-time staff had left.

Just prior to Christmas 2011, Stephanie announced she was going on stress leave. This surprised me as I hadn't noticed any change in her demeanour. I wondered, even worried, that I had been part of that stress, although part of me was relieved she was leaving. Like Robbie, she argued against most new ideas I had suggested. On the plus side, we had recently adopted one of her "anti" suggestions: As we started to plan for Christmas Dinner 2011, she spoke against it. "Rodney, you are always saying we are trying to replicate normal, everyday living situations for our clients. It's not normal to sit down with a hundred people for Christmas dinner."

I tried to think of a countervailing answer but couldn't. Saying, "but we've always put on a dinner," seemed lame, especially as I was the one always advocating for change.

Stephanie seized on my lack of response. "At Christmas time, we don't want to spend our own time holding a fundraiser to pay for the food. We're all busy with family," she said in a strong voice, which drew approving nods from the staff. Encouraged, she continued. "We could just put on a drop-in lunch and pay for the food with the money you received from giving those Living Life to the Full presentations."

"Stephanie's right," Lisa agreed. "It would be more normal for people just to drop by someone's house for lunch. A dinner for a hundred smacks of an institution." They had a point.

We ran the idea by 30 random clients. The count was 11 for big dinner and 19 for a drop-in lunch at the office. That Christmas, we bought finger food and juice from Costco and stopped work at noon.

The staff decorated the large meeting room, and about 40 people dropped by. The ever-resourceful Dawn Black had her staff drop by with 40 presents. So by good fortune, all our clients received a small gift. Not attending a fundraiser, or cooking a huge Christmas meal, was far less work for our staff. I felt a sense of relief — one less event to worry about. Why hadn't I thought of that before? Maybe it was just an ego thing for me, carrying on with tradition.

Paige also announced she was leaving after Christmas. Funny, whimsical, spirited, helpful Paige wouldn't be brightening up team meetings anymore. As she had lost her union seniority, I hadn't been able to find her full-time housing work. I would miss her. She was the first staff member to support my fledgling efforts to start the thrift store and get her clients to help.

A week after Paige's announcement, Trevor walked into my office with downcast eyes and looking very awkward.

"What's up, Trev?"

He looked at me and opened his mouth several times, but no words came out. Did he have a serious illness? Was his recent marriage in difficulty?

"I'm leaving in two months. I'm giving my notice."

*No, not Trevor!* "Is something up? Why are you leaving?"

He paused and cleared his throat. "I've been here ten years, Rodney. I'm completing my accounting designation in a month. In order to progress in my career, I need to move on."

Electric panic coursed through my body. Since my first day here in the fall of 2004, Trevor had been a rock-solid, supportive employee, giving sound financial reports and advice as well as fixing computer glitches. Soft-spoken and calm, he was one of the most helpful and dependable guys I had ever worked with. As usual, what he said made perfect sense. I wouldn't try to talk him out of such a logical move.

It seemed like we had stumbled into a season of people leaving and I decided to get an impromptu picture of everybody in the office at that moment. We assembled on the sidewalk in front of the Treasure Chest, and I asked a passer-by to take a picture of us all. A good intuition as more folks left shortly after.

*Staff and Volunteers in front of the Treasure Chest*

When I first started at CMHA, it was Trevor, Donald, and myself running the show. I'd enjoyed the easygoing, no-drama relationship between the three of us. Now the last reminder of that era was leaving.

"Okay, Trev. I'll miss you, but as you said, it sounds like a good move for your career. Thanks for giving me lots of notice and..." I caught my breath. "Thanks for all your help, mate." We avoided looking at each other. "I'll put an ad on Craigslist right away. Maybe you could help interview your replacement?"

"Yes, I was going to suggest that." He looked out of the window for a few seconds. "Thanks for understanding."

I nodded. "I'll miss you."

He smiled, turned on his heel, and left my office. I sat looking at the empty doorway.

We only had one qualified applicant for Trevor's position, so we hired her. She was in her early 30s and seemed keen, friendly, and competent.

Valued volunteers were leaving too. Jessica, who was a great help in setting up the Run and fulfilled many roles after, had finally found full-time employment with a large telecommunication company. I hoped the excellent recommendation I gave had helped her land the job.


I often awoke in the early morning thinking about work problems. My usual cure was to watch TV until I got bored and return to bed until around eight o'clock. On Friday, March 11, 2012, I awoke worrying about the next day's Women & Wellness event — visualizing a checklist to ensure we'd remembered everything. Once engaged, my mind wouldn't shut off. At 5 a.m., I threw on my dressing gown and trekked downstairs to the living room. As the TV came into focus, I watched incredible scenes of a tsunami devastating the Japanese coastline. A chill ran through my body. Was I experiencing *Groundhog Day*, or was it happening again?

Homes, houses, cars, businesses, and people were enveloped in a giant wall of water. In an instant, those people's worlds had been wiped out. After a few minutes, the announcer explained they were reshowing the scenes from exactly one year ago when the tsunami obliterated parts of the Japanese coastline. After watching such a devastating sight, worrying whether we had selected the right flowers for the tables at the Women & Wellness event seemed less important.

That was also the year Steve Jobs passed away at 56. What a difference his vision and work had made to the world. I received a MacBook the previous Christmas and was a fan. But although innovative and successful, he was still dead at 56, 9 years younger than me. If I'd died at 56, I would have never worked at CMHA. I would soon be sixty-five, so ancient that instead of having to merge daily into rush hour traffic to earn a living, a government pension would enable me to stay home.

I had worked for wages since age 16 and still remembered my first job baling rags. A few months after starting the job, my shirt got caught in the rag press machinery. In a flash, my neck was sucked up against the drive spindle until the fabric parted with a loud ripping sound. I lost some skin from my neck and was badly shaken. They gave me a cup of tea with extra sugar — the English cure-all for emergency situations.

That accident ripped away my youthful illusions of immortality. Not long after, my father passed away from pancreatic cancer. A month after Dad died, my best friend, Eddie, was killed in a motorcycle crash. I realized at a young age that life was perilous and uncertain, and I decided to charge ahead with mine while it lasted. At 21, I immigrated to Canada and got married. A few months later, the tug I was working on hit a reef in the Haida Gwaii islands and was crushed by a giant steel barge full of gasoline. Another reminder of life's fragility. I quit working on the tugs and became an apprentice boatbuilder. At 23, I bought my first house and became a father.

Charging ahead became a lifestyle. I gulped at each challenge, grabbed the bull by the horns, got tossed around, learned from mistakes, and moved on to the next challenge. Maybe at 65, I could slow down, should slow down.

After 49 years of employment, maybe the next challenge would be *not* working. Who would I be without wrapping my life around a job? What would I do all day? Being unemployed was hard to visualize. Work had been my school of life. On the other hand, working until I dropped dead from cancer or got hit by a tidal wave wasn't great either. Thoughts of not working percolated through my head — like slow-dripping coffee awakening my mind to other possibilities. Then I refocused on the job at hand.

We had over 70 preregister for Women & Wellness. On the day of the big event, I felt antsy knowing that I would not be there making sure everything went well — fixing unforeseen issues that cause panic at the last minute. On the other hand, standing back was a welcome relief. It was rewarding to see Lorna shine at the multi-layered tasks needed to produce the successful soiree.

The day after the event, she burst into my office with a big smile on her face and told me it had gone very well. "Ginny was amazing, so was Dawn. The stories people told were awesome. We raised $1100. Good considering entry was free and it wasn't a fundraiser. I made sure everyone had brochures."

I smiled. "Wow, you did a great job, Lorna. Definitely a good addition on your resume. Was anyone triggered by the stories?"

"Some women were teary. Carmela sat with one woman for about 20 minutes after the meeting."

Two weeks later, Lorna applied for a job in Kelowna and asked me for a reference. I would miss her. A rewarding bond is formed when working for a good cause with like-minded people.

Cool, calm, and collected Carmela was the next person to announce she planned to leave. She had successfully run Bluebird House for us, then retrained to be our branch's coach for the Bounce

Back program. She'd also chaired the Miles for Mental Health meetings for eight months and played a large role in its success. For some reason I never understood, Bev wanted to have all the Bounce Back coaches under one roof. Sadly, this was not to be our roof. All coaches would now work for the Vancouver branch on Quebec Street. Carmela had been a competent worker and a friendly, supportive team member since I joined the organization. The longstanding work relationships with people that leave tend to wither and die without the daily infusion of collegial contact. I would miss Carmela's cheerful, positive outlook.

With Adnam as housing manager, the weekly staff meetings lacked the undercurrent of tension when Jennifer had been with us. He went out of his way to befriend and connect with each staff member. He was young, gracious, and handsome; the staff seemed buoyed up by the individual attention he gave them. Our relationship started off well, almost like a father and son. He was in his early twenties and me in my mid-sixties. On drives out to Maple Ridge for housing meetings, he sometimes discussed dating dilemmas and the family challenges he faced.

He was a good public speaker, and after one presentation at a volunteer fair in the local mall, he came back excited. "I was speaking about the benefits of volunteering for our organization, and passersby stopped to listen." He was growing in confidence in this managerial position, his first full-time job since university. Sometimes, this new success stretched to overconfidence.

Fraser Health occasionally allotted us funding to buy furniture for our houses. New furniture uplifted the spirits of our residents by sprucing up their daily living conditions. Adnam was enthused by Ikea. "It's very modern in design, just what we need to smarten up the houses and lift up the clients' spirits. I'm going to take a look at the Coquitlam store — see if I can get a deal from the manager."

I explained that for big organizations like Ikea, you had to apply months in advance to the head office. Individual managers had no power to give discounts.

"I'll talk to the manager," he said, smiling. "I'm sure I can get us a deal."

We didn't discuss it further. Three weeks later, Suzy at Bluebird House phoned me. "Rodney, there's a bunch of furniture from Ikea here. Who's going to assemble it?"

I was shocked and asked Adnam why he had gone ahead with Ikea when I hadn't okayed it.

He explained that he wasn't used to reporting to people.

"You're the trainee housing manager. Trainee means you're new on the job, so you need to check with me before any big decisions or changes are made." I explained that even when he was past the trainee stage, we did things as a team. "Did you arrange for someone to assemble the furniture?"

He seemed surprised to learn that it needed assembling. I guess he'd only seen the finished product in catalogues. Somehow, the receipts had been lost, making it tricky to return. I found a handyman at $10 an hour to put the furniture together, but after assembling one piece, he decided it was too difficult. One day a week after work, I stopped by each house and assembled the furniture. Looking at the little instruction pics, trying to guess what they meant, was a struggle after my brain had been fried by a hard day's work. The furniture may have lifted our clients' spirits, but assembling it dampened mine.

Six months before the next Miles for Mental Health Run/Walk in May 2012, Adnam told me he was considering running for Mayor of Surrey.

I swallowed. "I admire your go-getter spirit, Adnam, but wouldn't you need a longer employment record under your belt?" I didn't want to appear ageist by pointing out there were no mayors of major municipalities in their twenties. "This is your first full-time job since university, and you've only been here six months."

"People told me I have a chance," he said, jutting his chin out.

"Okay. It's up to you. But you can't run for mayor and do this job."

"I think I could do it!"

"No. The housing manager position is a full-time position, plus you were thinking of taking on the Run as well." I recalled Jennifer mentioning he was ambitious.

Adnam pursed his lips and left my office without speaking. Later that afternoon, he re-emerged with a smile on his face and said he wanted to talk about the pay he would get for managing the upcoming Run.

"What would work for you?" I said.

"Well, there are all the volunteers to coordinate, the sponsors to be recontacted, prizes to be donated, a video to be made…"

"Yes, I agree, there's lots to be done, and by the way, count me out as the hamburger chef this time. Also, try and arrange for better weather than that downpour we endured last year." We both laughed. "For managing all aspects of the Run, I'm prepared to offer you twenty percent of the take or $4000, whichever is greater." I figured a percentage would provide him with the impetus to make it as successful as possible. "For the Run, you will sign on as a contractor, must pay your own taxes, and will get the title of Run Director." Being a contractor for the Run avoided any problems with the union about job descriptions or overtime pay.

He stared at me for some time. I continued, "Let me know in a week, so I can start looking for someone else if the answer is no."

Conveniently, the phone rang. After another long look in my direction, Adnam left the room.

With no Christmas dinner, and other people in charge of the Run and the women's event, the only event I was responsible for in 2011 was the Annual General Meeting in the fall.

We paid the residents at Bluebird and Barnabas Houses to make sandwiches. I found an engaging speaker, prepared the AGM report, wrote the program, and printed membership cards and brochures. For this AGM, I could relax. We were doing well on all fronts — a far cry from my first nervous AGM appearance in 2004 seven years before. Life at work was a lot more relaxed without the panic of trying to leap across financial chasms.

One of Trevor's last acts was to come into my office and let me know the Treasure Chest had made $100,000 profit in the past year — far in excess of what I thought possible and an incredible testimony to the hard work of Sandy, our volunteers, and the generosity of donors. In our first year of operations, the Treasure Chest made just over $12,000.

The only sour note that month was letting one of our most competent volunteers go. I knew by the dour look on Sandy's face as she stormed into my office that something was very wrong.

"You're not gonna believe this: Teresa was on the till, and all the money's gone again."

We were dumbfounded. This was the third time. After the second time she'd taken it home "by mistake" and brought the entire amount back the following Monday, we suggested she take a break for a month. She smiled and agreed without argument. That was Teresa, always agreeable, always helpful. Two months after coming back, she had done the same thing again.

Saddened and frustrated, Sandy and I agreed she had to go. Taking hundreds of dollars home by "mistake" on Friday and bringing it back Monday was officially going to be off the worry list.

We never learned why Teresa took the money home. Maybe the underlying message was that she wanted to leave but didn't want to tell us. If so, it was third time lucky. I missed her cheery face and chatting with her in the back room. We never found anyone as competent as Teresa, or as baffling.

Most volunteers signed in on time, completed their shifts with pride, and left. The daily ebb and flow of goods, customers, and volunteers continued as regular as the tides under Sandy's careful management. We were open from 10 a.m. to 4 p.m. Tuesday to Sunday. Having Mondays off gave us a chance to clean house, restock the shelves, and rearrange the display windows.

Customers were usually helpful and respectful, many bringing in donations as well as buying things. Rarely was I called to help. An exception was with one customer who had been caught stealing twice. The first time, I followed her out of the store and told her in a friendly manner that all goods had to be paid for. She had spiky bleached hair, bold jewellery, a strong European accent, and a grating voice. She stared at me with fiery blue eyes and yelled, "You crazy. I not steal from your shit store. You got all garbage here," and stormed off. The staff were watching through the window. As she was so belligerent, I told the staff to phone me if they saw her stealing again. That kind of robust anger could be damaging for someone with an anxiety disorder.

The second time I was called to stop her stealing, I said, "Excuse me, madam…" She looked up, poked her tongue out, and left. Two weeks after that incident, I got a call from Vi, our 91-year-old volunteer. "Rodney, that woman they call the Eurobitch is here again. She's stealing books. Can you come down?"

I didn't encourage the name-calling, but neither did I tell them it was wrong, and it kind of fit. I raced down the pine stairs two at a time and arrived just in time to see the woman stuffing books into her bag. "I've asked you not to steal in this store. It upsets the staff. Please put the books back on the shelf."

"I pay later. Just put in bag to carry."

"You've been seen stealing before."

"These people work here, all crazy in the head. Crazy people tell lies."

That really upset me! She'd insulted the people running the store — my people.

"Please put those books back immediately and leave the store, or I will phone the police," I said in a voice I hoped was calm and authoritative.

With a defiant smirk, she dropped the books on the floor and yelled, "You get everything for nothing. You should give for free. Why you open this store, just to make money?"

Customers stopped shopping, and staff turned to watch the commotion.

My angry side thought, *Yes, Eurobitch, just to make money.* My professional voice replied, "Please leave now and don't come back." It was more than likely this customer had her own mental health issues.

Our volunteers were proud their hard work running the Treasure Chest contributed hugely to our bottom line. People shoplifting in "their" store really upset them. I was more concerned about the negative effect her angry tirades might have on the staff than the loss of revenue. In fact, we sometimes gave things away to people who needed household items but couldn't afford them. When

Heather found homeless people housing, or our clients moved from a transition house to their own apartment, we often supplied cooking pots, plates, cutlery, bedding, and a microwave. Sandy had the staff make up "moving in" packages so we were prepared when they were needed.

After resolving the financial problems and raising our profile in the community through the Treasure Chest, the Run, and Women & Wellness events, it was easier to attract board members. Volunteers want to sit on the board of an organization that is performing well. Since returning to the ED position, I tried to build a board that represented the diversity of our community in addition to having beneficial skill sets. I put ads on Craigslist or Charity Village and forwarded candidates' resumes to the board for their approval. If I got a feeling that an applicant wouldn't be a good fit, I included my reasoning in the email. Having been burned by some previous board members, I was wary of who became my boss. The board never questioned my opinions; they could have also suggested new members, but this didn't happen.

By the beginning of 2012, we had eight competent board members — four women and four men from seven different ethnic origins and ages ranging from 23 to 69. An ED in a local nonprofit once said to me, "When I think of CMHA boards, it conjures images of elderly white women sitting around planning rummage sales to raise money." No more! I was proud of our board's ethnic diversity and talents. With a competent board and our finances in good order, the future looked stable.

As our organization's public profile expanded, I began receiving requests to give presentations on mental health topics.

I had written a presentation called "Practical Support for People with Mental Illness" based on the typical problems and real-life solutions we discussed weekly at staff meetings. I charged $75 for a 60-minute presentation to colleges. Not a lot of money but I was glad to share my knowledge with the mental health workers of the future through practical rather than theoretical ideas.

After giving this presentation to a group taking a Community Mental Health course at a local college, I wrapped up the class by asking how the students thought people with mental illness should be treated. I wrote their answers on the board: with respect, kindness, understanding, support, good medication, etc.

"These are politically correct and kind answers," I commended them.

A woman of about 45 sat in front of me; I asked her if she had a son or daughter.

"Yes, my daughter's 20."

"How would you feel if she told you her boyfriend had a mental illness and she was bringing him home for dinner tonight?"

She looked aghast and responded with a barrage of questions. "Would he drool? What on earth would we talk about? Would he eat normally?"

I wiped the previous answers off the board and asked each of the 12 students in the room how they would feel about having a guest with mental illness come to dinner, date their parent or child, or come to live with them. Inspired by the honesty of the first woman, they all gave candid answers. I wrote their revised answers on the board:

Would they drool? Would they steal, have proper table manners? Would things get crazy? If they forgot to take their meds, would they be violent? Was mental illness catching? Could you trust them? What would we talk about? Did they shower?

I thanked the class for their honesty and scanned the faces in the room. "When a person gets diagnosed with a serious mental illness, they usually get hospitalized, diagnosed, and medicated. By the time they get out, my experience has been that they are often turned away by their families and have lost their jobs. Former friends often ignore their calls. Not only do they lose much of their social network and have to cope with the symptoms of their illness, but they have to face the prejudices you see written on the board.

"If the world thought about each of you in these negative terms, what would that do to your self-image and the ability to achieve, or even make, life goals?" I was glad to see most people nodding and taking notes. I wrapped up by saying that while the medication is usually beneficial, each client should be encouraged to find opportunities for social inclusion. "Your focus should be to help your clients open their minds to becoming active players in their own well-being." This got everyone's attention as though it were new information. "You could be the only one in your clients' lives who encourages and believes in them. It could be the spark that gets them believing in themselves. I'm leaving this class by believing all of you have the ability to do that. Pay it forward."

# Life Changes

The insistent clanging of the phone jarred me awake at 6 a.m. I reached clumsily for the phone, knocked it to the floor, and retrieved it. It was Ali, my younger sister in England.

"Sorry to phone so early but Mum's had an accident. She's in hospital."

The unwelcome news caused a sinking feeling in the pit of my stomach.

"She's had a bad fall and hit her forehead. Her whole face is black and blue. They don't think there's any brain trauma, but the doctor said she'll be there for at least three weeks."

As Mother was in her 80s, I dreaded her having serious health issues a continent away. "Okay, thanks for letting me know."

"Well, there's more." Ali explained that although she hadn't been to see Mum, she'd had a long conversation with the social worker at the hospital. They both agreed it would be better if Mum went into a care facility rather than returning home.

"What? Why? That's a bit sudden, isn't it?"

Ali informed me that Mum had been on a steady mental decline. Despite the live-in caregiver she hired, Mum spent much of the day riddled with anxiety and frequently phoned Ali with delusions: Her friend Reg was holding her hostage at his house; the bank was stealing her money; the caregiver was stealing her food; she couldn't remember who was coming for dinner and had been waiting outside for them.

My always-organized sister had been researching care facilities for at least a year and found a suitable home for people with dementia close by so she could visit.

"Mum would have a better life if she were in a home for people with dementia."

I held my forehead as I thought about Ali's words. It made sense. At this stage, the important thing was Mum's quality of life. Suffering continual anxiety was stressful for her and everyone around her. At least in a home, she would have 24-hour professional care and lots of people her age to chat with.

"Another thing, Rod, I'm going away to France for a couple of weeks. I wondered if you could come over, stay at the house, and clean it out ready for sale. Maybe you could visit Mum at hospital in the afternoons?"

For the last eight years, Ali had handled most of our mother's needs and had only asked me for help once. How could I refuse?

"Clean it out ready for sale" was said quickly, a short sentence that triggered an unpleasant tightness in my chest. I'd always known that one day, 28 Claremont Road would no longer be the family home, but it didn't stem the feelings of loss flooding into me.

Dad had been so proud to move us into our new house, with its panoramic views of the town, countryside, and sea, just before my sisters were born. It had been the Baker home for over 50 years — a solid brick anchor. When Mum left, it would be put up for sale to pay for her care, and that would mean the end of our family bungalow.

"Al said he could probably come down and help," Ali added.

My brother sharing the responsibility would be welcome.

"You'll need to come right away, Rod. You could get the house sorted out, then when she leaves the hospital, I was hoping you could ride with her to the new care facility. The hospital provides transportation."

"Yeah, okay. I'll get back to you. Thanks, sis."

The call woke Anna. She overheard and gave me a hug. There

was nothing urgent to keep me at work, and she booked me a flight for London leaving in two days.

I went to work early that day and made preparations to be away. Adnam beamed when I asked him if he could look after things for a couple of weeks. He'd expressed interest in becoming ED when I retired and saw this as a fortunate chance to gain experience and add to his resume. In the last few months, he'd asked me twice when I planned to leave. I gave vague replies but felt the nudge. "Move over, old man."

The flight to England was a nine-hour, mind-deadening drone punctuated by occasional plastic capsules of food and beverage. En route to my last-ever visit to our family home, a heavy numbness settled into my soul.

Although the train from London to Newhaven whipped along at its usual 90 miles-per-hour, the staring cows and slow brown rivers seemed to linger in the window. The smell of electric trains in moist air hit me as I opened the door at my station. I walked the familiar mile home in light drizzle, my suitcase clicking on the paving stones. Forgotten memories snapped into focus: I passed by the tree where I'd first kissed a girl goodnight and the corner where Eddie and I had crashed our homemade go-kart into the trees.

The key was in the usual place, under a brick by the coal bunker. I opened the door. The house smelled of cooked vegetables and Mum's Avon perfume. I lowered myself onto the living room couch in the strange silence of her missing voice. I gazed at 50 years of memorabilia weighing down shelves in the living room: a herd of ebony elephants marching across the mantelpiece, red and gold encyclopedias that I'd used for school homework, the bronze bust of Nefertiti that I'd brought home from Egypt on my second trip at sea.

A family had lived here once — my family. Now the last member was leaving. She didn't know that — wouldn't be able to comprehend. I barely could myself.

My younger brother, Al, arrived the next day. It was a relief to see him. Good to have help in emptying out our house. It was a peculiar thing to do. We didn't know what to say.

"Shall we do the loft first, Al?"

Lofts are convenient storage spaces for things no longer needed but not discarded.

"Okay, I'll go up and start chucking stuff down. You take it outside."

Family history clattered onto the hallway tiles through the hole in the ceiling: my first motorcycle helmet, green with white wings painted on each side; my sisters' twin dolls, Looby Loo and Penny Lane, a gift from Aunty Pat on their eighth birthday. Three battered suitcases plummeted down, followed by the shabby black cardboard one I had gone to sea school with. Brightly painted papier-mâché masks my sisters had made at school crashed onto the floor. A cloudburst of memories rained down. I wanted him to treat things more gently, wanted to say "Stop!" but didn't. Picking up the remembered things of my youth, I carried them one by one to the big yellow steel bin sitting in the driveway that Ali had arranged for us.

"Okay, that's done. I s'pose we'll visit Mum now?" he said, swallowing as his blue eyes stared somewhere past my shoulder.

"Yeah. Ali said her face was banged up."

"Yeah. I heard that." Al nodded. "Maybe we could pick up some fish and chips for lunch first?"

"Good idea." I needed something to fill the empty space in my stomach.

Brighton Hospital was an austere five-storey brick building.

When my mother had my twin sisters, she'd held them up at a third-floor window so I could see — two small bundles of white who would soon be living in our new bungalow. Ten-year-old kids weren't allowed in the hospital; fifty-five years later, I was visiting again — this time allowed in.

A nurse stationed by the door of the dementia ward gave us a friendly smile and asked who we were visiting.

"Mrs. Baker."

"Down there, dear. Sixth bed on the left."

The ward was full of single beds with blue blankets. Some oldies were wandering around; others lay silently in bed.

The dark blue bruise on our mother's face from her forehead to her chin gave her a ghoulish appearance as she stared vacantly at the ceiling.

"Hi, Mum. It's Al and Rod, come for a visit," Al said in a loud voice.

She flinched and stared at us for a few seconds. "Goodness, what are my big boys doing here?" Her face lit up with a smile. "I'm in a sort of hotel, but it's not very good. I can't find my clothes."

We tried to chat for a while, but with the lack of common memories due to Alzheimer's, the conversation quickly dried up. Resourceful Al pulled out his laptop, set it on her bed, and started scrolling through family pictures. It put a big smile on her face. She remembered everybody. "There's my brother Ian standing by his new car." After a while, she grew tired. "Why aren't those people talking to me, Alan?"

"They're just pictures, Mum."

She looked puzzled. "Can they see me?"

"No, Mum, but *we* can see you. And the good news is we'll be back to see you again tomorrow."

Al's cheery words revived my plummeting spirits. She smiled at the reassuring news. We hugged her and left.

Each morning, we cleaned out a room in the house — three bedrooms, a kitchen, and the living room. We kept most of the photographs. Ali had arranged for a company to remove anything of value that we didn't want. I took the wrought-iron welded house name that Dad had made and a few other things that would fit in my suitcase. Al kept a stamp album. After sorting out each room, we visited Mum each afternoon. We made lighthearted bedside conversation about nothing much, but inside, I felt deceitful for not mentioning we were emptying her home of all the things she loved.

On the fifth day, we started on Mum's bedroom. I came across a wooden box that held every letter I had ever written home: at 14, postcards from a school camping trip in the Lake District. At 16, I'd written from sea school followed by letters from all over the world from my time in the merchant navy. After I emigrated at 21, there were long letters describing my life in Canada that tapered off over the years to Christmas and birthday cards. Despite our often-fractious relationship, the carefully kept letters showed she cared. Maybe I shouldn't have left home at such a young age. I sat on the bed and couldn't stop the tears running down my face.

My brother looked at me. "What's up?"

"I dunno, just...just." I didn't need to explain my feelings to him. He probably wouldn't get it. I didn't see letters from him to Mum. Al left the room. I sat until the tears ran dry. My shirt was wet. I stepped outside, sat on the brick steps, and looked at the view.

On the morning of our seventh day together, Al left. I watched through the window. It was foggy as he walked down the front path of the family home for the very last time — past the red hot pokers and the mountain ash tree onto the street. He didn't look back. I wondered how he felt. We hadn't discussed it. Soon it would be me walking down that path — the lone remaining witness to the full cycle of our house: When we were waiting for this house to be built, Dad had rented a flat in the adjoining town of Peacehaven. We visited each week to watch the progress.

"That's where the kitchen will be, and your bedroom will be here, Rod," Dad said, pointing at empty spaces. I was ten when we moved in and remember being surprised that my leather-soled shoes echoed on the tiled floor of the empty house.

At the end of our family's tenure at number 28, all the furniture was gone, and I slept in a sleeping bag on an air mattress I'd brought with me. Each morning, I caught the green number 12 double-decker bus to the hospital to visit Mum. We played Scrabble. Somehow, the word game part of her brain still functioned. Each afternoon, I stopped at the pub on the walk to the bus. Food, washed down with beer, helped settle my churning stomach.

I used the pub Wi-Fi to check in with the office. Adnam assured me that everything was running very well in my absence. Consoling to hear something was normal.

As instructed by the hospital, I arrived on my mother's last day there at 9 a.m. Mum was due to be moved at 10 o'clock. She was dressed, and the bruise on her face looked better.

"Hello, darling, are we going home today?"

I tightened my lips and stared at the floor. "Actually, we're going up to stay in a house close to Ali today," I said in a loud, confident voice.

She looked confused. "When am I going home?"

"You've had an injury, Mum. You're not ready to go home yet.

You're in hospital."

"Don't be ridiculous. I've never been in hospital a day in my life. I'm perfectly fine."

"The doctor said you're not ready to go home."

"What doctor? I'm a grown woman. He can't tell me what to do."

Mum was still her feisty self.

At a loss for words, I pulled our suitcases into the elevator and down to the transport ambulance in the parking lot. The uniformed driver said hello to Mum, helped her into her seat, and buckled her up. An elderly woman was already seated in the vehicle. She gave a weak smile as we entered. Inside the ambulance, a faint odour of antiseptic blended with the driver's aftershave.

"Are we going home, Rod?"

"Not yet, Mum. We're going up to see Ali."

"I want to go to my own home. I have to look after my garden."

I explained again, slowly, that she'd been ill and wasn't ready to return home. She waved off my explanation.

"Don't be silly. I want to go to my own home."

About every 15 minutes, she repeated, "Are we going home now? I want to go to my own home." I guessed that was the length of her short-term memory. After a while, I failed to respond. Her words hung unanswered in the air but echoed in my head. The other passenger gave me a mournful look.

At work, I always found words to cheer up a family who were distressed by the cognitive decline of the loved ones they were visiting. No such insights came to mind for my own mother — just guilt that I was the main actor in the deception and sad for Mum. She had lost her memory and now was losing her home. Two cornerstones of her identity.

The driver stopped at the city of Guildford and helped the elderly passenger out of the ambulance and down the path to the front door of her terraced home.

Mum pressed her face to the window. "See, that lady is going to her own home." She stared at me and pursed her lips angrily. The five-hour trip from Brighton to Halesworth burned a permanent crater of remorse into my psyche.

I heaved a sigh of relief as we pulled into the courtyard of the care facility, a stately ivy-walled mansion. A cheery woman in a blue uniform came to greet us.

"You must be Mrs. Baker. Welcome to Bountiful House, my name is Adriana. Pleased to meet you both."

I took Mum's arm. She was weary from the long ride and weak from being in hospital. Adriana led us upstairs to my mother's room. Ali had decorated it with family pictures and some of Mum's favourite ornaments and paintings. She didn't seem to notice.

Mum looked around suspiciously. "Who's paying for this?"

"The government is paying," I replied.

She nodded approvingly. "That's nice of them."

"I'll let you unpack, Mrs. Baker, then one of the staff will show you around," Adriana said.

I helped Mum put her clothes away in this small room that was replacing her bungalow with a garden and view of the sea. One of the workers came to take her on a tour of the facility, and I went down to the office to sign some papers.

Ten minutes later, there was a commotion outside the door, and my mother burst in looking outraged.

"Rod, you can't leave me here. These people are all deranged." She was right, but what she didn't realize was that with her serious dementia, she was one of them.

Adriana took charge. "Now, Mrs. Baker, calm down. I'll have one of our staff make you a nice cup of tea and find some biscuits. Perhaps you'd like to play some Scrabble? Your daughter, Alison, told us that you're rather good at that game."

That was enough distraction for her, and Mum followed the staff member out of the room.

My legs started to buckle, and I put a hand on the office desk to support myself. Adriana moved toward me, offering a hug as solace till I caught my breath. I was embarrassed; her collar was wet with my tears. She'd probably seen this a hundred times before, but it shook me to my core. She waited until my breathing was even and handed me a tissue.

"I'm sorry," I mumbled, but it came out more like a groan.

She smiled and nodded. "I realize it's upsetting, but your mother will feel better tomorrow. That's one good thing about dementia, they often can't remember why they were upset."

I chickened out of saying goodbye to Mum and caught a cab to Ali's house. She was still away in France. The house was along a narrow country lane bordered by low green hedgerows. Her garden was bursting with sunflowers, hollyhocks, and roses, all glowing in the late evening sun. Surrounding fields of barley rippled in the wind. Peaceful but lonely.

Staring out of the kitchen window, I was racked by guilt for leaving Mum at the care facility and telling her she couldn't go home *yet* when I knew she was *never* going home.

I sent emails to distract myself: the first to Ali, letting her know everything had gone to plan; then to Adnam telling him I'd be back in two days; and the last to Anna describing the day's events. Writing was safer, helped sort out my thoughts. I set the alarm on my phone, slipped under the patchwork quilt on the guest bed, and fell into a fitful sleep.

Arriving at Heathrow the next day, I surrendered to the process of passport inspection and electronic-wand waving before passing through the portal of those to be elevated.

The Airline Gods were benevolent and awarded me an emergency exit seat. I'd enjoy the luxury of stretching my legs to their full extent for the next nine hours as we leapt across the chasm between continents, the great separator of families. The rush of acceleration pulled me back in my seat as we hurtled down the runway and shot skyward into the clear morning air.

I thought of my first flight to Vancouver 44 years before — a hopeful 21-year-old setting off on the adventure of a new life in Canada. On this flight, I was at the latter end of that adventure and pondered what lay ahead: would my life lapse into a slow oblivion like my mother, would it end abruptly like my son's, or would I enjoy good health for a few more years? One thing for sure: at 65, I had a lot less life to live than when I was 21. Maybe I should retire, experience life without working. The change from being in charge of everything to being in charge of nothing would be dramatic. No longer valued by others for my daily work, I would need to find ways of valuing myself. Had the busyness of work been a way of hiding from myself? How would I feel having every day to myself? Happy, empty, numb?

Since leaving school at sixteen, not working had been a temporary problem, not a chosen goal. Having time for myself had meant it was the weekend or a holiday. The lack of wages would be another big change. I would have no income other than a government pension.

"Would you like something to drink, sir?"

I flinched and looked up. A smartly dressed young flight attendant smiled and awaited my answer.

"Yes, please. I'd like a beer." I enjoyed the feel of the cold liquid swishing down my throat. It felt slightly decadent to be streaming through the atmosphere at 900 km/h, 30,000 feet above the earth at -30C, and still be able to drink beer — a moment of suspension from the pain of the recent past and the challenge of an uncertain future.

Since starting at the Simon Fraser Branch eight years before, I had solved a nonstop revolving door of problems. After such turbulent times, the prospect of calm waters ahead would lack the thrill of accomplishment that had become my daily caffeine. The sole remaining challenge was Bev's determination to have some branches amalgamate. At 65, I wouldn't be selected to run an amalgamated branch. It would probably be an uber-confident 40-something-year-old with an earring — a social-media whiz with an MA in nonprofit management, unlike myself who just guessed at solutions and soldiered through. After running my own branch, I didn't want to work for another ED.

If I retired, maybe I could use my counselling degree to work part-time as a counsellor. Instead of writing boring funding proposals, I could write a book. Rather than sitting at a computer all day, there would be time to exercise. We could get a dog and take it for walks. I accepted another beer, Heineken, one of my favourite brands. I sipped and mused: We could move to a smaller house and be mortgage free. If it needed fixing, my woodworking skills would be helpful.

By the time the plane cruised over the jagged peaks of Rockies and started the long descent into Vancouver, the idea of retirement was growing roots, sprouting: I visualised myself telling the staff, the board, the volunteers, and our clients that I was leaving. Before committing to a decision, I decided to discuss it with Anna.

After such a draining trip, it was wonderful to get a hug from Anna and be driven home, where I could relax and sleep in my own bed. Sitting on the comfortable leather couch in the living room, Anna poured us a glass of wine. I recounted the whole traumatic experience: emptying the house, the hospital visits, the ambulance ride, and leaving my mother at the care facility. The conversation petered out.

"Is there something else?" Anna's canny sixth sense was at work.

"What do you mean?"

"By the look on your face, it feels like there's something going on in your head."

I had planned to tell her in my own time, the right time. Sometime. She continued to look at me with big eyes.

"It crossed my mind that I might…might retire."

The words hung in the air.

"Baker, really? That's a big decision."

I laughed nervously. "Yeah, it is. What do you think?"

"Great. I never liked that place anyway," she said, topping up our wine glasses.

Anna, like many Italians I knew, didn't have much of a filter. I laughed at her honesty. "What would I do, though?"

"Baker, you'll find something! Listen, I was thinking about making pasta carbonara tonight with grilled zucchini as an appetizer."

"Sliced thin with oregano sprinkled on top?"

"Yes."

The food of life would continue whether I worked or not. As for finding new meaning in my life, that would be the next experiment.

## 2012 — Saying Goodbye

I arrived at work early, entered through the thrift store, started up the stairs but stopped to look back. Three years before, this space had been nothing but a cement floor, dirty windows, and flickering lights. In contrast, new laminate floors held shiny chrome racks full of goods. Paintings for sale lined the walls. The store's pristine appearance was ready to welcome the first shoppers of the day. I looked at the spot just inside the front door where Sandy had said, "This wasn't about meeting for coffee, was it, Rodney?" when she realized I wanted to open a new store and hoped she would run it. I recalled Trevor saying the Treasure Chest had netted $100,000 that spring — an amazing accomplishment for an operation run by volunteers and organized by a part-time manager. Revenue from the store covered our funding shortfalls and allowed us to pay back the $40,000 from mortgaging Bluebird House to cover the deficit that arose when I was in Italy.

I made myself a coffee and jotted down some notes for the staff meeting. During emotional moments, I often lost the thread of what I planned to say. I wanted the staff to be the first to know I was leaving, then I would tell the board. I sat in the staff room, drinking coffee and scanning my notes. The box of a dozen donuts was the table centrepiece.

Lisa wandered into the room. "Great! Donuts. You forgot the napkins again. I guess it's a guy thing. My husband's the same."

"How was your trip, Rodney?" Adnam asked.

How to explain that trip? "I got everything done, thanks."

I waited till everyone was seated. People sipped their coffees and reached for donuts. We were back to free coffee. I'd started buying it again. The coffee was a tiny perk for the difficult work they did every day, now that we could afford it.

I usually launched into a round-table check-in as soon as we were seated, but that day, I sat silently. People looked at me. I looked at my notes and back at the staff. I swallowed, took a breath.

"I've decided it would be a good idea for myself and maybe the organization if I resigned my position." The 10 staff, usually a chatty, witty, or combative bunch, fell silent. All eyes looked at me. I looked down at my notes. "I'm going to tell the board that I plan to give my notice in three months' time. I'll stay for the next Miles for Mental Health Run/Walk in May and then leave."

Adnam broke into a broad grin at my announcement. Most of the others looked shocked.

Kevin blurted out, "Why are you leaving?"

"Good question. I feel my work here is done. Everything is going well. There are a couple of annual events to connect with the community, the Treasure Chest is doing great, and there are no financial problems. I have given what I can give here."

Kevin continued staring in disbelief.

"It's time for someone new, and younger, to take over, someone with better knowledge of social media and more energy to take this branch to the next level. As you are the people who do the work that keeps this place going, you deserved to hear first."

Lisa pulled her hair back with both hands and glared at me with hard eyes. "How the hell are we going to prevent the wrong kind of person getting the job like last time you left?"

"Guys, I think that had to be a one-off, but I hear you. When I talk to the board tonight, I'll bring up your concerns. I'm going to drop in on the transition houses tomorrow to tell all the residents I'm leaving."

"I'll come with you, Rodney. As the housing manager, I'd like to reassure them they'll still be in good hands," Adnam said.

"Sure, okay." I would rather have done it alone, made it more personal, but I could see the value of the housing manager adding reassurance in the face of unexpected news.

The day drifted by slowly. I felt like a becalmed sailboat wallowing in the doldrums. I looked around the office and remembered prepping the studs for the drywallers. I'd left the original odd-coloured chartreuse window trim which went well with the new buff wall paint. The window looked down three stories onto the street and the Chinese restaurant where I sometimes went for chicken chow mein. We had been at this location for three years, but the memories of moving in remained fresh. Soon this would be someone else's office. The new ED would have no knowledge of the struggles we'd been through to make this happen. It would all just be here.

I phoned Sandy and asked her if I could drop by her house.

"Anything wrong, Rodney?"

"Nope, just gonna be over that way." I bought a large bunch of red roses. Their perfume was overwhelming as I drove to her house.

She looked both happy and perplexed as she opened the door. "What, why?"

I thrust the roses toward her and got straight to the point. "I'm leaving in three months. Just wanted to bring you a small thank you present." The words flew out of me. I didn't want to get into a long speech I couldn't finish. We'd been comrades in arms for over six years. We both knew she had done her best with the store and I'd done my best to support her. Together, we'd made the Treasure Chest work.

"Do you want some coffee, Rodney?"

We always had coffee. We drank it in the back room of the Treasure Chest while we plotted and planned. It was a familiar ritual in an unfamiliar situation. We sat in her kitchen at a pine table.

"When exactly are you leaving?"

"Right after the Run. Will you stay at the Treasure Chest?"

"Ha, maybe not. I stayed last time you left, and it was a big mistake." We reminisced about the four store locations and some of the interesting folks who had worked there.

We fell silent and stared at our coffee cups.

"You gonna put those roses in a vase? I didn't bring them all the way here for them to dry out."

"I will as soon as you leave," Sandy said with a sad smile. "Now go. Don't be late for your board meeting."


I sat at the head of the table, waiting for the eight directors to file into the room. The mismatched chairs we'd used eight years ago at my first board meeting were recently replaced by nine smart-looking grey-cushioned ones donated to the Treasure Chest.

"I have some news which will pre-empt the normal meeting agenda."

People looked a little surprised and gave me their attention.

"After careful consideration, I have decided it is time for me to leave this organization."

It was as though the air was sucked out of the room. Everybody stared at me, some with their mouths open. To fill up the silence, I used the notes from the staff meeting to explain my rationale. After all the great support the board members had given me, I felt guilty abandoning ship.

"Well, that's a shock," Graham said. "Maybe you could sit on the interview panel to hire the next ED?" he asked with a smile. "Given that you have insider experience."

"Sure. I think the staff will be glad to hear that. They've expressed concerns about you hiring another ED like Veronica."

There was a general buzz of talk and serious faces as they digested the information.

By the end of the meeting, we agreed that I would write a job description and send it to the board for approval. As we left the room, the mood was friendly but sombre.

The next day, Adnam was late. I waited 20 minutes, failed to reach him on his cell phone, and left without him. One of his few faults was tardiness. Visiting our four transition houses to say goodbye brought out the joker in me. The Riverside House manager made some tea and put out some cookies like any convivial visit. With a smile, I told the residents that I'd recently become a senior citizen and was retiring while I still remembered their names. In jest, I deliberately got a few names wrong. They laughed, and I continued. "I'm sure you lucky guys will be getting a much younger ED with a fresher memory and fewer wrinkles."

Sarah, the lone woman resident, looked worried. "Will it be somebody friendly, Rodney?"

"Yes, that's part of the job description," I kidded. "Must be super friendly, like cats and pink houses. We've got you guys all covered."

She smiled ruefully, but my breezy approach worked. I figured it would be hard for them to be down if I was up. I used it in the other three houses.

Saying goodbye to these clients was like chopping off little bits of myself. The challenges and successes of their lives always came up in our weekly staff meetings. I knew I would probably never see them again. Past EDs visiting clients during a new ED's era wasn't usually accepted practice.

Preparations for the Run were in full swing. Adnam was doing double duty as housing manager and Miles for Mental Health Run/Walk director and enjoying both positions. He shone in the public eye, which increased his energy and work output. I decided to lessen my involvement — just give a short welcome speech to participants, thank our sponsors, and take part in the walk.

There were few responses to our ads for a new ED. Although expensive, the board decided to continue advertising in the *Vancouver Sun* every week until suitable candidates were found.

Most of my focus was spent trying to clean up all the files under my purview, all 99 of them. For every aspect of my responsibility, I'd created a file as a repository of information. My private notes needed upgrading to be understood. I wanted the incoming ED to have the best information available and reviewed each file for clarity and content.

As I scanned through all the files, I kept getting lost in past endeavours: a 20-page proposal to run a mental health day program in an adjacent city. A file called "House Repairs" containing pictures and descriptions of all the repair work we had ever done to the transition houses.

It took a week to get the files in order. I was tempted to round off the 99 by making a final file numbered 100, called "Getting the 99 in order." I decided to keep copies on my personal computer to remember the many projects we had ventured into. I had learned so much and wanted to retain the knowledge and the memories.

We received five applications for the ED position, three of which were viable: a woman with a good resume and some experience as ED of a nonprofit from the town of Mission; a woman in her 40s currently working in nonprofit management who lived in the adjacent town of Burnaby; and Adnam. More candidates would have been better, but the pay wasn't high and the responsibilities many. The problem with the woman from Mission was that she hadn't worked in 18 months and it had been eight years since she had run a nonprofit.

Adnam was confident and knew our organization but was in his mid-twenties and had only one year's experience in nonprofit management. He had been talking up his bid for the ED position to our staff. They all encouraged him and assumed his becoming ED was a certainty.

While staff members were impressed with Adnam, it was the interview team he had to convince. By acclamation, the interview panel awarded the position to the woman from Burnaby.

Given his age and lack of experience, Adnam did very well to come a close second. When the president informed him he hadn't been selected, I saw him leave the building. He didn't return for the rest of the day. I wondered if he was okay and also worried that he may have quit and I'd have to take over the Run, just two weeks away. Fortunately, he reappeared the following day and carried on doing both jobs with his usual competence. I felt for him. It's never easy to have your aspirations dashed.

I told the staff I didn't want a big send-off. They obliged with a farewell party at Barnabas House in New Westminster. All the staff and about 30 clients came. The president of the board presented me with a fancy clock and read out the inscription: "With thanks to Rodney Baker for outstanding work as executive director of CMHA-SF." Everybody clapped. I turned red. My reward had been the work.

The Miles for Mental Health Run/Walk would be my swan song with CMHA-Simon Fraser Branch. It felt rewarding to spend my last day taking part in an event I helped create. I awoke on the morning of the event to find sunshine, unlike the devastating downpour of the previous year.

I arrived at Queens Park just before the event began and chatted with Adnam until he signalled it was time to start. I hopped onto the stage, picked up the mic, and thanked all the participants for showing up and our donors for their support.

I put my bib on, took my place at the starting line, and chatted with the other participants. I felt a tap on the shoulder. It was Kevin.

"Wanna walk around the course together?"

"That would be great!" It felt satisfying to end my CMHA career with Kevin at my side.

We walked close to the trail where I had towed two-year-old Steve on his little red toboggan, the first winter he had seen snow. I was 25 then and on my way to a new career as an apprentice boat builder. Forty years later, I was passing the same location — walking away from my final career.

"You're very quiet, Rodney," Kevin said.

"Kev, you've been hearing me running meetings and rattling on about stuff for over seven years. I'm just giving you a break."

We both laughed.

My last day of work had been happy and easy. I left the park and drove toward home. As I turned onto the freeway, the familiar high-rise came into view — the one that always triggered feelings of grief over Steve's death. The construction tower crane, like the ones he used to work on, was long gone. But driving by the high-rise still conjured up sad thoughts and emotions. Now that I'd quit my job in New Westminster, I'd rarely take this route; that was okay.

I arrived home and sat alone in my home office, between lives: My work at CMHA was over — the next adventure yet to begin. I felt relieved, sad, happy, empty, proud, and a little shaky. Kaleidoscope images flashed by — Comedy Courage, Riverside House, Sheppard House, the Run, the Treasure Chest, Italy, England, Christmas dinners, Outreach, helpful volunteers, courageous people, difficult people. I wondered how it would all fit into one story.

Anna spotted me from the kitchen. "Baker, you're home."

"Yeah, get used to it." We both laughed.

"Do you want to eat now or later?"

"Maybe in an hour. I was thinking I might start to write a few notes."

"Notes on what?"

"The outline of a book."

"You've never written a book before."

"You'd better be nice to me. You're going to be in it."

## Afterword 2020

In 2015, the Simon Fraser Branch merged with other branches to form the Vancouver Fraser Branch.

In 2017, the last Miles for Mental Health Run/Walk was held in Queens Park.

I have kept in touch with some of the people I worked with:
- Ada works part time for a nonprofit and has her own accounting practice.
- Barney left Fraser Health in 2011 and works for the Lookout Society.
- Carmela leads a team of 11 Bounce Back coaches for the Vancouver Fraser Branch.
- Debbie Sheppard, who donated her commission so that we could buy Riverside House, continues to sell real estate in Maple Ridge.
- Heather carried on her amazing work as an outreach worker until 2017 when the Vancouver Fraser Branch decided to discontinue the program.
- Jackie, mother of two and star Comedy Courage comedian, has a business selling health products.
- Jennifer, who orchestrated our original Miles for Mental Health Run/Walk, got married, moved to the US, had a baby daughter, and started a successful real estate enterprise in Seattle.
- Jessica, the competent Run volunteer, works as a senior product manager for a telecom company and still uses her barbecue skills.
- Kevin still works for CMHA in New Westminster as a housing support worker.
- Paige managed a thrift store in Maple Ridge for a few years after leaving CMHA but now works for a medical supply company.

- Suzy, the competent transition house manager, left CMHA, ran her local hospital thrift store, and raised revenues from $5,000 to $108,000 per annum.
- Sandy, the manager who brought the Treasure Chest operation to new heights, enjoys her grandchildren and still brings donations to the Treasure Chest.
- Sharon, the competent Treasure Chest volunteer coordinator, passed away in 2014. Sandy had often visited her in hospital.
- Trevor, the trustworthy accountant, has a three-year-old daughter and is the controller at Woodbridge Homes.

I work a few hours a week as an addiction counsellor for the North Shore Medical Centre and have written four books since leaving CMHA. My dog, Fargo, took me for walking breaks between bouts of writing and passed away as this book was finished.

The Treasure Chest is still operating at 435 6th Street in New Westminster.

## Other books by this author

*Constant Traveller R801168 — At Age 16 I Went to Sea*

(shortlisted WIBA)

*I Need My Yacht by Friday — True Tales from the Boat Repair Yard*

(Semi-finalist Chanticleer Book Awards. Positive review in *Pacific Yachting*)

*Um, Where is Belize? — A Journey into the Unknown*

**All books available on Amazon or at Lions Bay General Store**

**Your review of this book on Amazon would be appreciated**

Made in the USA
Middletown, DE
23 November 2023